The Captain's Cookbook

Captain Walter Kaprielian
who compiled, edited, wrote, designed
and illustrated this book
with the help and
encouragement of many
good friends.

He stands here on the bridge of
the "Blue Beard" ready to go out for
a day of offshore fishing off
Montauk Point, New York.

The Captain's Cookbook

by

Holt, Rinehart and Winston
New York

Walter Kaprielian

Acknowledgements:

Many thanks to many wonderful
friends who helped make this book possible

To the Captains, every one

My staff, and the management
of Ketchum, MacLeod, and Grove for their
patience, paper, and the space I took over

To Walter Adams, Tom Burgess, Paul Kimatian,
Georgia Carroll, Dinaz Boga, Katsuji Asada,
Lynda Gianforte, Suzanne Anoushian,
and Leo Rogers for hours of their valuable time.

Jack Samson and his fine staff

Al Ristori of the Garcia Corporation

Air Jamaica
The Bahamian Ministry of Tourism

The Murray Hill Photoprint Company

Set-to-Fit Typographers

Denis Karlin for the photos of me

and to my terrific family
for eating a lot more seafood than
would be considered normal.

to the sea, who has fed me
in so many ways

the best
fisherman of
them all →

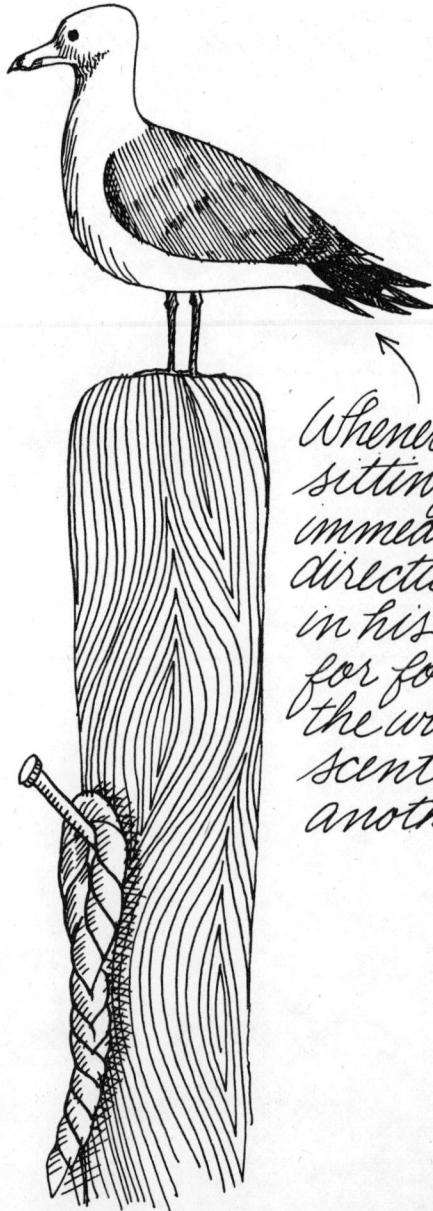

Whenever you see a
sitting seagull, you'll
immediately know the
direction of the wind. For
in his constant search
for food, he always faces
the wind, waiting for the
scent that will signal
another meal from the sea.

Table of Contents

A preface

The idea behind this cookbook was not a sudden one.

It evolved from the questions of many friends, relatives, guests, and customers who, after a successful day with me, out at sea, would look at their catch and ask, "what's the best way to make them?"

Most cookbooks have a tendency to intimidate me. They seem to make assumptions of knowledge I don't have. My attempts to cook by them have been successful, but when it comes to sea food, nothing has been as satisfying as the meals I have shared with men I have known who earn their living working the sea.

This cookbook is an attempt to capture those delicious experiences and share them with you.

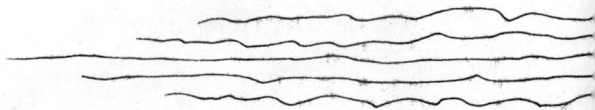

This cookbook is also an attempt to prove that seafood cooking need not be complex to be good. On the contrary, the simpler, the better.

The recipes have all been contributed by charter boat and private captains and mates from all coasts of the United States, the Virgin Islands, the Bahamas, and Jamaica. Every one is terrific!

They are all easy to make, and are illustrated in a step-by-step "how-to" manner for you to follow.

Approach them without fear. There is hardly a thing you can do wrong. Substitute species if a recipe appeals to you but the specified kind is unavailable. You will not be disappointed.

Use these recipes as a basis for new ones. Improvise, alter, create. Most of all, enjoy what the sea provides. Good cooking!

The Captain's Cookbook

Sport-Fishing Boats

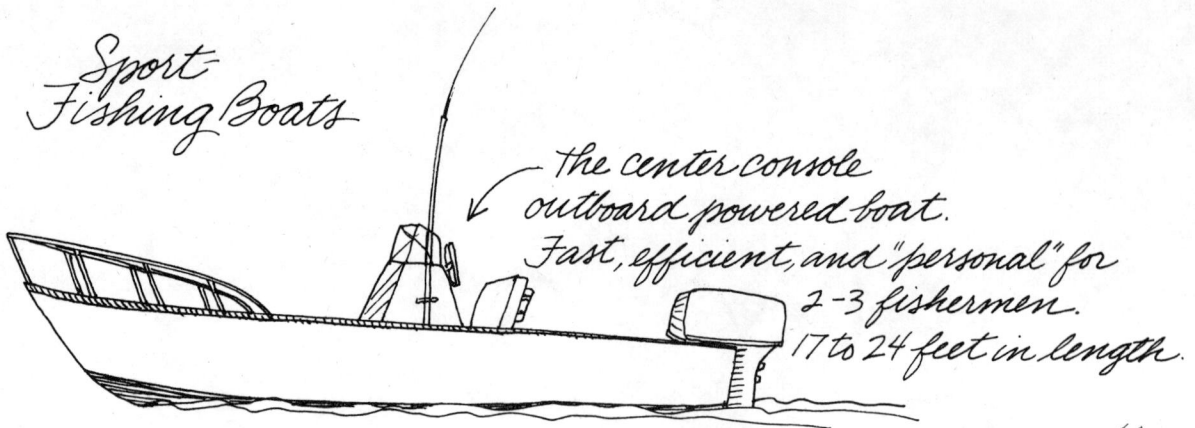

the center console
outboard powered boat.
Fast, efficient, and "personal" for
2-3 fishermen.
17 to 24 feet in length.

the Sports fisherman.
Anywhere from 25 to 50 feet in
length. Most popular for
inshore and offshore
trolling with 6 fishermen
or less →

BLUEBEARD

The Party boat ranges from 40 to over 100 feet.
Mostly used for bottom
or drift fishing.
Customers line railings
all around boat and
fish from there.

Some Basics.

No more than an ordinary kitchen will be required to prepare anything in this book.

With the exception of a few very inexpensive utensils you might not already own, you should have everything to prepare a gourmet delight from every recipe shown.

The next few pages should help prove that there is no big secret to successful seafood cooking.

Basic tools and utensils.

1. A sharp knife is the single most valuable tool.

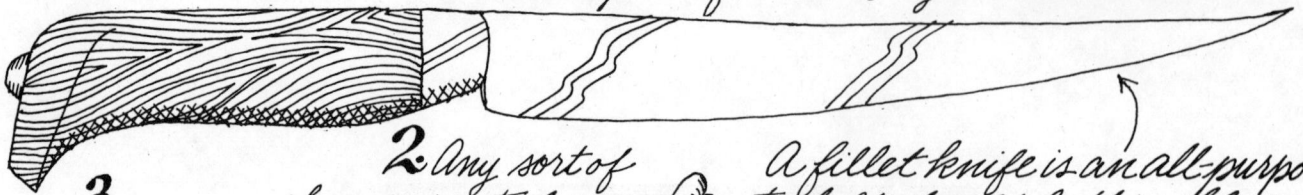

A fillet knife is an all-purpose tool. It should be thin bladed. Stainless steel is very nice, but not not necessary as the plain steel (the kind that turn black) seem to hold an edge longer. Never use a fillet knife to open shellfish. It's bad for the blade, and worse for your hand.

2. Any sort of sharpening tool you have around to keep your knife keen edged.

3. A scaler of any kind.

dull

even duller here.

4. Hard as it may be to believe, a dull-edged knife called a clam knife. It's usually about seven inches long, and about half an inch wide. Used only for opening clams, oysters, mussels, etc., without cutting your hand when it slips (as it inevitably will).

5. A common scrubbing brush for scrubbing sand from shell-fish. It can be wood, plastic, or anything that can take heavy use.

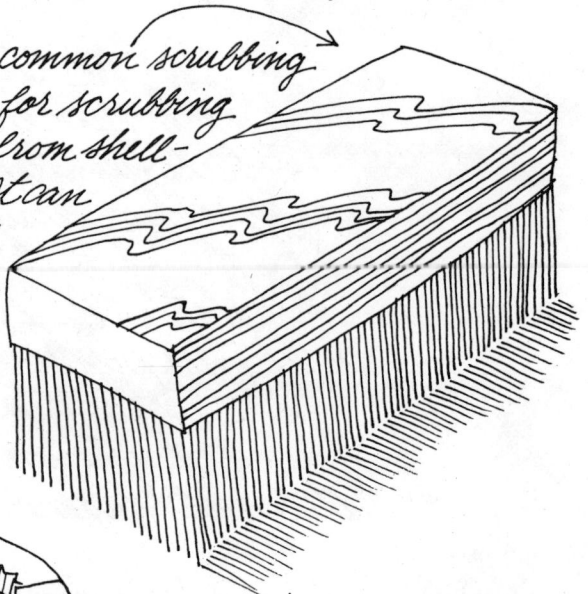

6. A set of nutcrackers and a nut pick, (you can find a set at your grandmother's house) for cracking shells and getting meat out of hard-to-reach places.

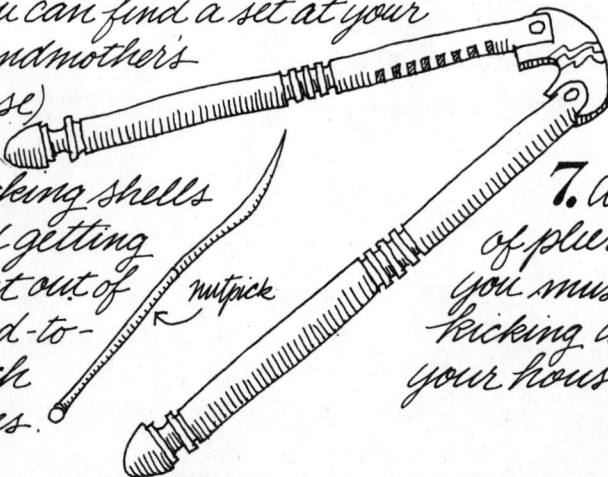

nutpick

7. A pair of pliers that you must have kicking around your house, car, or garage.

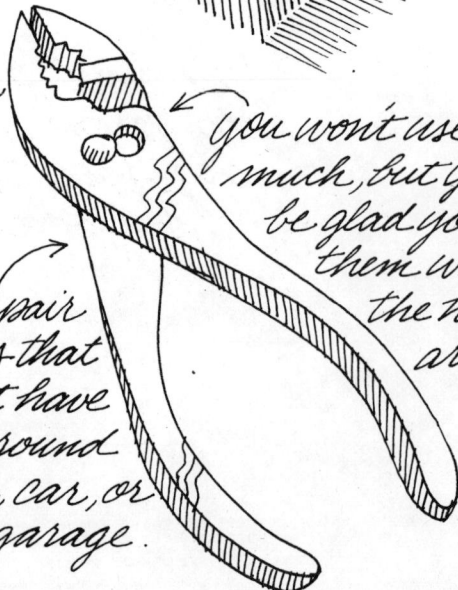

You won't use these much, but you'll be glad you have them when the need arises.

8. A basic pot with a lid that fits. Its size should be dictated by the number of Guests you're cooking for.

or a steamer

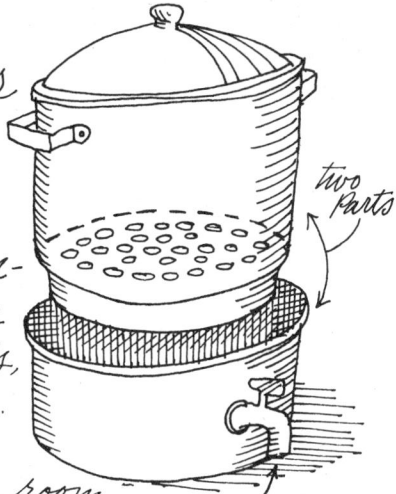

two Parts

spigot to remove clam broth.

9. A good skillet, either black iron, or teflon coated.

The size is again a matter of average need.

A steamer is not as much a necessity as a convenience when making lobsters, clams, mussels, corn, or steamed fish. It is not expensive, and if you have the room to store it, it may well be worth having.

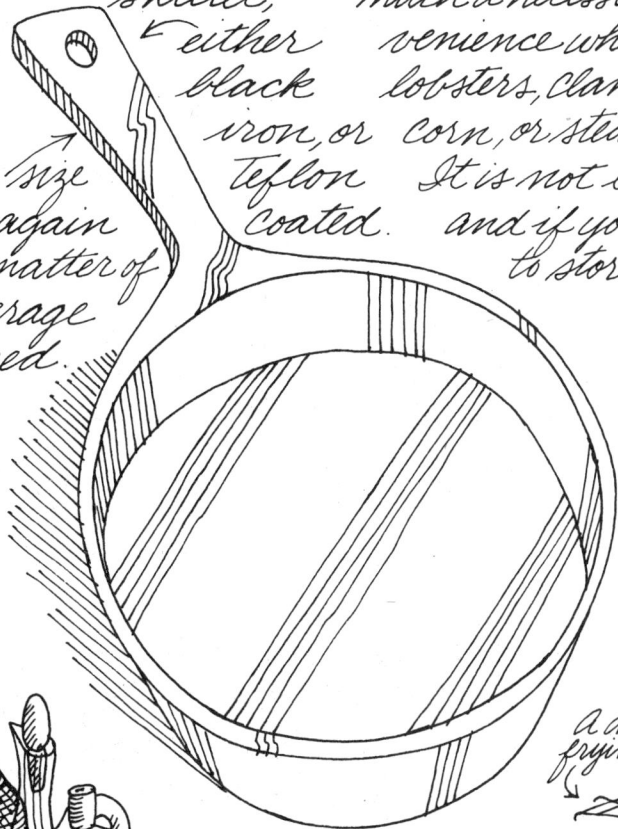

10. A basket for deep frying. It can be round or square, and will need a matching container to hold the oil.

a drain ring for frying fits on ledge.

or what I have found to be a good substitute for both a deep fryer and a steamer... A Wok.

You will use a lot less oil in a Wok, and it will stay hot much longer.

11. the basic spices and miscellaneous goodies around the kitchen

How to find good sources of seafood.

1. The nearer you are to water, the greater your chances are of finding a good source. Look for fishing boats, fish stores, or seafood restaurants in or near harbor or waterfront areas.

2. Look for fish stores in fish-loving ethnic areas. Chinese, Japanese, Italian, Jewish, Puerto Rican, and Scandinavian neighborhoods are good places to start looking. The best conch I've eaten outside of the Bahamas was bought in a Puerto Rican neighborhood right in the middle of New York City.

3. Invest in a good meal at a quality seafood restaurant and then ask if the manager can recommend a source that meets his high standards. This usually pays off. If the place itself will sell fish on a retail basis, you'll probably pay a premium, but it may be worth it.

4. Commercially frozen fish are available in most retail stores. Don't look for bargains here. Lobster tails, shrimp, king crab legs, sole, and swordfish, are usually available and are the only things I can recommend.

5. Try to find out the seasons and species indigenous to your area. This will insure your knowing if the species you are interested in purchasing could possibly be fresh.

6. Best of all, make friends (or at least a deal) with a fisherman... and offer to take the fish from him "as is". If you do, you'll be first on his give-away list, as most people ask, "Is it cleaned?"

Substitutions:

Mussels and clams can be substituted for each other in a steamed or sauced form.

Mussels, clams and oysters can be substituted for each other in recipes for them in a stuffed form.

Bay scallops and ocean scallops can be substituted for each other with adjustments in cooking time to compensate for their size difference.

Lobster and Crab meat can be substituted for one another in sauces, soups, and stews. Any species of either can be substituted for any other species.

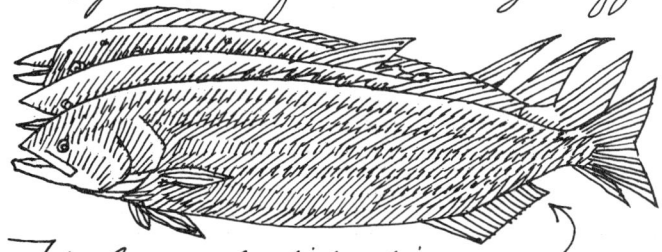

Fish substitutions:

As far as the author is concerned, there isn't a recipe in this book that cannot be made well with another species with totally different flesh characteristics. We have, though, separated them into groups by color, texture and flavor.

1. Cod, Whiting, Ling, Croaker, Weakfish (Sea Trout) have a soft flesh that cooks up white, flaky and very mild.

2. Striped Bass, Snook, Redfish (Channel Bass), Rock Cod, Red Snapper, Mutton Snapper, Dolphin, Grouper all have a firm flavorful white flesh.

3. Flounder, Fluke, Sole, Blowfish have a delicate white meat that is tasty yet mild.

4. Tuna, Bonito, Albacore have a red meat-like color and texture until cooked. then the flesh takes on a lighter color and flaky texture with rich flavor. Salmon has an orange flesh that is delicate in texture yet flavorful.

5. Bluefish, Mackerel have a soft oilier flesh, rich with taste.

6. Swordfish, Marlin, Mako Shark have a firm, distinctive texture and taste all their own, as does the Yellowtail that has a rich dense white tasty meat.

What to look for when purchasing seafood.

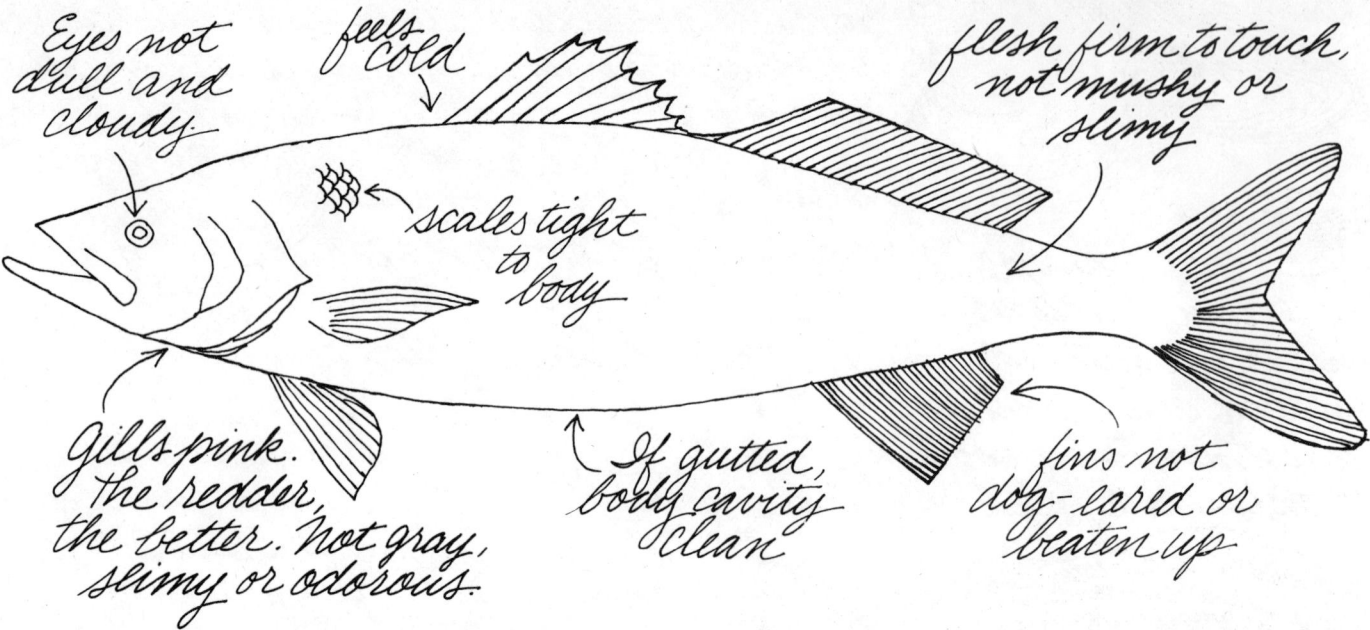

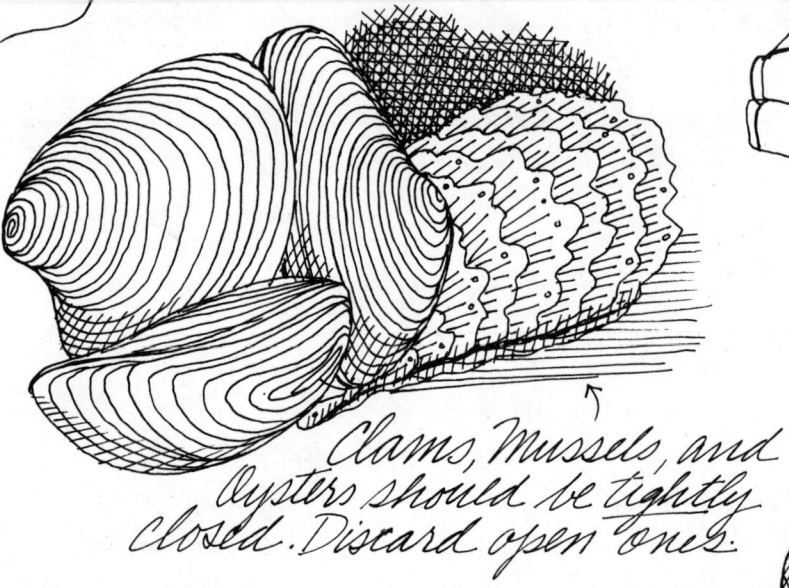

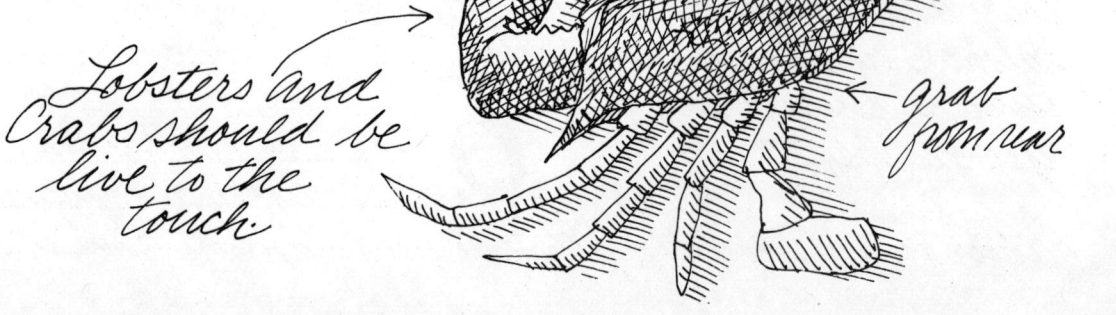

Eyes not dull and cloudy

feels cold

flesh firm to touch, not mushy or slimy

scales tight to body

Gills pink. the redder, the better. Not gray, slimy or odorous.

If gutted, body cavity clean

fins not dog-eared or beaten up

All seafood has a smell, but it should not be a repulsive or foul one.

Shrimp should be well-iced. I personally don't recommend freezing as you are probably re-freezing

Clams, Mussels, and Oysters should be tightly closed. Discard open ones.

Lobsters and Crabs should be live to the touch.

grab from rear

Mollusks

Clams, Mussels, Oysters, Scallops, Conch, Abalone, and all their varieties grace our shorelines. They can be rightfully called "Fruits of the Sea," for each has a delectable flavor all its own, especially when fresh picked.

Raw, steamed, boiled, broiled, fried, chowdered, sautéed, or sauced, there is hardly a thing you can't do with them.

The next few pages hold some basic information to help you understand and take advantage of these shellfish at their very best.

Mollusk facts.

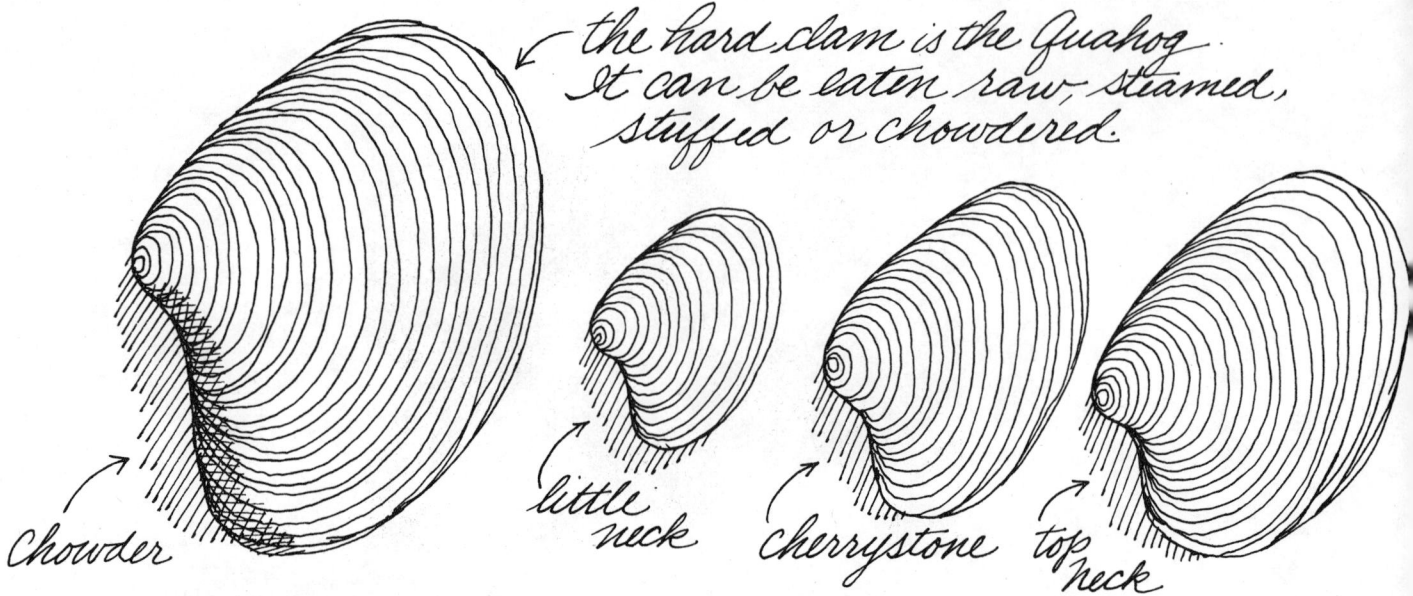

the hard clam is the Quahog.
It can be eaten raw, steamed,
stuffed or chowdered.

Chowder

little
neck

cherrystone

top
neck

These are all the same clam in various
stages of growth. All should be scrubbed
clean to avoid sand in your food.

put knife here

To open a live clam, hold as per
diagram and apply steady pressure
to top of clam until muscle of
clam relaxes.

(apply pressure with first two
fingers of left hand over top
of clam knife blade.)

For purposes other than eating raw,
steam for a few minutes, then
insert knife
into
slightly
opened
clam.

press here

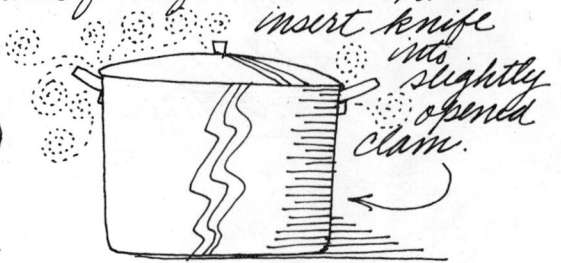

Save the liquid for
flavoring... (see some of
the clam recipes later
in the book).

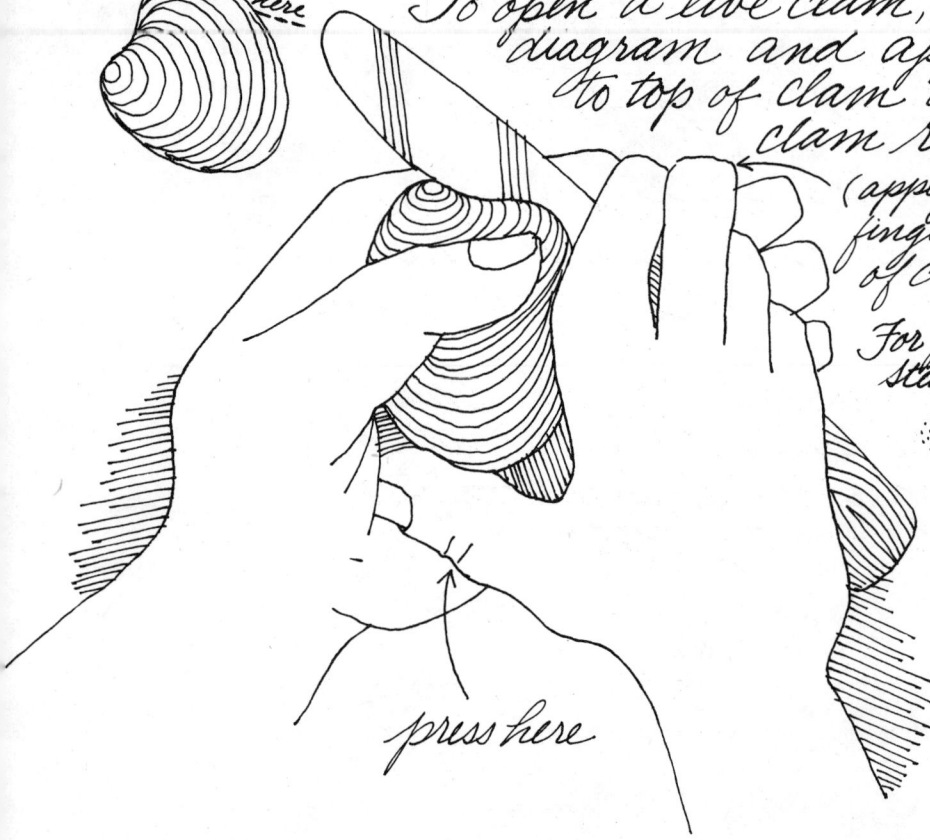

The lowly Mussel
The most underrated
and inexpensive of all
the Mollusks.

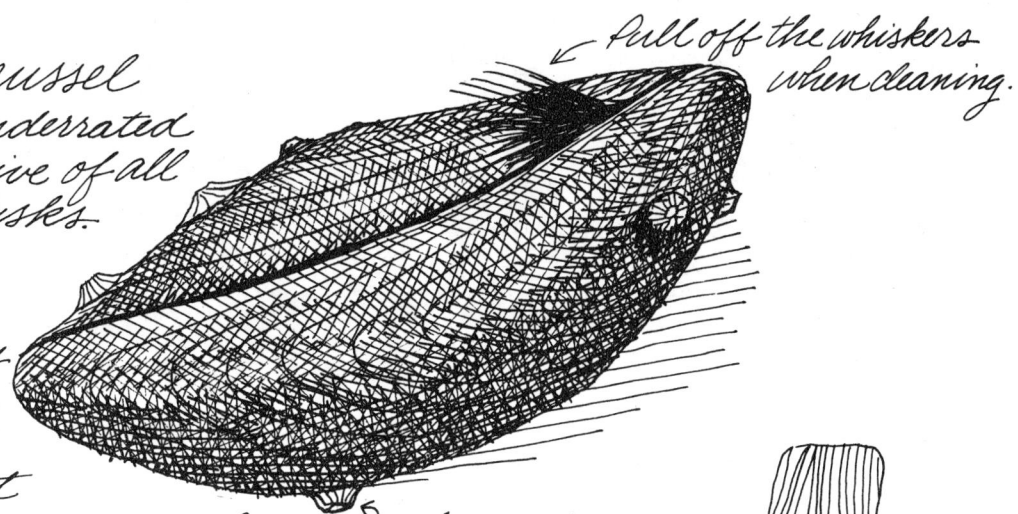

Pull off the whiskers
when cleaning.

there is hardly
a thing you can
do wrong with
them except not
scrub them well.

Break off barnacles as
they act as reservoirs
for sand.

Discard any
partially open
ones or any that
float After
being left
in water.

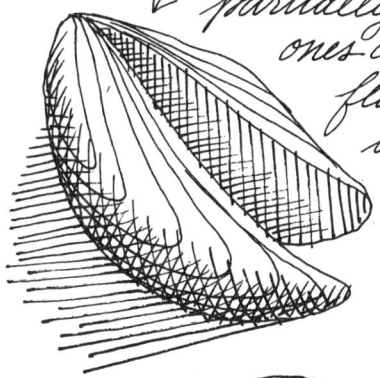

Mussels are
found
in clumps on
pilings or
rocks.

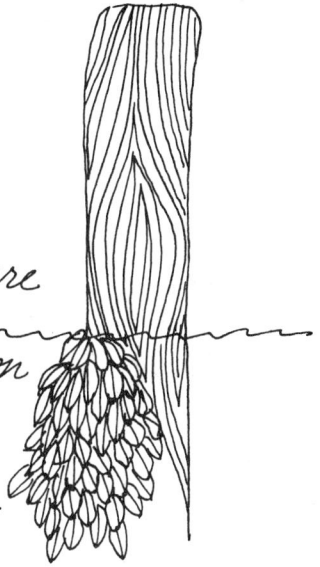

The Steamer (also called
the Soft Clam)

As kids we called them "Piss clams"
because they'd shoot water out
at you if you stepped on
the sand near where
they were buried.

Most
commonly used
with

broth

lemon
and
melted
butter

the neck is usually
filled with sand.
Pay special note
to de-sanding
instructions
in recipes.

removed
from shells,
skinned, dipped
in batter and
deep fried.

the Oyster,
the king
of shellfish

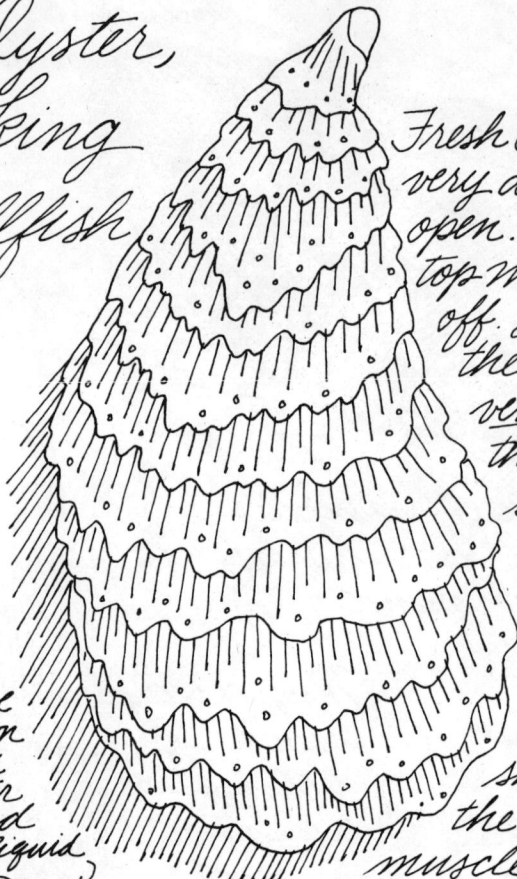

Fresh Oysters are very difficult to open. The convex top must be pried off. Sometimes if the oysters are very chilled they will open slightly so you can insert a knife and slide it around the shell to cut the holding muscle... or break edge with a pliers and slip knife into opening to free top.

side | view

Bottom holds body of the Oyster

top→

Stick end of knife into hinge and twist.

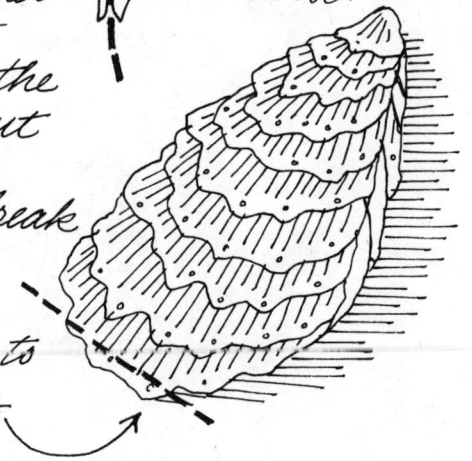

Lay oyster concave side down to hold Oyster and liquid.

the delicious Bay Scallop looks just like the Shell Oil Company symbol

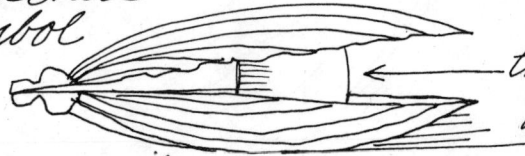

the part you eat

Strange as it may seem, the part you eat is the muscle that holds the shells together.

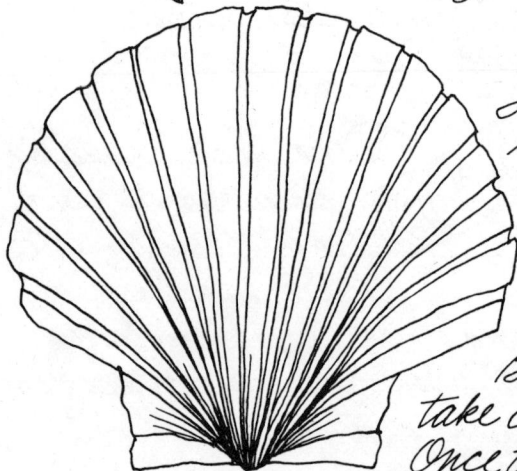

Should you ever get whole Bay Scallops in the shell, you must take care not to cut the muscle in half. Once the knife is inserted, it should slide across the inside top of the shell to cut the muscle off where it is attached.

slide across inside top.

How to clean them.

The first thing you want to do is get rid of sand, both externally and internally

The scrub-brush is indispensable for removing surface sand. Use it briskly under running water on all shellfish.

the "Steamer" is the worst offender as far as sand goes. Besides the surface sand on the shell and neck, there is sand in the neck itself that must be ejected. Here are a few methods for removal.

On Mussels there is a "whisker" that should be pulled off.

1. Place clams in a net bag and hang overboard for a day or two. Do not let bag touch bottom.

or **2.** Put clams in a bucket of salt water in which a handful or two of cornmeal has been thrown. Change water twice a day, for two days.

or **3.** Method 2 can also be used with fresh water. If you have no cornmeal, change water as often as feasible from scrubbing to cooking.

Conch - a Caribbean favorite. Can be purchased cleaned at well-stocked fish markets or those that have a large Caribbean ethnic trade.

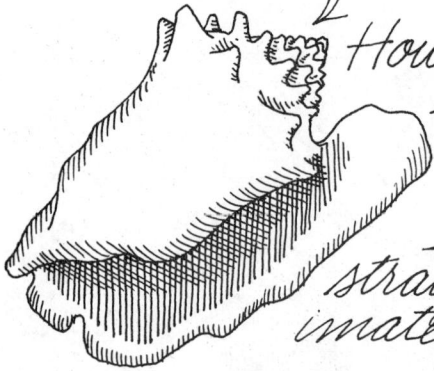

How to clean a Conch (should you be lucky enough to be where they are found).

1. You will need a hatchet and a small, sharp, straight-bladed knife approximately 5 inches long.

5"

2. Lay Conch down on a solid surface with its opening facing down.

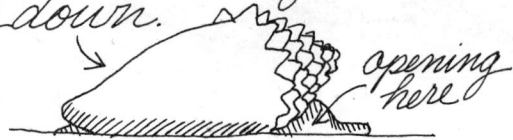

opening here

3. Knock a hole (using the hatchet) between the ridges of the spiral points, halfway between the blunt end and the widest point. Do this on the top-side opposite the opening.

hit here

opening here

4. Insert knife in hole behind muscle that keeps Conch in shell and cut it.

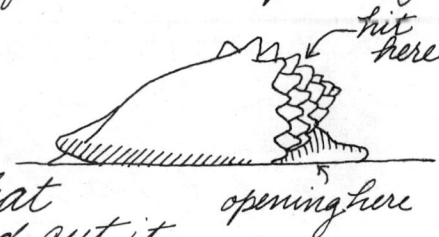

5. Grab "foot" (hard brown shell-like piece at opening) and pull out. Its skin is black or dark grey.

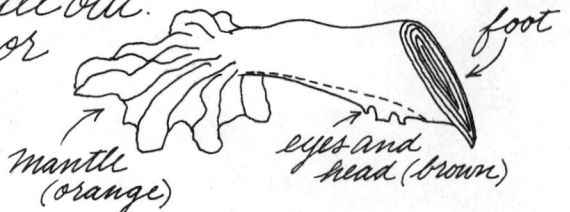

foot

mantle (orange)

eyes and head (brown)

6. Using the "foot" as a handle, cut off head and eye stalks and the orange mantle. Skin remaining Conch. The body will be white underneath. Devein and finally cut off the hard foot. You're ready to look at recipes.

Simple (but delicious) eating.

Raw:

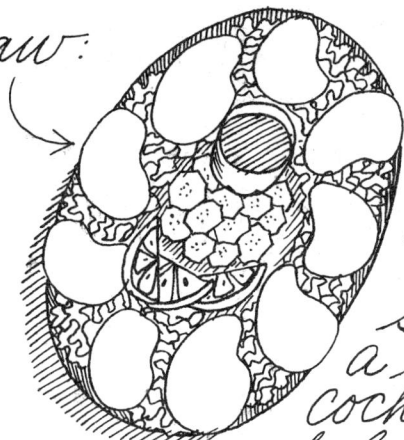

Oysters and hard-shelled clams can be enjoyed raw on the halfshell. They are commonly served cold, often on a bed of ice, with cocktail sauce, wedges of lemon and oysterette crackers.

Tabasco Sauce and extra Horseradish should be available to suit personal tastes.

Steamed:

Clams and mussels are excellent when steamed until their shells open. The liquid in which to steam them is a matter of taste and experimentation. Start with a half inch of plain water and go from there.

BEER

1969 Chabl

Water

TOMATO SAUCE

Broth

The broth, or liquid left from the steaming should be used to "dunk" the shelled mussels or clams in. It not only rinses the last vestiges of sand away, but imparts a flavor that sets it up for its last "dunking" into a bath of melted butter into which some fresh lemon has been squeezed.

Butter & lemon

Fried:

Whether breaded, battered, egg-dipped, or floured, all shellfish are delicious when fried!

Recipes vary, but basically the shells are removed, the bodies dipped and deep-fried in cooking oil heated to about 315°F.

A hint when frying soft clams (Steamers): Slice neck lengthwise. This will enable you to pull filmy skin from clam and also make neck tender.

Another hint: A Wok is the most economical way to deep fry. It uses a lot less cooking oil.

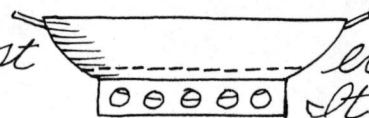

Miscellaneous:

Broth

The broth can be used as a soup base. It can be put in the water used to boil Linguini to further flavor the pasta. It can be used as a basting liquid when baking fish.

Mussels and Clams can be dropped whole into Chowders about ten minutes before serving. They will cook, open, and flavor the soup as well as make it look terrific.

Try this Drop a whole shucked Clam (juice and all) into a Bloody Mary

Miscellaneous bits and pieces.

Abalone, a west coast favorite, is protected by California law from being shipped to other states. Canned and frozen Abalone from elsewhere is available, and a recipe for a tasty hors d'oeuvre is in this cookbook.

Drop whole scrubbed clams or mussels into simmering red or white spaghetti sauce. Cook until the shells open, then serve with the spaghetti.

Scallops are frozen best when placed individually on a cookie sheet or baking pan, then frozen till hard, removed from pan and stored in plastic bags.

Put oysters, clams, or mussels right on grill on a charcoal fire. When they pop open, remove from fire with tongs or gloves and serve with melted butter.

Fresh bay scallops can be marinated in the juice of lemons or limes with chopped or sliced onions, salt and pepper, for a half hour, and eaten raw. Delicious!

If you need to mince clams in a chopper for a recipe, shuck them and freeze individually on a baking pan. When almost hard, put through the chopper. It's easier and a lot neater.

Surround a fish you are baking with a row or two of scrubbed mussels or clams about 15 minutes before the fish is done. They will cook and open and add their juices to the juices in the pan. Baste once or twice and serve. It makes a beautiful looking (and tasting) platter to bring to the table.

Clam broth makes an excellent replacement for water in canned condensed clam chowders.

A simple "to taste" mixture of ketchup, horseradish, and a dash of Tabasco makes a nice cocktail sauce.

Try almost anything!

Captain John Vitalich has fished the
waters of the Pacific from Chile to Alaska,
the Galapagos Islands, Australia, and the
neighboring South Pacific Ocean.

Formerly the skipper for the famed Zane Grey,
his specialty has always been big game.

John now runs the "Ciervo," a handsome
50 foot Sportsfisherman that's moored at
the Lido Yacht Anchorage in Newport Beach,
California. His recipe is for a
Southern California favorite, Abalone.

Baja Abalone Ceveche

1. Get a can of cooked Abalone and slice into pieces approximately an inch long, ½ inch wide, and ⅛ inch thick.

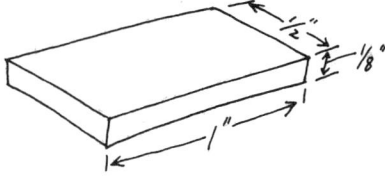

2. Combine all of the following ingredients in a bowl or pyrex dish.

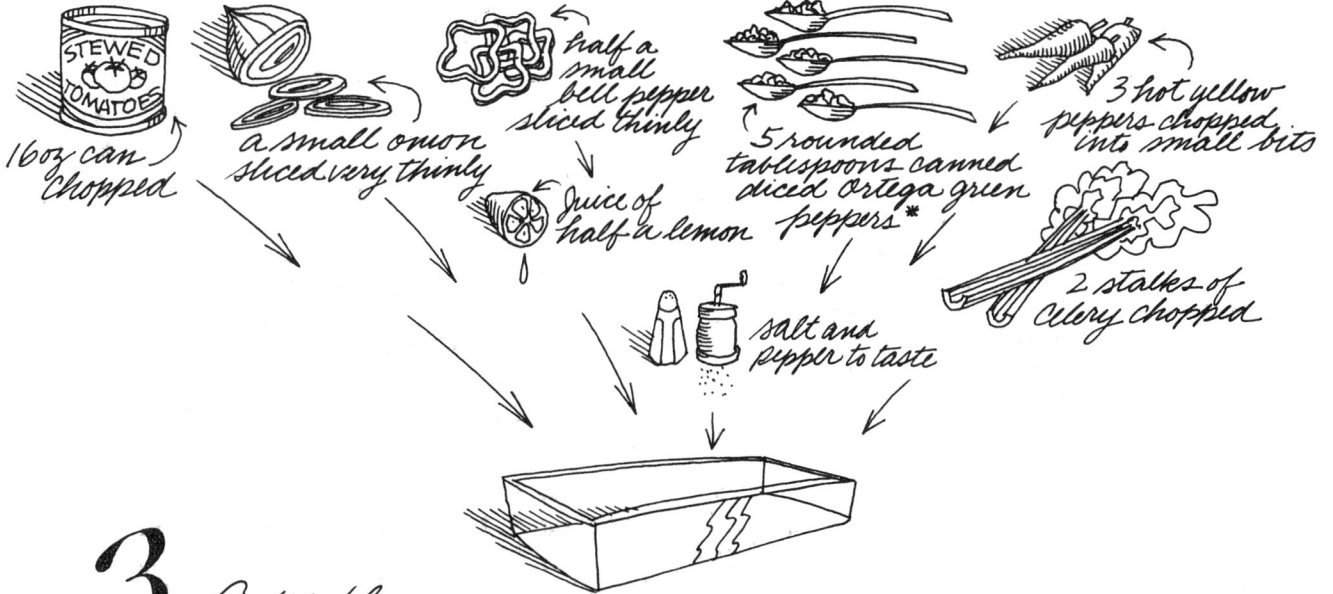

16oz can chopped STEWED TOMATOES

a small onion sliced very thinly

half a small bell pepper sliced thinly

Juice of half a lemon

5 rounded tablespoons canned diced Ortega green peppers *

salt and pepper to taste

3 hot yellow peppers chopped into small bits

2 stalks of celery chopped

3. Add the Abalone, mix, and refrigerate for at least 2 hours before serving.

Makes an excellent hors d'oeuvre.

* If unavailable use 2 more finely chopped yellow peppers.

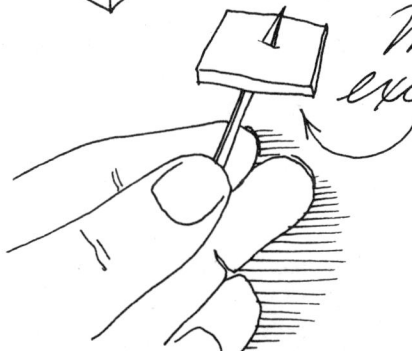

"Happy Hour" is the name of Captain Walter F. Johnson's 40 foot Chris Craft Sportsfisherman that is based at the Belmar Marine Basin in Belmar, New Jersey.

Captain Johnson's recipe for Clams à-la-Casino is another delicious version of this many-recipied taste treat.

Be ready to make seconds.

Clams à-la-Casino, South Jersey Style

1. Open two dozen Cherrystone Clams half-shell style and place in shallow baking pan

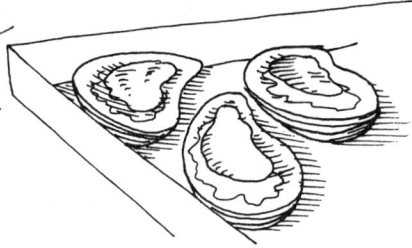

2. Chop up one half pound of onions, a half pound of green peppers and a half pound of raw bacon

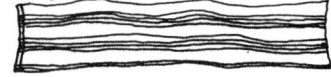

Chop all ingredients very fine.

3. Combine all chopped ingredients and stir lightly to mix.

4. Spoon mixture on to raw clams

5. Top each clam with a teaspoon of melted butter and black pepper to taste.

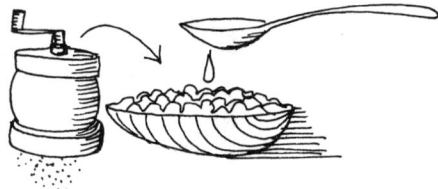

6. Bake in a preheated oven at 400 degrees for 30 minutes and serve. Watch how fast they disappear!

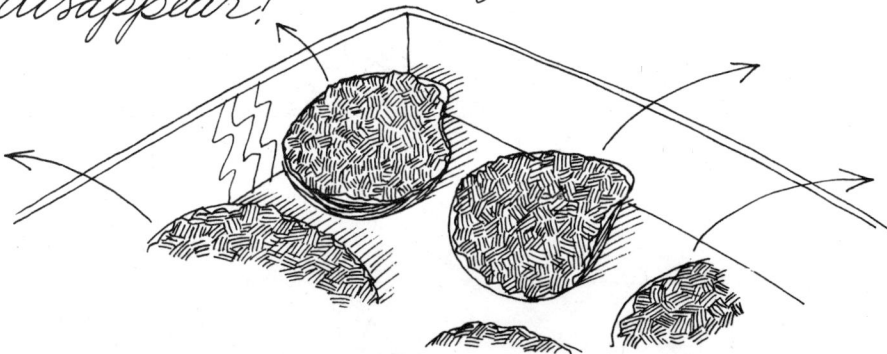

Captain Bob Killey, Senior (shown above) and
Captain Bob Killey Junior (out fishing) are well
known in the Montauk, New York, area
for their fishing know-how.

Bob Senior is Dockmaster at the Montauk
Marine Basin and also runs the "Ghost". He's a
master at night Striped Bass fishing and
daytime lobster trapping.

Bob Junior runs the twin diesel-powered
31 foot Bertram called "Twilight" and makes
his father proud with his offshore
successes with Swordfish, Giant Tuna, and
all the species of East Coast Sharks.

Clams Casino the way Captain Bob Killey likes them best.

1. Take four dozen Cherrystone clams, shuck them, and save both the liquid and half the shells

2. then take three medium onions and a pound of bacon

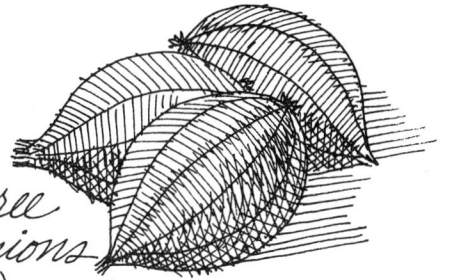

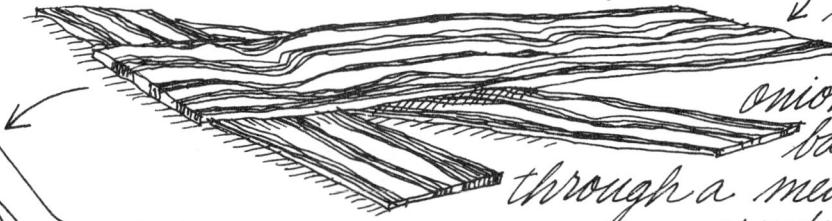

and put the shucked clams, the onions and bacon through a meat grinder

Not a blender

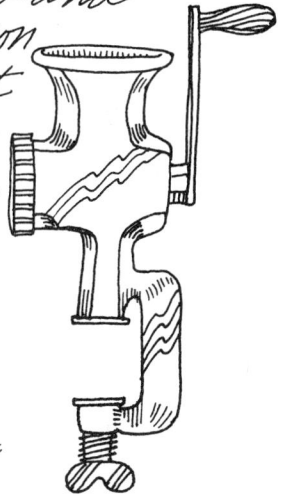

3. Brown the onions, bacon, and clams. Add the clam juice and

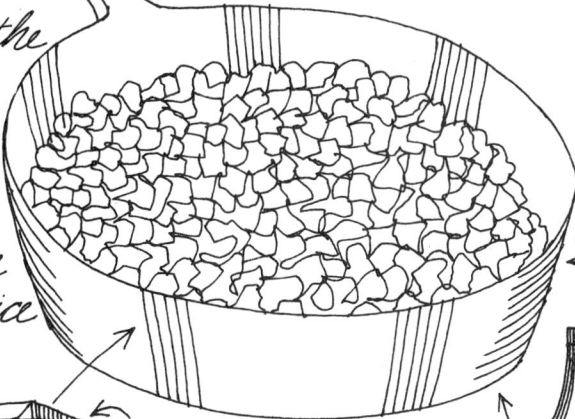

also add

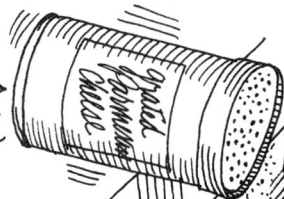

to taste

a dash of tabasco

use enough to give mixture a stuffing quality

Seasoned Bread Crumbs

4. Stuff into the empty Cherrystone shells

5. Place on baking tray, sprinkle with grated Parmesan and bake 20 min. at 350°... Wow!

top with

Captain Glen Frankel runs the "Blue Water"
a 38 foot, twin-engined Egg Harbor that
specializes in offshore fishing out of
Montauk, Long Island, New York.

Although Glen's first love is fishing for giant
Sharks and Tuna, at the end of a long day,
his second love is a big bowl of new
England Clam Chowder. Here's his recipe.

New England Clam Chowder à-la Captain Glen Frankel
(this recipe serves twelve)

1. Place 12 chowder clams in a pot and cover three quarters of the clams with water.

2. Steam clams until they open. remove from shells, chop into small pieces and put aside. Save the broth.

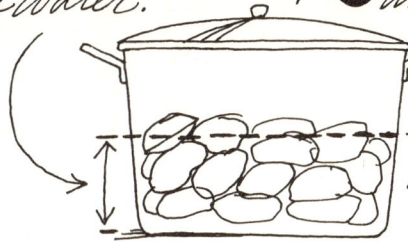

3. Peel, dice, and boil 3/4 of a pound of potatoes. Drain and put aside with clams and clam broth

4. In a large pot, render a quarter pound of salt pork or Bacon.

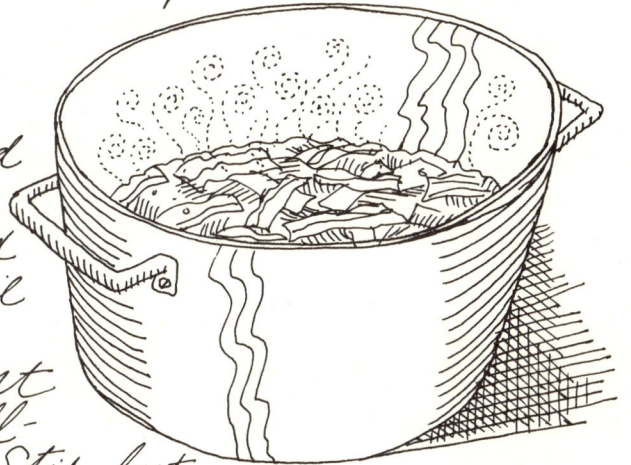

5. Add a half pound of diced onions and cook until they are transparent. Add 2 oz of all-purpose flour. Stir but do not let brown.

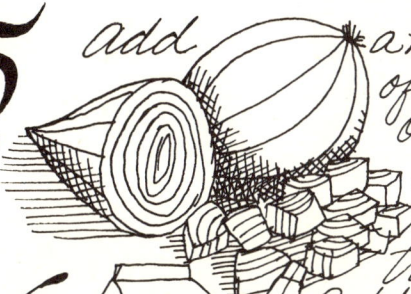

6. Add one qt. of Clam broth and let simmer

1QT CLAM BROTH

7. ONE PINT MILK   Cream 1/2 PINT   Heat milk and cream in a separate saucepan and add to clam broth mixture

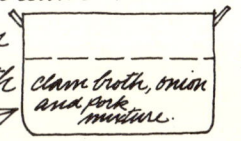

clam broth, onion and pork mixture

8. Season with 1/8 tsp of white pepper, 1/2 Tsp of Worcestershire sauce, and simmer for 45 minutes

9. Add potatoes, chopped clams, dot with butter, serve and enjoy!

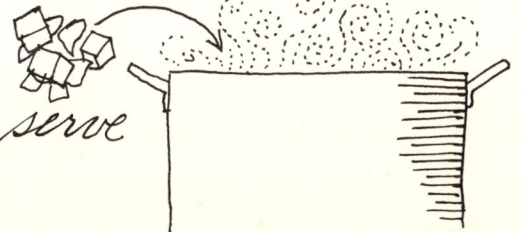

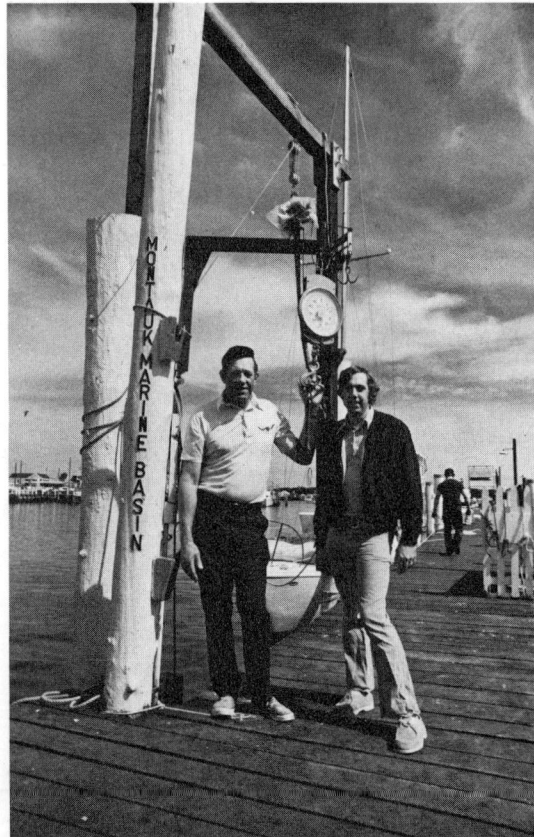

Captain Carl Darenberg is sort of a legend on the Eastern end of Long Island. He's been fishing there for over 30 years now.

When it comes to catching fish, whether its Giant Tuna and Swordfish or the tiniest of Snappers, he's a tough man to compete with. Carl owns and operates the Montauk Marine Basin.

He's shown here with his son Carl, Jr., who is also a Captain and runs the "Fortenate" out of their marina.

You'll rave about this recipe.

A Darenberg family favorite is Soft Clam Pot Pie
(Serves six.)

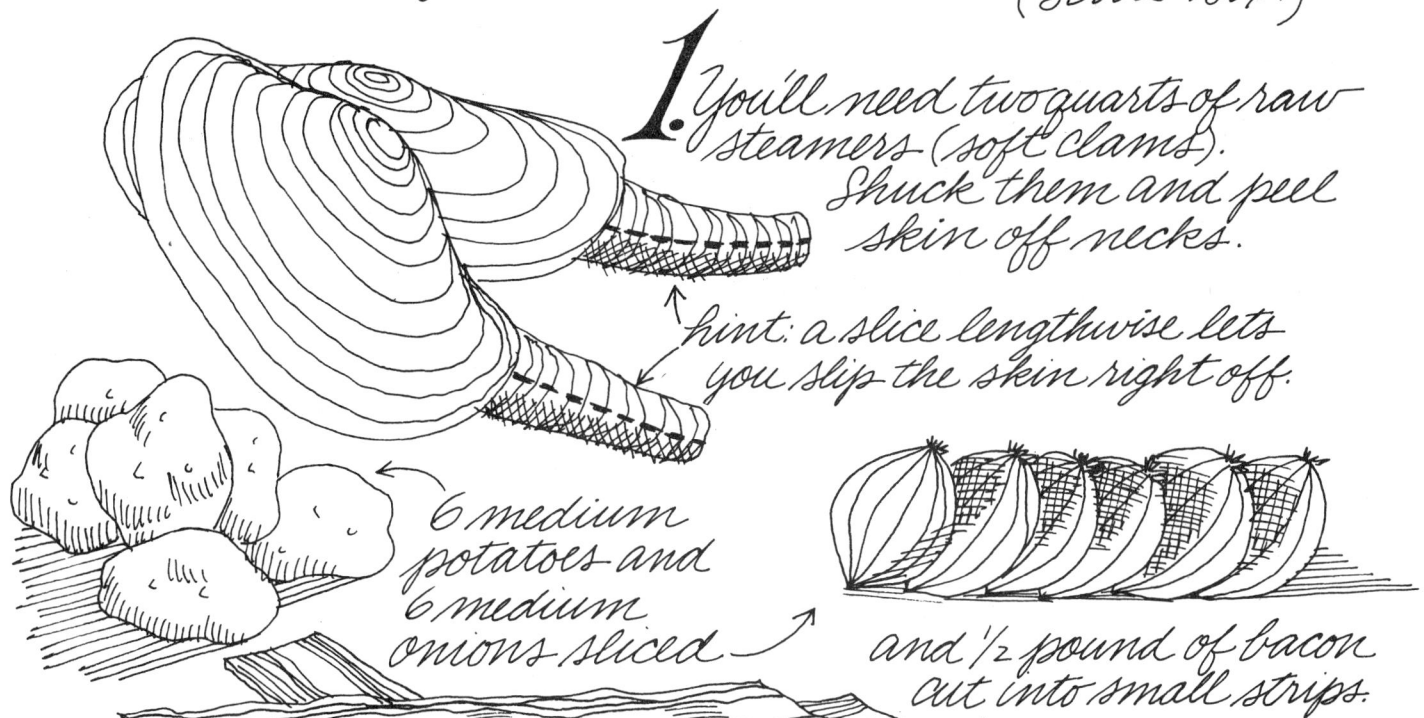

1. You'll need two quarts of raw steamers (soft clams). Shuck them and peel skin off necks.

hint: a slice lengthwise lets you slip the skin right off.

6 medium potatoes and 6 medium onions sliced

and ½ pound of bacon cut into small strips.

2. Sprinkle a tablespoon of flour onto the bottom of a 14" greased casserole dish.

clams
bacon
onions
potatoes

to ½" from top
in layers

3. then add a layer of sliced potatoes on the bottom, then a layer of onion, then bacon, then clams. Continue till you're about ½" from top of dish.

4. Sprinkle top with ½ tsp. of leaf thyme, ½ tsp. salt, 1 tablespoon of flour, ¼ tsp. pepper and ½ cup of clam juice.

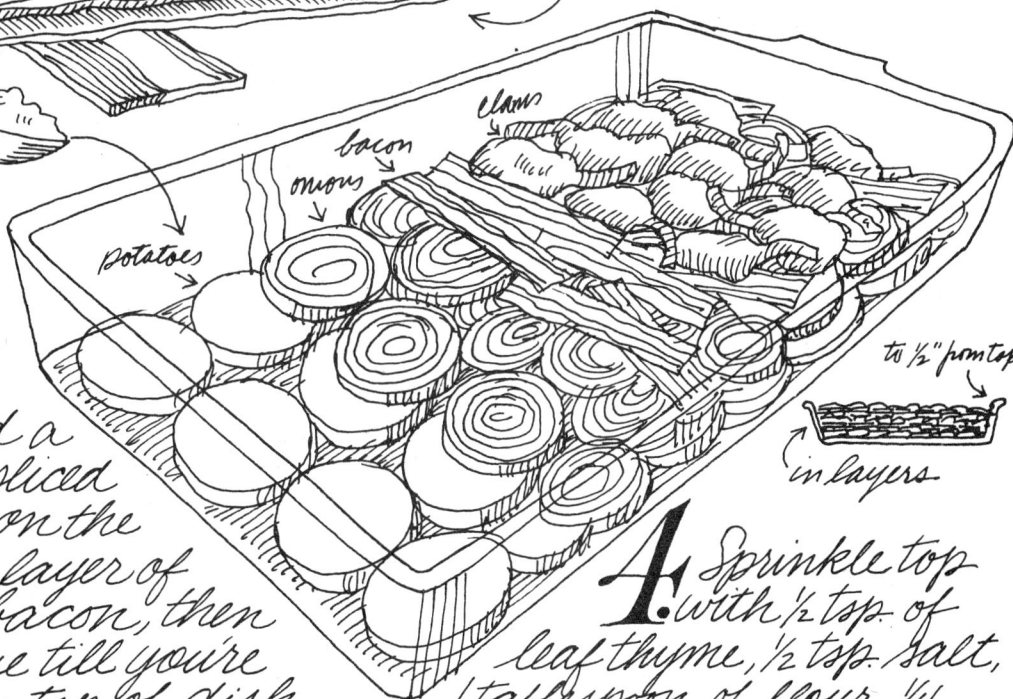

5. Cover with your favorite pie crust mix and cook in a moderate oven at 350° until the potatoes are soft to a fork. Approximately 45 minutes to an hour... It's terrific!

Captain Sam Collins has been chartering
since 1938. He now runs a beautiful 40 ft
Rybovich Sportsfisherman called "Big Blue"
out of the Rybovich Boat Works in
West Palm Beach, Florida.

He fishes the Waters of Florida
and the Bahamas for everything
from Marlin down to Bonefish.

Captain Sam contributes his
recipe for a chowder made from
Conch you'll really like.

A delicious West Palm Beach Conch Chowder
by Captain Sam Collins

1. Take two pounds of finely chopped Conch and place in a bowl that contains

Water ½ cup

the juice of three limes

chopped conch

and marinate 30 min.

2. Drain and place in a cooking pot

with 1 cup ← water

and cook over medium heat until tender.

3. While the Conch is cooking, sauté ¼ cup of finely chopped salt pork or bacon in a skillet until slightly brown,

then add one large onion finely chopped and one large pepper finely chopped and sauté.

4. Now add the ingredients of the skillet to the Conch pot plus

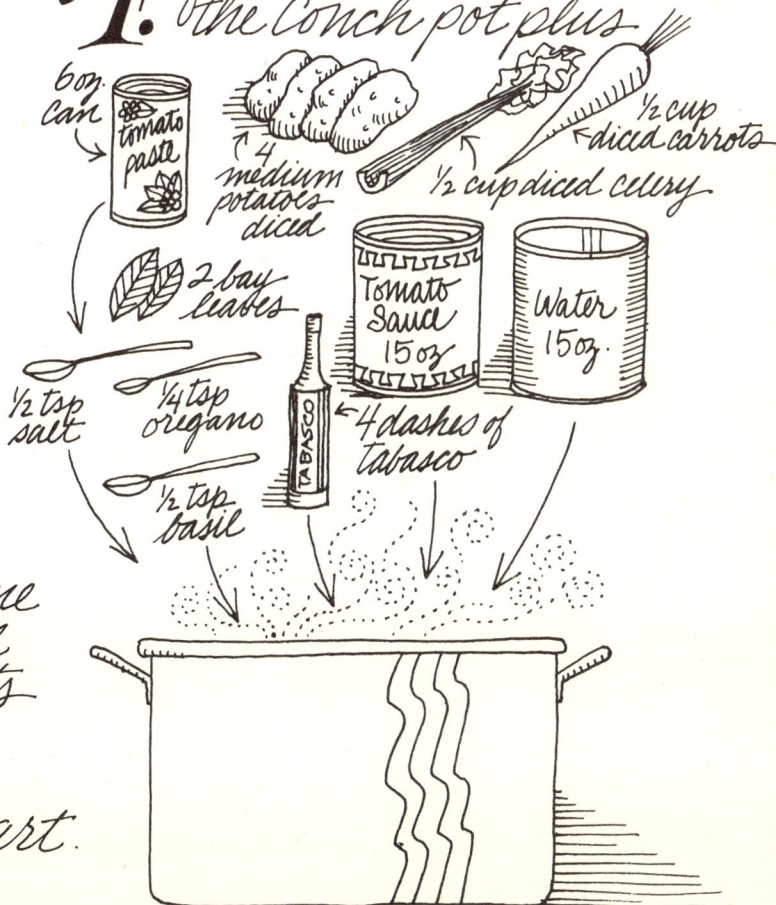

6 oz can Tomato paste

4 medium potatoes diced

½ cup diced carrots

½ cup diced celery

2 bay leaves

Tomato Sauce 15 oz

Water 15 oz

½ tsp salt

¼ tsp oregano

½ tsp basil

TABASCO 4 dashes of tabasco

5. Simmer for one hour or until potatoes and carrots are tender. Do not overcook so that vegetables fall apart. Serves 8-10.

Captain Arthur Moxey is the skipper of the 43 foot "No Limit" that is moored at the Nassau Yacht Haven on the island of Nassau in the Bahamas.

Captain Moxey specializes in all sorts of deep-sea fishing and serves his guests all sorts of native foods during their charters with him.

His Conch Chowder is a perfect example of what to expect, and it is absolutely great!

Conch Chowder Bahamian Style

1. Take a dozen cleaned Conch and beat well with a mallet to tenderize. Then boil for 25 minutes.

2. Cut boiled Conch into small pieces, and put aside.

3. In a large frying pan fry ½ pound of salt pork. Add to the pan

two 8 oz cans

one pound of peeled, sliced onions

two sweet peppers cut into rings

two stalks of celery chopped

Cook until vegetables start to soften.

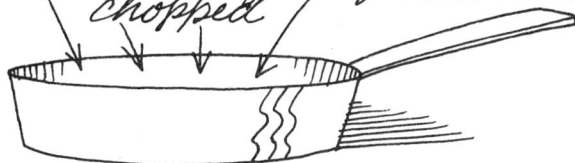

4. In a separate pot, place a layer of peeled, sliced potatoes. Then a layer of broken-up "Pilot Bread" biscuits

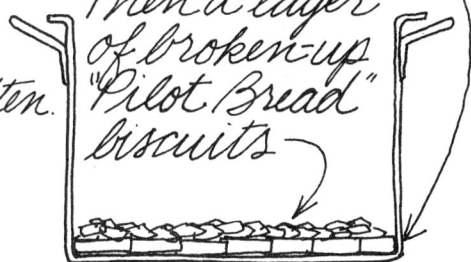

(substitute any good brand of dry biscuits if Pilot Bread is not available).

5. Then a layer of Conch, and on top of that, a portion of the fried-up step 3.

6. Repeat all layers again (until all of Conch and step 3 is used).

step 3
conch
bread
potatoes
step 3
conch
bread
potatoes

7. Season pot to taste with salt, pepper (black) and optional red pepper. Add 2 cups of water, rest lid on pot and place over a medium flame for approximately half an hour. Lid should not completely seal pot.

8. Serve while hot and get ready to dish out second helpings. Recipe will feed 6 well.

Captain Milton Pearce has held ten world records for fishing but by his own admission, he's more famous for cooking than for fishing.

He runs his 42 foot Pacemaker called "Bahama Thunder" out of the Nassau Yacht Haven in the Bahamas.

Captain Pearce's recipe for Crack Conch is so "melt-in-the-mouth good" it will convert you to a Conch lover the very first time you try it.

Crack Conch Bahamian

1. Take one Conch per person and pound to a pulp without breaking apart.

...then season with salt and pepper

2. Dip beaten Conch in FLOUR and then in well-beaten eggs (4 per 8 Conch)

3. Place each Conch in hot fat and brown quickly.

4. Remove from pan and place in deep casserole dish

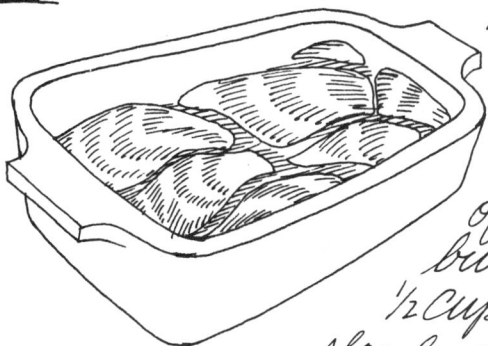

5. Mix ½ cup sherry, 2 teaspoons Worcestershire sauce, the juice of 2 limes, ¼ pound butter, half a green pepper (chopped) ½ cup of mushrooms, BUTTER and simmer slowly until heated and pour over the Conch.

← chopped or sliced

6. Salt and pepper to taste and bake at 350 degrees for half an hour. It will melt in your mouth!

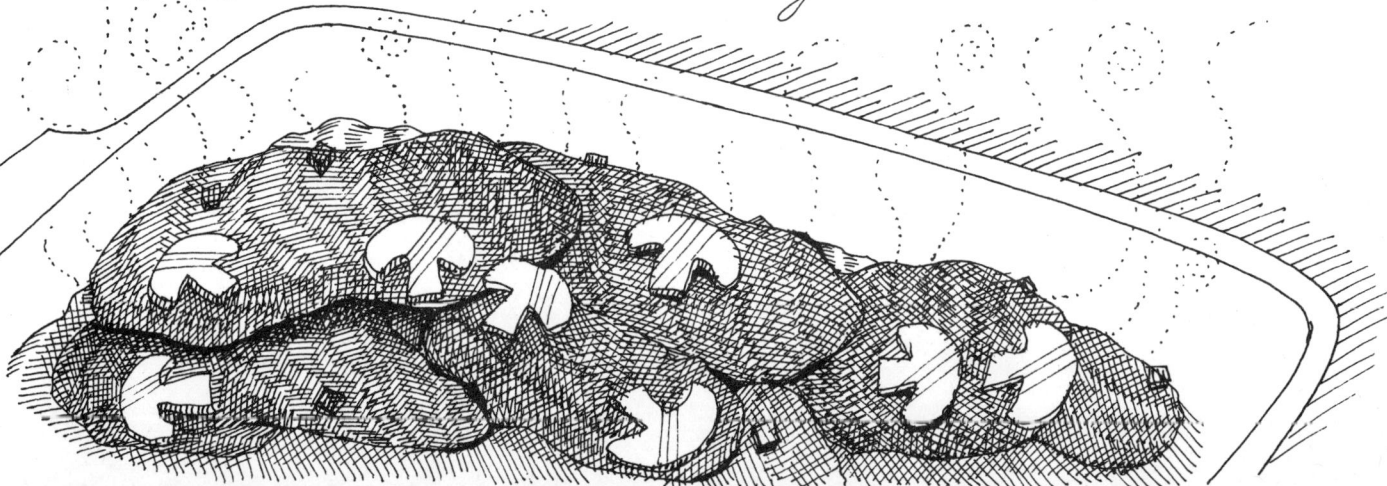

Captain Jack Morrow has been sportfishing
for twenty years off Florida and the Bahamas.
He's also fished the waters of New England,
the Carolinas, Georgia, and as far
south as the Virgin Islands.

Captain Morrow is presently running
a beautiful 50 foot Rybovich Sports
fisherman based in West Palm Beach,
Florida. It's called the "One Bull".

His recipe is for a tasty refreshing
saldd made with Conch.
You'll make it again and again.

Conch Salad, a great West Palm Beach favorite. Mix it up fresh! (Serves 6)

Dice up 8 Conch (it will look like more than this.)

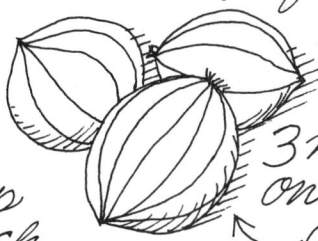

3 medium onions diced.

3 tomatoes diced.

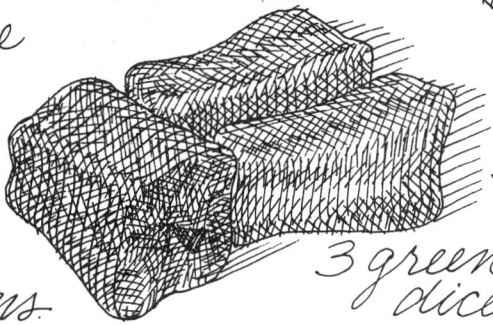

3 green peppers diced.

1½ teaspoons.

lime juice.

¼ cup.

¼ cup.

1 teaspoon salt.

6 tablespoons.

1/8 teaspoon black pepper.

As much as you want to make it as warm as you want.

Combine all ingredients in a salad bowl and refrigerate several hours before serving.

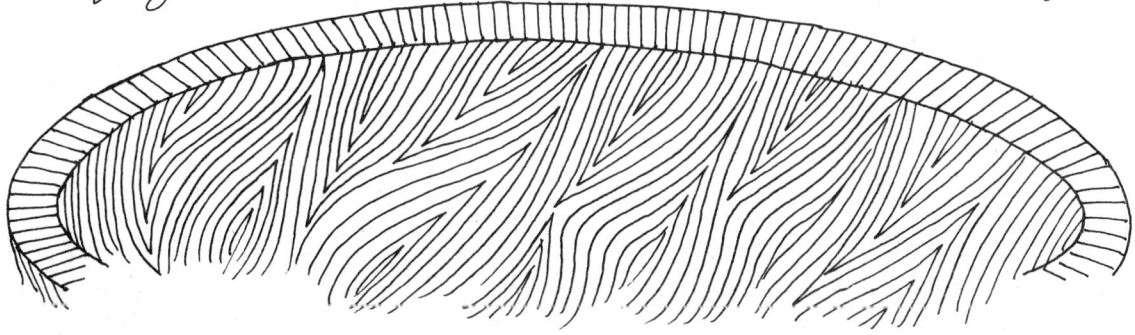

Author's recipe: Mussels steamed Italian style in a zesty tomato sauce. Serves 4 Mussel lovers.

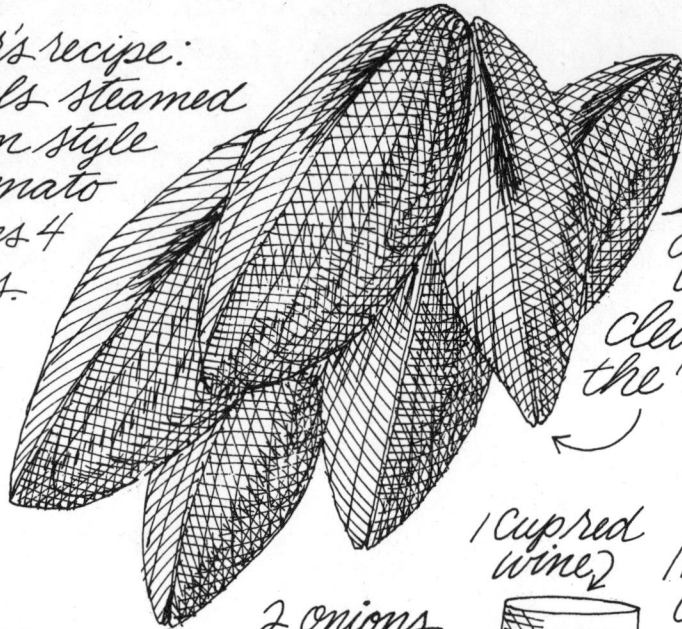

1. Take 3 pounds of fresh Mussels. Scrub them clean and cut off the "Whiskers".

2. Get

One large can → tomatoes

1 Can tomato paste

2 onions chopped

1 Cup red wine

1 Bell pepper chopped

Salt, pepper, and → garlic powder, oregano — to taste

a few teaspoons of olive oil

3. Combine all in a large pot. There won't be this much →

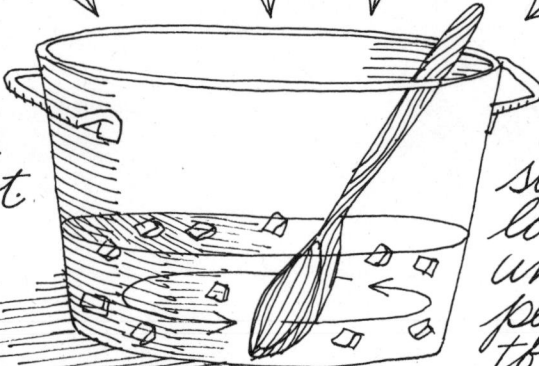

Stir and let simmer on a lowish flame until onion and pepper start to soften.

4. Place Mussels right in the sauce. Cover and steam until all shells open. Shake or stir every so often. Liquid from Mussels will dilute sauce but flavor it beautifully. Serve in big bowls with big towels. Enjoy!

Author's recipe — Mussels steamed in white wine.

1. Scrub them free of sand, algae, and barnacles, then pull off the "Whiskers" as close as you can.

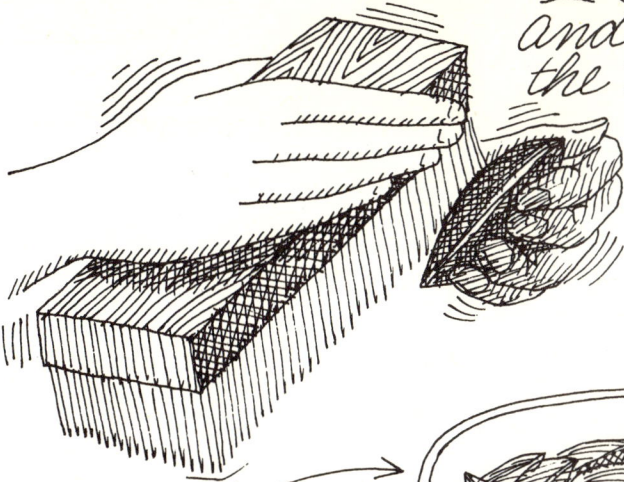

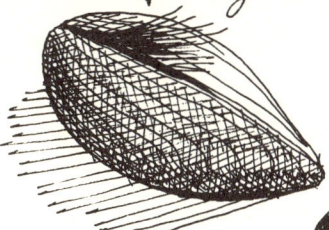

2. Place them in a pot that has a good tight-fitting lid.

3. Add enough dry white wine to cover half of a medium-sized mussel on the bottom of the pot.

4. Steam over a medium flame until all the shells pop open. Shake pot a few times while cooking.

5. Serve with wedges of lemon and a sprinkle of parsley.

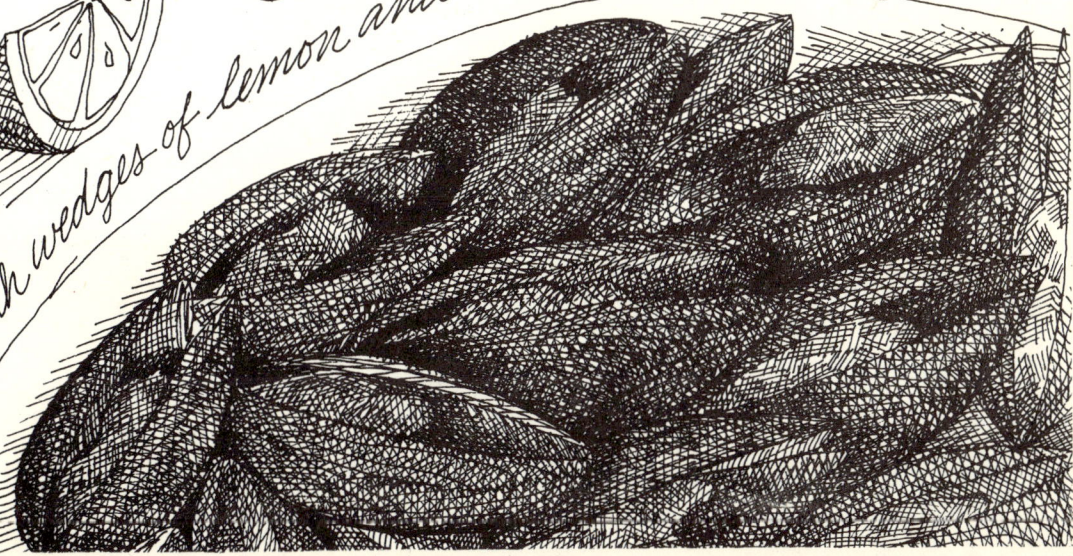

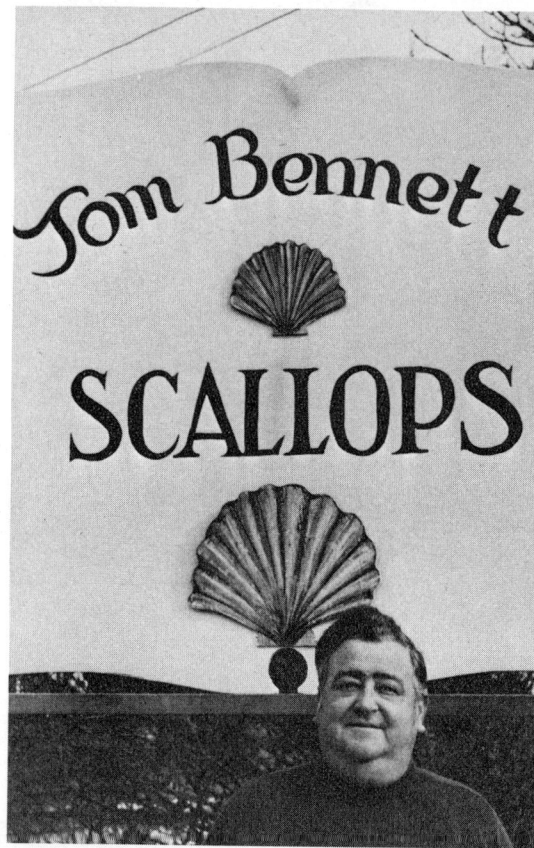

Tom Bennett was born and raised in Amagansett, Long Island. He's spent 18 years of his life in the business of catching, buying, and selling various forms of seafood. The last 13 years have been devoted exclusively to the handling of the delectable Bay Scallop from his operation on Montauk Highway in Amagansett.

Tom's family and a crew of 14 are kept quite busy during the Scalloping season and many of his Scallops find their way to the finest restaurants in Long Island, New Jersey, and Massachusetts.

Scallop Stew for four with fresh Bay Scallops

1. In a large saucepan melt 1 tablespoon of butter and sauté one pound of fresh Bay Scallops for about 5 minutes

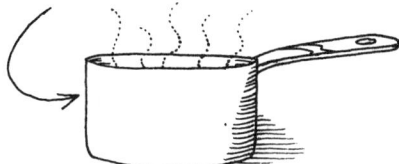

2. Add 3 cups of milk to the scallops in the saucepan and simmer slowly for 10 minutes

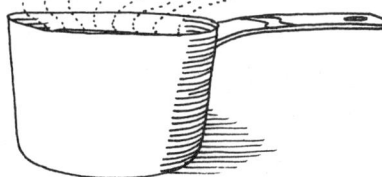

3. Season with salt and pepper.

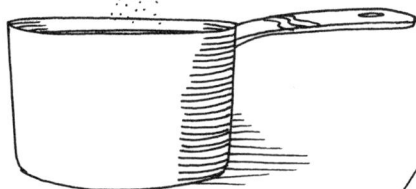

4. Serve garnished with parsley.

Steve Dellapalla stands in front of his "shucking house" which is only about two hundred yards from where he was born on Route 27 in Amagansett, New York.

A professional scalloper for over eleven years, and a professional netmaker all his life, Steve's world has revolved around the farming of the sea.

He sells succulent bay scallops commercially along the whole east coast and is quick to tell you many ways to enjoy them. Here's one terrific way.

Bay Scallops Broiled with Bacon

1. Rinse and drain a half pint of fresh bay scallops.

2. Take eight strips of bacon and cut each strip into six pieces

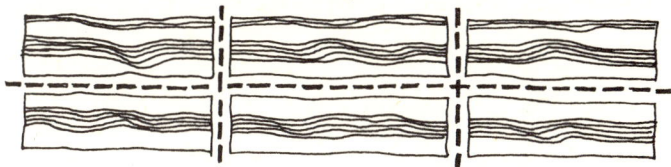

3. Wrap each scallop with a piece of bacon and pin with a toothpick

4. Place scallops on their sides in a broiler tray

5. Broil for 2-3 minutes on one side under a hot broiler then turn each scallop over and broil for 2-3 minutes on the other side.

6. Serve and enjoy hot!

Captain C. Robert Johnson runs
the "Hannah J", a 29 foot fiberglass Bass boat
built in Rhode Island. He sails from
the Falmouth Foreside anchorage
in Falmouth, Maine, where he
charters for Bass, Bluefish, and Mackerel.

Casco Bay, Maine, yields beautiful
medium-sized Scallops in the winter
months. Bob's recipe for slow-
cooked Scallops is a treat.

Bay Scallops cooked in White wine, Maine Style.

1. Melt a half stick of butter slowly over low heat in a frying pan.

BUTTER

2. Add white wine until there is about 1/4" in bottom of pan and slowly warm.

VIN BLANC

3. Squeeze in some lemon to taste, and black pepper.

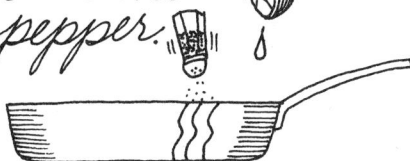

4. Add Scallops to the wine, butter, lemon, and pepper mixture.

5. Slowly warm, not really cooking, as they can become tough. Turn Scallops in warm liquid slowly. Test by tasting.

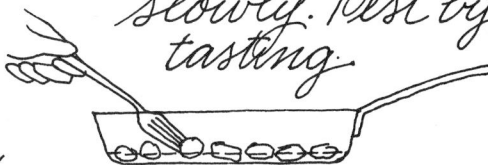

6. Serve on warm plates with parsley on top.

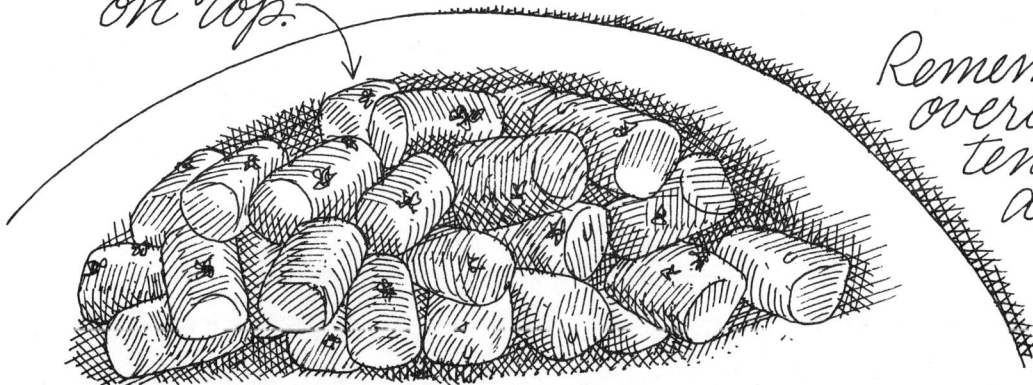

Remember, do not overcook. It's tender and delicious.

Author's recipe   An Oyster appetizer that is also terrific when made with Clams.

A dozen opened Oysters or at least three per person

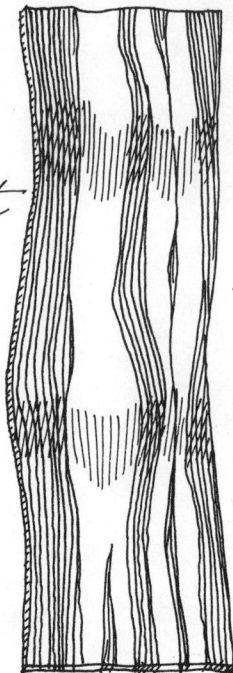

One Oyster-sized strip of bacon per Oyster

and some seasoned bread crumbs

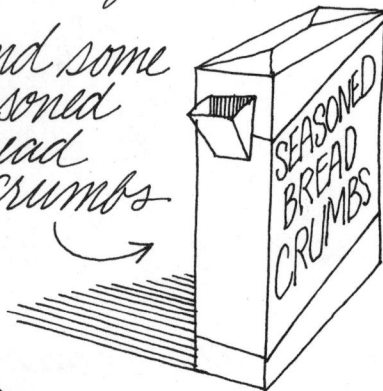

SEASONED BREAD CRUMBS

1. Place opened Oysters in a tray. Take care not to lose the liquid in the shells

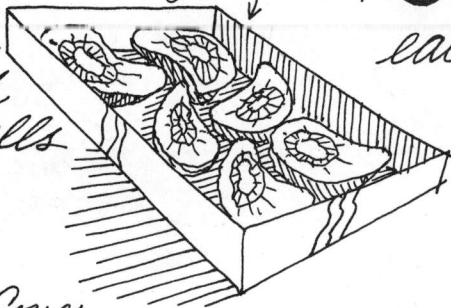

2. Fill each Oyster with bread crumbs

SEASONED BREAD CRUMBS

3. Cover each Oyster with a strip of bacon

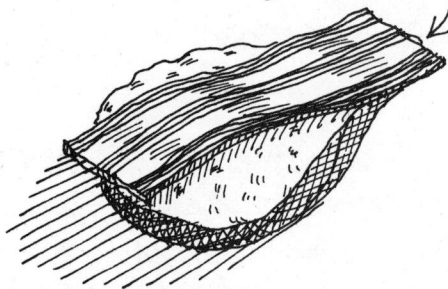

4. Broil until bacon is crisp, and get ready to make seconds!

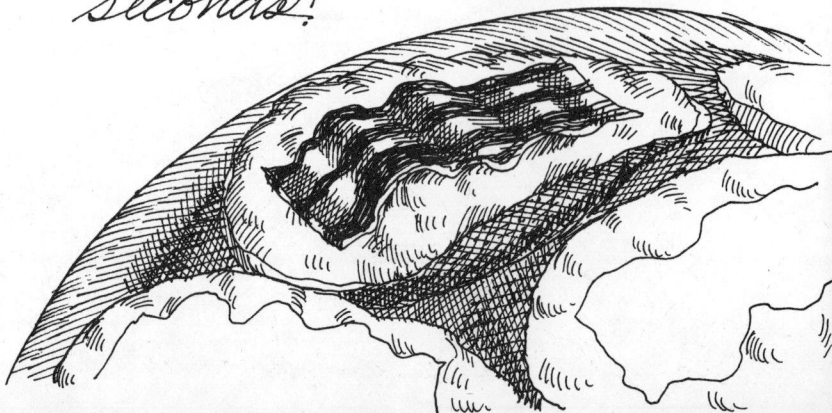

The Shrimp

In volume, by far America's
favorite shellfish, eaten by young
and old alike in all forms.

Whether the tiny variety found in
colder waters, or the jumbo, almost
lobster-like varieties, shrimp
have found their way into the hearts
and menus of almost every
culture and society.

Read on, and then see what
your creative mind might cook
up for these versatile creatures
of the deep.

How to prepare Shrimp.

Shrimp are usually sold headless. Preparing them is very simple as there is hardly anything you can do wrong with them.

1. they are easily shelled by hand.

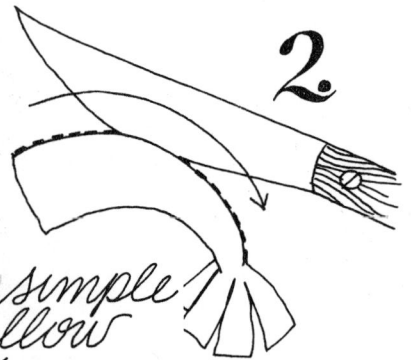

2.

Shrimp can be served in a multitude of ways. The "Shrimp Cocktail" is simply boiled, shelled Shrimps on a bed of lettuce, served with a sauce.

A simple, shallow cut across the curved back exposes the vein to remove. (Do so with the edge of knife or toothpick.)

Basic Boiled Shrimp

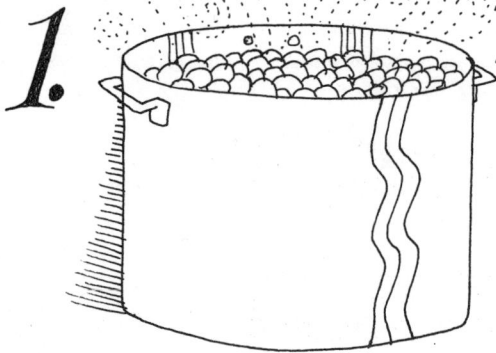

1. One tablespoon of salt to a quart of water. Bring water to a boil.

2. Put in Shrimp

3. Reduce heat and simmer for five minutes

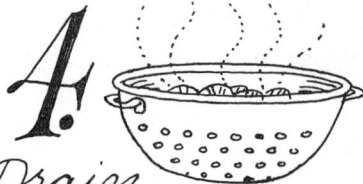

4. Drain and serve... some like it chilled, some hot.

Mmm good!

Fried Shrimp (Tempura Style).

1. Shell, devein, and rinse the amount of shrimp you want to make. Whether you leave the tail on when de-shelling is just a matter of taste.

2. Prepare a batter with a mixture of:

1 egg   water   FLOUR   SOY SAUCE ← a dash

medium thick consistency

3. Dip Shrimp first into flour then into the batter.

4. Deep fry in oil that is heated to 375°F.

use a frying basket   or   a wok →

Sautéed Shrimp

1. Leave Shrimp in shell! Rinse well.

2. Sauté a clove of garlic in butter. Use enough butter to cover the bottom of your pan.

3. Sauté Shrimp in garlic butter until tails are crisp. Try one as a test. Shells will peel right off. Serve with lemon.

Shrimp Miscellaneous:

In a red Spaghetti sauce: Drop shelled, deveined shrimp into simmering sauce about 10 minutes before serving.

In a white Spaghetti sauce: Sauté whole shelled and deveined shrimps (or cut them up into smallish pieces) in butter and garlic, then put into white sauce before serving.

In chowders and fish stews: Drop shelled, deveined shrimp (whole or in pieces) into the chowder about 10 minutes before serving.

On rice: Place shelled, deveined shrimp on top of cooking rice about 10 minutes before heat is removed. They will steam on the rice, then stir in. (Mussels and clams work well this way too, except put them in 5 minutes earlier than the shrimp. I like to combine them all.)

In salads, of course: Add whole or cut-up boiled shrimp.

In noodles (regular or Japanese style): Cut up shelled, deveined shrimp and add to cooking noodles about 10 minutes before serving.

In stuffings for both fish and poultry: Cut up shelled, deveined shrimp and add to your stuffing mix.

Yakitori style: Place individual shrimp (shelled or unshelled) lengthwise on bamboo skewers and hold in deep, hot fat (with or without batter) until done. Serve immediately.

Author's recipe

Roasted Shrimp in the shell. A great looking, great tasting first course. (Serves about 6.)

1. Take 2 pounds of medium or large-sized shrimp. Do not shell. Hint. If frozen, defrost and sprinkle a handful of flour on them. Scrub thoroughly and wash off. (It takes away that sometimes "fishy" smell.)

2. Make a pasty marinade of:

1½ tsp garlic powder

GARLIC POWDER

CUMIN
1 tsp

SALT

1½ tsp

¾ tsp red pepper

3 tblsp lime juice

3. Combine spices and lime juice. Add Shrimp and marinate for one hour.

4. Transfer Shrimp to a broiling pan or skewer on bamboo sticks. And broil about 5 min. on one side, and 5 min. on the other. The shells may char but the meat will be fine.

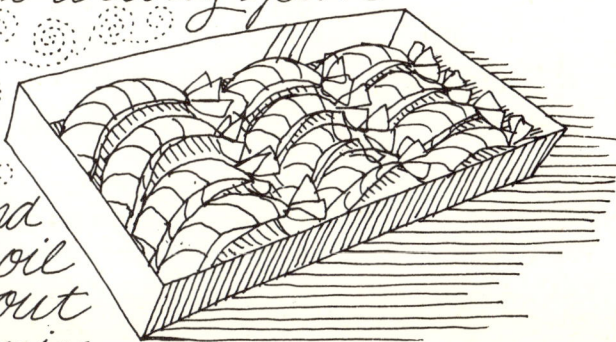

48.

Captain Billy Wagner is known as the "Cajun Conch" because he fishes primarily the southeast Louisiana coast and the Florida Keys in a big 38 foot Bertram Cabin Cruiser. It's named the "Shearwater".

Captain Bill, his daughter, and youngest son are shown here with a beautiful Tarpon his daughter took off the Florida Keys.

Look for him at the Duck Key Marina or Coral Key Village, and you may find him in the galley cooking up some of his Crawfish Delight.

Crawfish Delight. You can make it with shrimp, crawfish, or Florida lobster meat.

1. Prepare one cup of shelled shrimp, crawfish, or lobster meat. (Drop shrimp, crawfish, or lobster into boiling water for 3 to 5 minutes, and shell.)

2. Combine

CREAM OF SHRIMP SOUP — 1 can condensed

½ CUP MILK

Hellmann's Real Mayonnaise — 1 cup Mayonnaise

2 cups cooked thin noodles or vermicelli.

3. Add shrimp, crawfish or lobster.

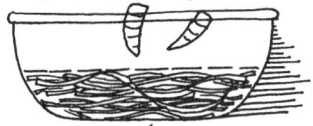

4. and place in a buttered baking dish.

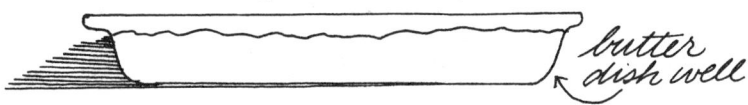

butter dish well

5. Cover with grated cheddar cheese.

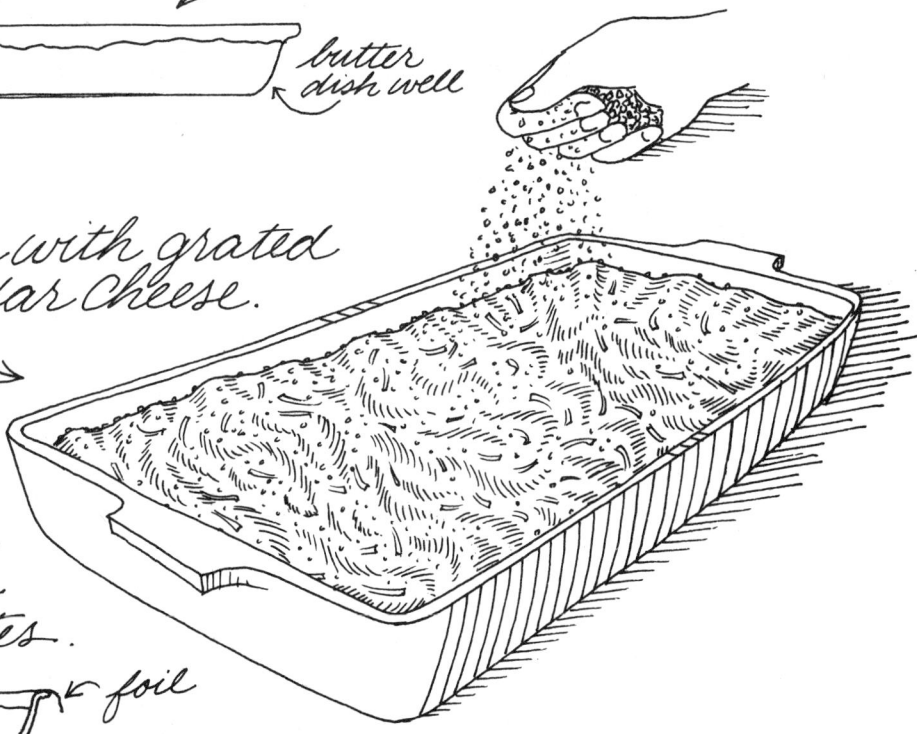

6. Bake covered in 325° oven for 30 minutes.

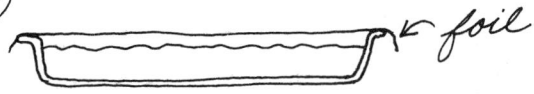

foil

Serve 4 with a tossed salad, green vegetable, crusty rolls, and Key Lime pie.

Captain Robert Parsons and his wife
Bev are a husband and wife team that run
the 60 foot Bertram called the "Len II."

They spend part of the year at the Kona Kai
Club in San Diego fishing for Albacore and
Swordfish, and the other part of the
year in Baja fishing for Marlin and
Roosterfish. What a life!

Their recipe is for jumbo shrimp
and it's jumbo good!

Jumbo Shrimp Mexican Style

1. Drop as many jumbo shrimp as you feel you'll need in salted, boiling water. After water boils again, lower heat, simmer five minutes and drain.

2. Shell and devein shrimp leaving part of the shell extending from tail to pick → them up by.

3. Boil 2 cups of white rice and put aside

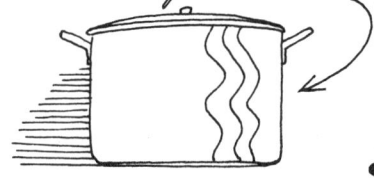

4. Partially cook and drain one pound of bacon strips cut in half →

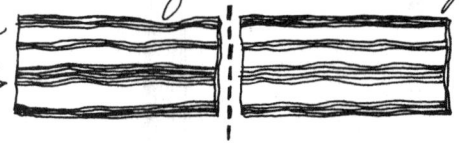

5. Make a basic white sauce by mixing

BUTTER 2 tablespoons
FLOUR 2 tablespoons
MILK MILK 1 cup
SALT

6. Heat mixture slowly and grate into this sauce one cup Chihuahua cheese and one cup Oaxaca cheese. (Substitute Jack cheese if others are not available).

7. Lightly butter a large serving dish or pan. Fill with rice and pour cheese mixture over rice. →

8. Place jumbo shrimp and partially cooked bacon on rice and place in broiler until bacon is crisp. Wow!

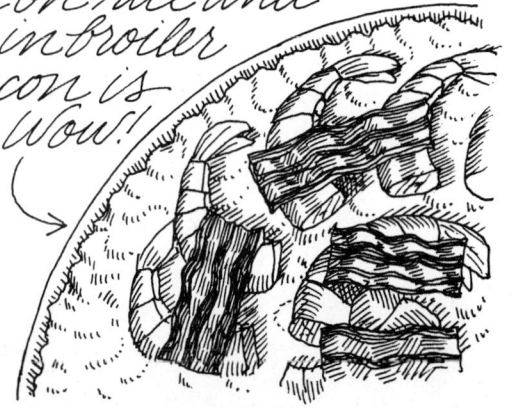

Captain Jules and Betty Langston live
an enviable life on board their beautiful
custom-built Sportsfisherman the "Fiesta".
They spend the five summer months
at Hatteras, North Carolina, the Blue Marlin
capitol of the world, and the five winter
months at the private resort Ocean Reef
Club in the upper Florida Keys. The months
between are spent going from one to the other.

Originally from Louisiana, Captain Jules'
favorite recipe is for a Shrimp Creole that in
Hatteras is called Pamlico Sound Medley.
We call it just plain terrific!

Pamlico Sound Medley (Shrimp Creole).

1. Melt one stick of margarine in a large pot then add

MARGARINE

4 cloves of garlic finely chopped or crushed

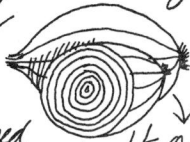

1½ Onions diced

1½ Green peppers diced

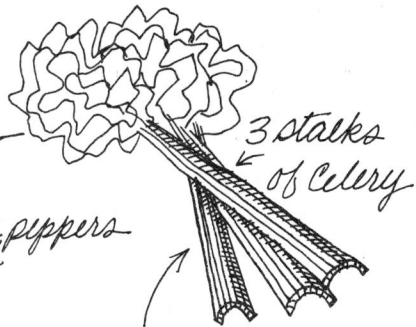

3 stalks of Celery

dice, tops and all

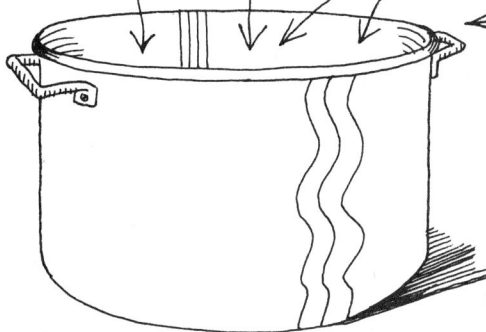

2. Cook slowly, stirring often until tender, then add:

TOMATO SAUCE — 1 can 16 oz

BOUILLON — 1 can 10 oz

4 bay leaves

Sliced MUSHROOM — 1 can 4 oz

PIMENTOS — 1 can (diced)

1 pkg → FROZEN SLICED OKRA

¾ tsp chili powder

1 tsp salt pepper thyme basil chopped parsley

Cook over low heat for 2 hours

3. While basic mix is cooking, take 2 pounds of un-shelled shrimp and add to enough boiling salted water to cover. Cook 8 min., pour off water and shell.

4. After cooking 2 hours, add the 2 pounds of shrimp and a half pound of crabmeat. Simmer 10 min and serve on rice. Mmm! Feeds 6 to 8.

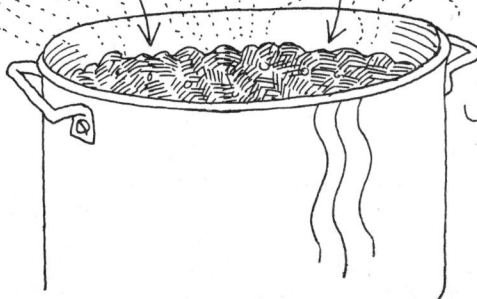

Captain Bruce Barnes is the Captain
of two very different fishing boats.
One is the 105 foot "Qualifier 105"
shown above. It specializes in 7-day
trips to Mexican waters out of
Fisherman's Landing in San Diego.

The other is a 48 foot Sportsfisherman
called the "Silver Fox" that can take up
to six people in air-conditioned
comfort on executive-type charters from
Marina Cortez, also in San Diego.

Captain Barnes' salad is a "Must".

"Escondido Salada" from Southern California that is absolutely fantastic.

1. Mix together:

½ cup mayonnaise

½ teaspoon dill weed

¼ teaspoon salt

juice from half a lemon

Mix in small bowl and put aside.

2. In a large salad bowl, combine two hard-boiled eggs, chopped, one large ripe avocado, chopped, one stalk of celery chopped, two lobster tails, cooked and in bite-sized pieces, twelve large boiled shrimp in bite-sized pieces, (or one small can) and one ripe tomato chopped.

3. Squeeze in a half lemon over the chopped salad and mix.

4. Mix in dressing. Season to taste and serve with corn chips. Muy Bueno!

5. An Economy Salada can be made by substituting two cans of white Chunk Albacore for the lobster and shrimp. Its equally enjoyable.

Crabs and Lobsters

Whether it's the Dungeness crab of the
West Coast, the popular Blue Claw of the
East, the Alaskan King, the huge-clawed
Maine lobster, or the long-antennaed
Spiny lobster of Caribbean fame,
these denizens of the deep provide
some of the most succulent flavors
of the sea to those lucky-enough
to partake of them.

Boiled, broiled, steamed, stuffed,
split, baked, creamed, bisqued,
chowdered, sauteed, stewed, chilled,
picked, sauced, or smoked, their
flesh is worth every minute it
takes to pick and pull it from
the nooks and crannies of
their shell-covered bodies and legs.

One wonders who first was brave
enough to consider eating one of these
sea monsters. One also smiles to
think of how this bravery was rewarded.

Crabs... most common are the Blue Claw
hardshell variety on the East Coast
and the Dungeness Crab on the West Coast.

How to prepare.

Boiled... throw live crabs into a large pot
of rapidly boiling water (add a tablespoon of salt
per quart of water and ¼ cup of white vinegar).
You can also add spices if
you wish. Some people use Cayenne
pepper or "Old Bay" seasoning (1 teaspoon).
When water returns to a boil, let
boil 5 minutes, then simmer 15 more.
They're done.

salt

VINEGAR

Steamed... Place crabs on a raised
rack at least 2 to 3 inches high.
Add equal amounts of water and vinegar
to a point just below the rack.
Bring to a boil and place rack over
the water.
Steam for about 20 minutes. They will
turn bright red.
They're done.

hold
from here

Watch out
for these

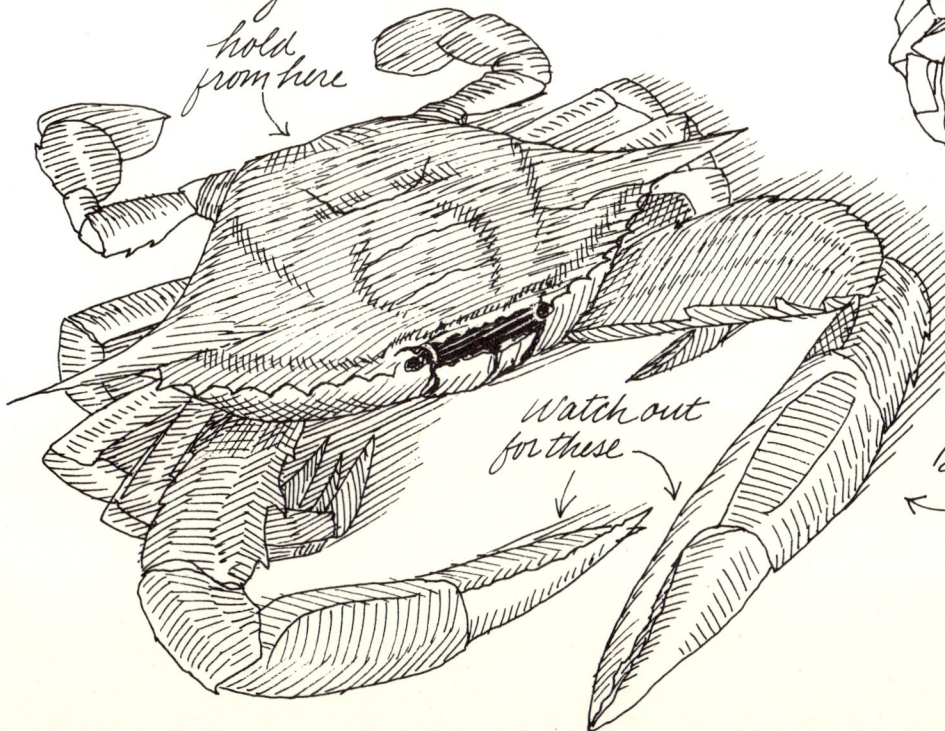

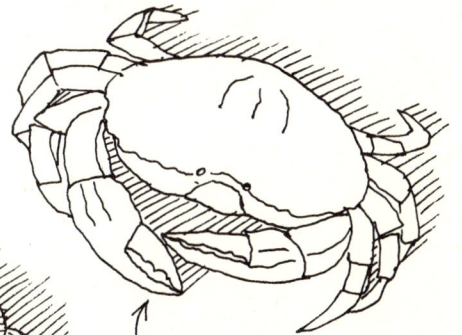

Dungeness
(is actually a larger
species than the
Blue Claw).

How to clean a hardshell crab.

1. Break off two large claws with a simple twisting action. These can now be cracked with the use of a pair of nutcrackers or a wooden mallet.

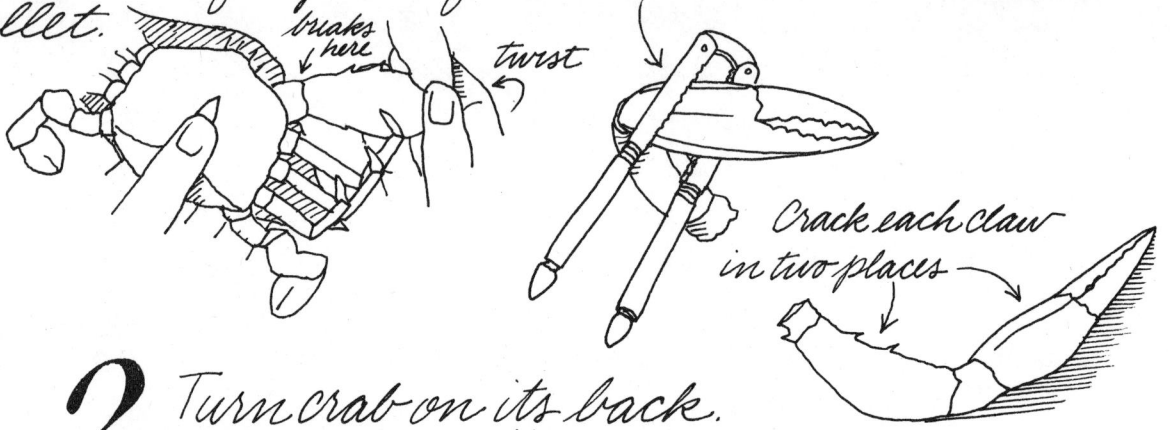

breaks here

twist

Crack each claw in two places

2. Turn crab on its back. You will notice a pointed flap on the underside. Lift with fingernail and pull back until complete upper shell comes off with it. You can wash and save top half of shells for later use as individual baking dishes.

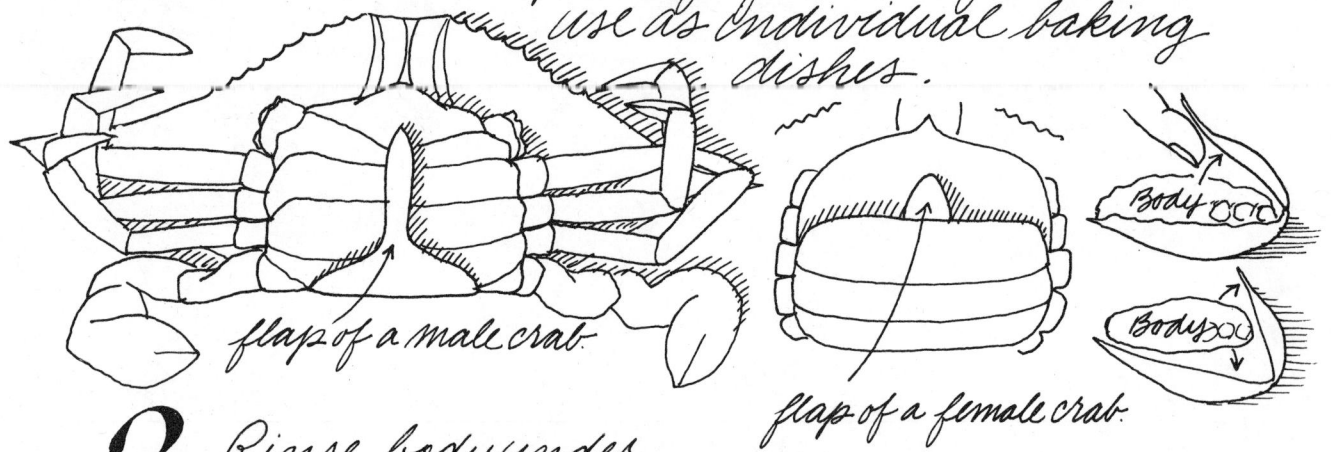

flap of a male crab.

Body

Body

flap of a female crab.

3. Rinse body under running water. Push out all soft spongy matter in center cavity and feathery gills on top of both halves of body. Break body in half and you're ready to grab a nut pick and start!

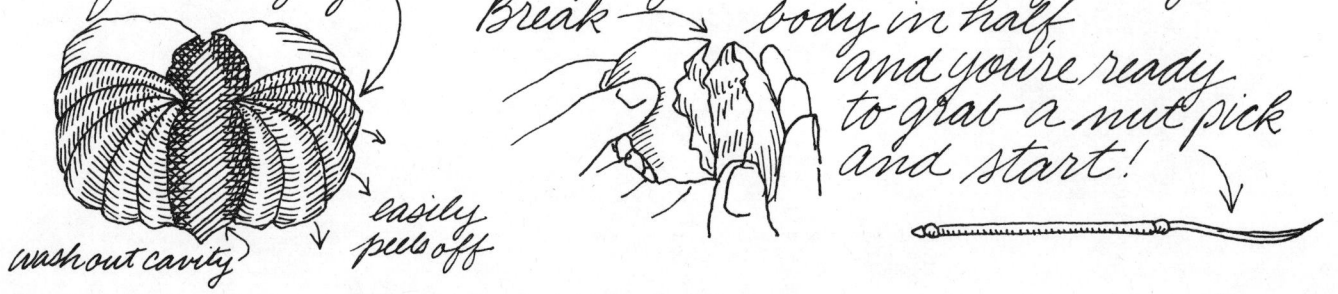

wash out cavity

easily peels off

Soft Shell Crabs

Very delicate, very delicious. You eat the whole thing... and love every bit.

How to clean.

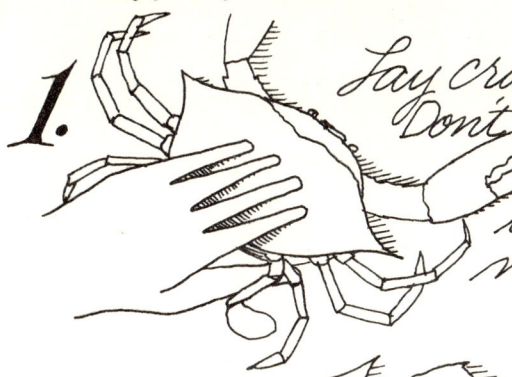

1. Lay crab on cutting board. Don't be afraid as it is in its "shedding" stage and is so soft it can do you no harm.

2. Take a sharp knife and quickly cut off "face" of the crab. This will kill it and allow you access to its insides to remove entrails and gills.

3. You can now easily lift up "points" on each end of crab, insert your finger and remove feathery gills on each side and soft intestinal sac in center.

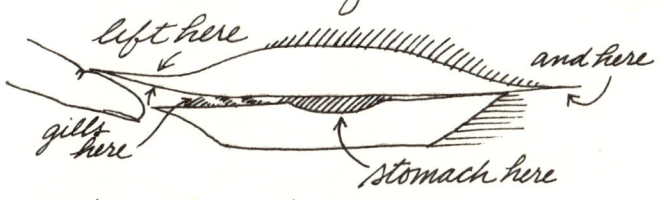

lift here
and here
gills here
stomach here

4. Rinse in running water and pat dry with a paper towel. Dip in egg, then in flour. You can now saute in butter, deep fry in 375° oil, or broil. The choice is up to you. All are equally delicious.

5. Serve on toast with crisp lettuce and a Tartar sauce.

Captain Ralph Blair's "Eva Mae II" is a 44 foot Pacemaker Sportsfisherman that sails from Charleston, South Carolina, in search of Blue Marlin, Sailfish, Dolphin, and King Mackerel.

The Gulf Stream is where this boat and its Captain feel most at home, but this delicious favorite of Ralph's doesn't come from the Gulf Stream, it comes from the bays. Its crabmeat, prepared in a very special way.

"Crab Imperial" from South Carolina

1. Take one pound of Crabmeat and make sure all shells and cartilage have been removed. Hold aside.

2. Melt one tablespoon of margarine or butter.

3. Add in one tablespoon of flour, then slowly add ½ cup of milk, stirring constantly to keep mixture smooth.

4. Cook, stirring mixture over medium heat until it comes to a boil and thickens (2-3 minutes).

5. Mix in one teaspoon instant minced onion, 1½ teaspoons Worcestershire sauce and two slices of white bread, cubed with crusts removed.

6. Let mixture cool and add ½ cup mayonnaise, the juice of half a lemon, a teaspoon of salt, and a dash of pepper and blend.

7. In another pan, melt a tablespoon of butter until lightly browned. Add crabmeat and toss lightly. Combine with sauce mixture and stir well.

8. Spoon mixture into individual shells (or greased 1 qt casserole), sprinkle with PAPRIKA and bake at 450° for 10-15 minutes. Fills six 5 inch shells. lightly browned on top. "mmmm."

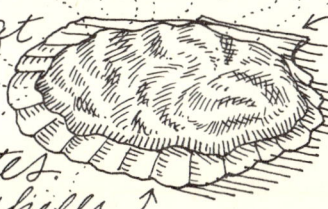

Captain Wayne P. King was first mate on his father's charter boat, the "King George", for twenty years.

He now owns and operates the "Capt. Joe" out of Freeport, Long Island, N.Y., and specializes in both ocean and bay fishing for the many species of fish that inhabit Long Island waters.

Captain Wayne's favorite "Crab Witch's Brew" will add a new spark to an old crab-lover's taste buds.

Crab Witch's Brew (nice 'n spicy).

1. Take a large pot that will hold a dozen hardshell crabs (or more) and about 4 quarts of water. Use one that has a cover.

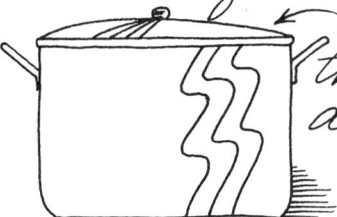

2. Put into pot of water, one tablespoon of salt for each crab, 2 heaping tablespoons of "Crab Boil*" or "Shrimp Boil" mixed spices, the tops (leaves) from one bunch of celery (or 2 sticks cut up), ½ teaspoon celery salt, 1 teaspoon black pepper, and 2 tablespoons of Red Hot or Tabasco sauce.

3. Bring mixture to a boil and stir for 5 minutes. Add ½ cup of white vinegar after boiling has occurred.

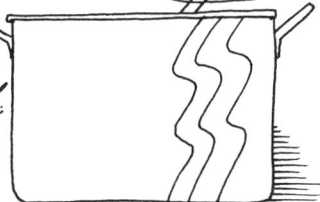

4. Wash off crabs in fresh water and dump in boiling brew. Cover and boil on low heat for 12 minutes. Watch that it doesn't spill over.

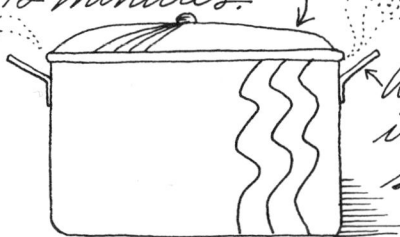

5. Serve on platter hot or cold. They'll be "out of this world!"

* A packaged potpourri of spices available where seafood is sold. "Old Bay" is a popular brand on the East Coast.

Mitch Zetlin was the Mate on the "Moustache" for six years. He now fishes the waters of Maryland and Virginia except for a two week offshore trip to Long Island waters every August.

Mitch is shown here with a near world record Blue Shark of 205 pounds he caught on 20 pound test line while fishing off Montauk, New York, on the "Colleen".

His recipe for Mock She-Crab Soup is followed by another one that is also the author's favorite, Chinese Cracked Crab.

An old Maryland favorite: Mock She-Crab Soup

You'll need a pound of fresh crabmeat or the meat picked from six or more crabs →

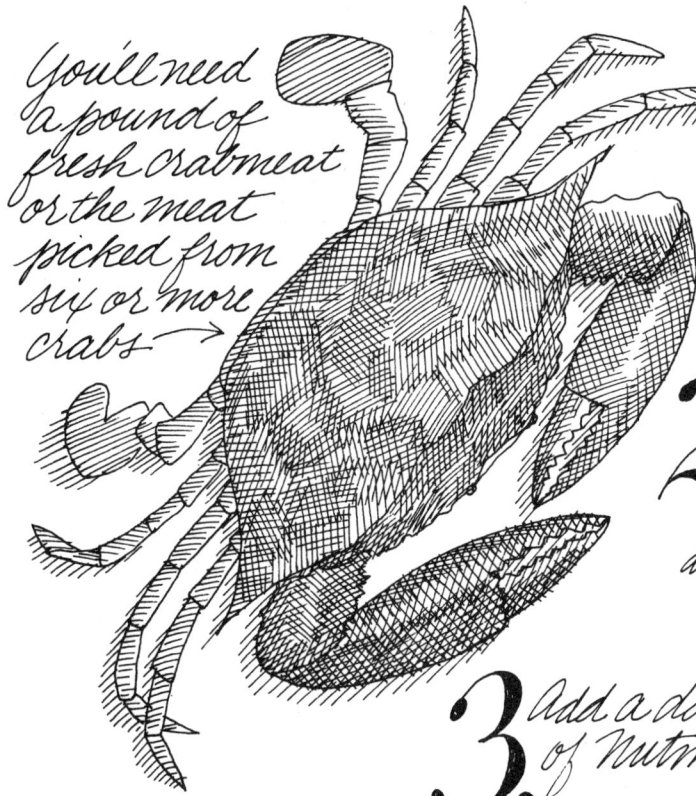

1. Combine half-and-half, evaporated milk, and crabmeat.

two 13 oz cans →

evaporated milk

evaporated milk

HALF HALF 1 qt ←

2. Force two hard-boiled eggs through a sieve. Add a tablespoon of Old Bay seasoning * if available or else spice to your tastes

any kind →

3. Add a dash of Nutmeg → NUTMEG

heat, but do not allow to boil, stirring regularly until flavors meld.

4. Immediately before serving, add one quarter cup of Sherry Mmmmm!

Sherry

1/4 cup

5. the flavor of the soup may be enhanced by making it in advance and letting flavors blend while refrigerated for a few hours before reheating.

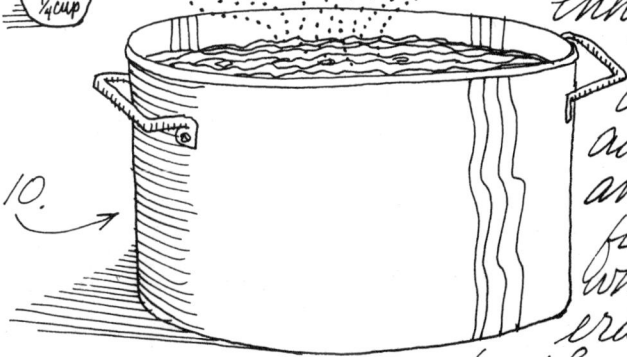

Serves 10.

* more easily found in fish markets than in supermarkets in most areas.

Chinese Style Cracked Crab à-la-Mitch Zetlin

1. Boil live crabs just until killed. Do not cook.

2. Clean crab in cold water. Break off claws. Turn over and lift off top shell by lifting flap and ripping upward. Wash out body viscera and feathery areas on the body.

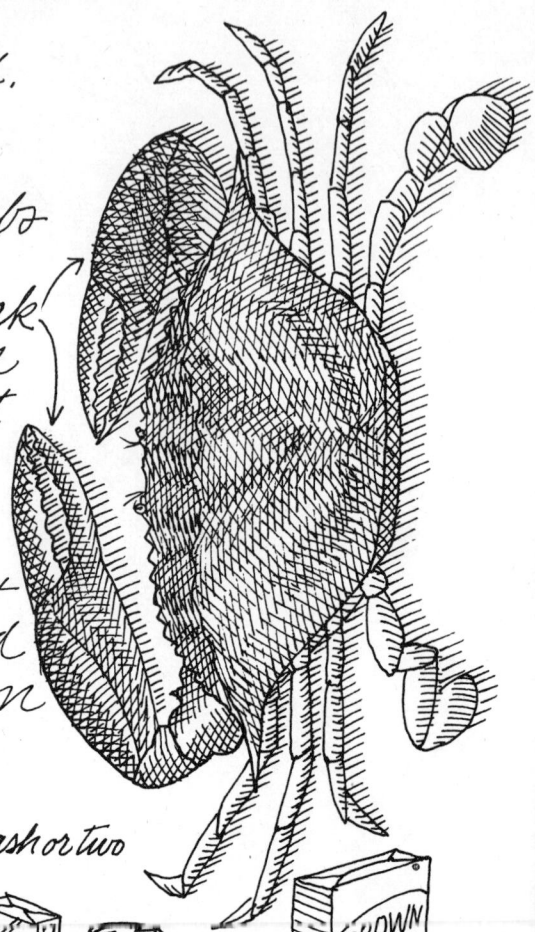

3. Crack claws with small mallet or nutcrackers

4. Take Crab pieces and fry in peanut oil for 3 to 5 min.

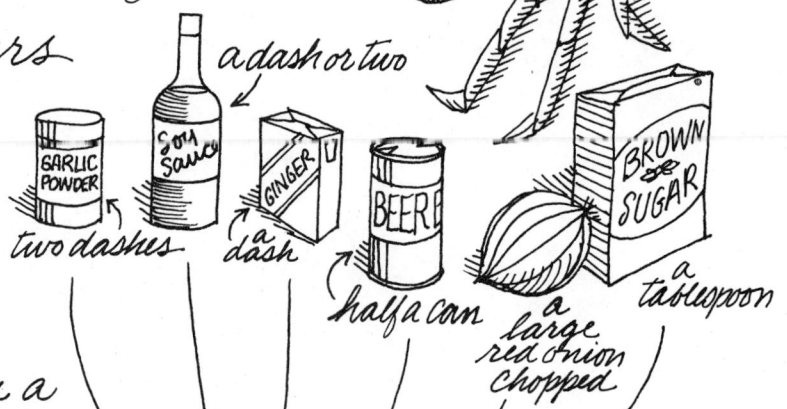

careful of popping oil

GARLIC POWDER — two dashes

Soya Sauce — a dash or two

GINGER — a dash

BEER — half a can

a large red onion chopped

BROWN SUGAR — a tablespoon

5. In a Wok or a skillet, combine ingredients and cook until onion softens a bit.

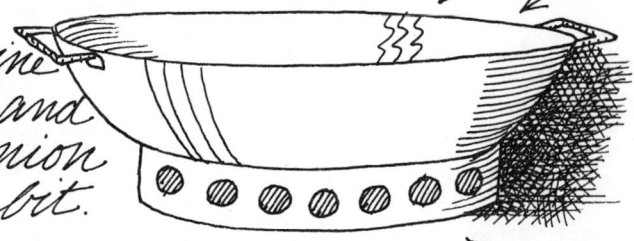

6. Dump in fried crabs. Stir in sauce so it gets into shells. Garnish with chopped scallion

Climb in and enjoy!

Lobster... most popular of the shellfish, no matter where it is found. Also the most versatile. There is hardly anything you can do wrong to it, except overcook it.

the Maine or Northern lobster is recognized by its big Claws. If it only has one, it's called a "cull".

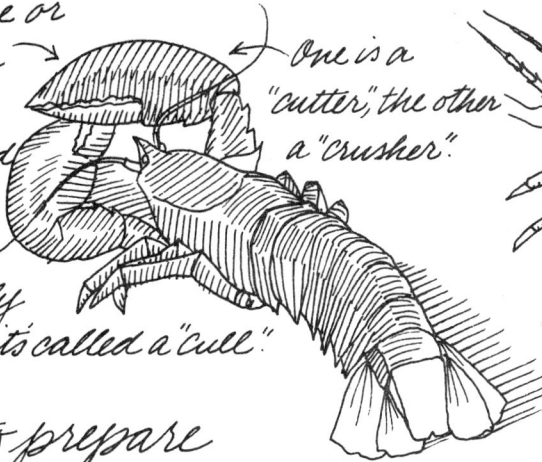

One is a "cutter", the other a "crusher".

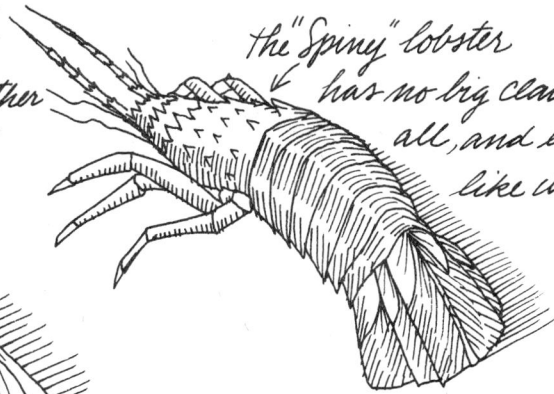

the "Spiny" lobster has no big claws at all, and looks like its name.

How to prepare

Boiled... Plunge lobster head-first into a large pot of salted, boiling water (add one tablespoon of salt per quart of water).
Bring water back to a boil and time.
A lobster of 1¼ to 2 pounds should cook about 10 to 12 minutes. Over that size, add about 3 minutes a pound.

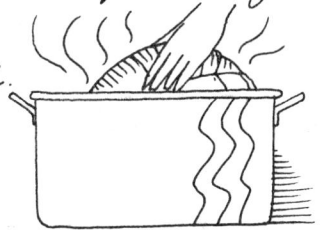

Steamed... Place lobster on raised rack in a steamer. Bring water to a boil, cover, and steam for about 20 minutes (for a 1-2 pounder).

Broiled... there are two methods. the first is to parboil lobster for 7 minutes. Split, clean (see cleaning instructions), lay on its back, brush with butter, sprinkle with bread crumbs (stuff if you wish), and broil for 5-7 more minutes.
The second is to split the live lobster (see cleaning instructions), lay lobster on its back, brush insides as per previous method and broil 20-30 minutes per 1¼ to 2 pounder.
In both, cut away membrane from both sides of tail to expose all of meat to the broiler.

How to clean a lobster for broiling.

1. Lay lobster on a cutting board (back down). Take a sharp knife and cut it right down the middle lengthwise.

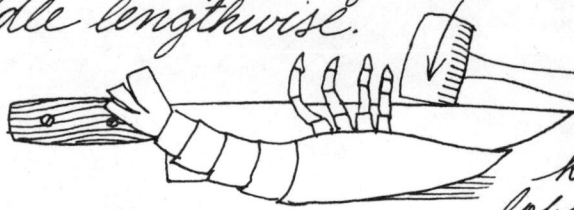

← this can also be done by laying a large knife on underside of lobster and hitting it with a wooden mallet.

2. Spread split lobster apart. Reach right behind the eye section in the head. You will find a smallish sac there. Pull out and discard.

3. Also remove black vein running under meat from head to tail. Do not remove the coral (red roe found in females) and the Tomalley (the greenish part) as they are quite edible.

4. You're ready for the broiler. You may choose to cut away the membrane on either side of the tail for greater exposure to the broiler. Do this with poultry shears.

5. Salt, pepper, butter (and maybe bread crumbs if you like) and you're ready to go.

Author's recipe — *Lobster Fra Diavolo*

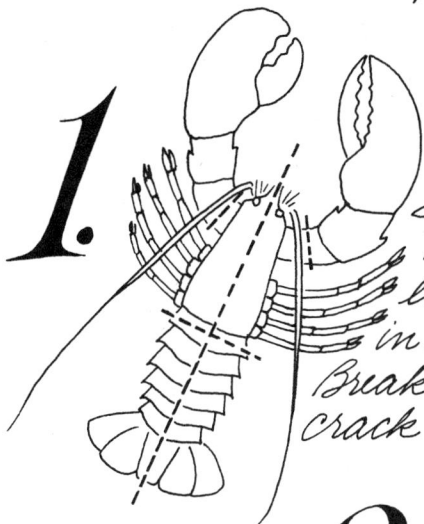

1. Split 2 1½ to 2 pound lobsters. Cut in half again. Break off and crack claws.

2. In ⅓ cup of olive oil, sauté 2 cloves of garlic minced, one medium onion minced. Use a deep pot or sauce-pan with a lid. Sauté for only 2-3 minutes.

3. Now add lobster pieces. Sauté flesh side down for 3 minutes. Remove and put aside.

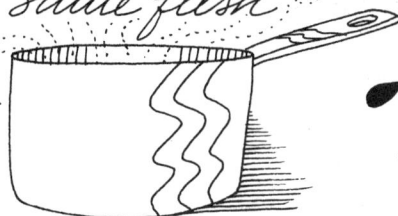

4. Add to oil, garlic, and onions — 2 tablespoons of chopped parsley, a 35 ounce can of Italian tomatoes (crushed). ¼ teaspoon crushed red pepper. A tablespoon each of oregano, basil. 1½ teaspoons salt, and let simmer for 30 minutes.

5. Add lobster and cook for 10 minutes more, then

6. Serve over pasta with a red wine and big napkins!

Captain Bobsy Holder runs the
39 foot twin diesel-powered Avenger called
the "Jupiter" out of Montego Bay, Jamaica.

Bobsy is a Blue Marlin specialist
and has won the International Marlin
Tournament held annually at Port Antonio,
Jamaica, so many times it's embarrassing.

This is his favorite recipe for Curried
Caribbean Lobster. You'll like it.

Jamaican Curried Lobster the way Captain Bobsy makes it in the galley of the "Jupiter".

Buy or catch 4 spiny lobsters that are alive and kicking.

A pot as big as necessary with a lid. →

1. Plunge lobsters head-first into boiling water. Add one teaspoon salt to each quart of water. Boil for 20 min. If you are using maine lobsters (1½ to 2 lbs) boil only 10 minutes.

2. Split down the middle on the inside and pull out all the meat from the lobster.

Break tail from body and set aside for stuffing.

3. Season the meat with salt, pepper, and a large chopped onion.

4. Sauté all in butter for 6-7 minutes, sprinkling in curry powder to taste.

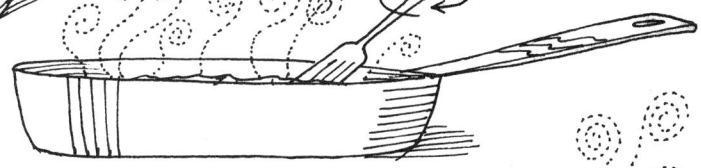

5. Place back in lobster tails. Garnish with chopped parsley serve and enjoy! →

Captain David L. Moree, Sr., specializes
in marlin fishing out of the
Yacht Haven Marina in Nassau, Bahamas.

His boat is a big 48 foot Chris Craft
named the "Island Lady."

Captain Moree's recipe for lobster
can be adapted for the Maine lobster
too. No matter which one you use
it will come out delicious!

Bahamian Stuffed Lobster fit for a King

1. Boil Caribbean "Spiny" lobsters for about 20 minutes (or Maine lobsters for about 15).

2. Lay lobster on its back and split in half lengthwise with a sharp knife, and clean out stomach sac and vein.

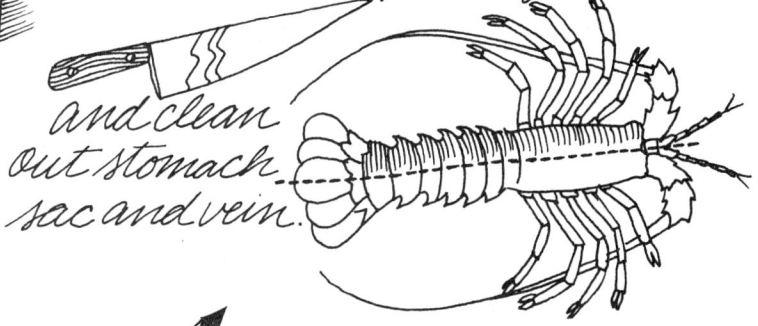

3. For 6 lobsters, chop one onion, a sweet pepper, and a stalk of celery and fry in oil until brown. Add a leaf of Thyme after frying.

4. Mix ingredients with a medium-sized package of instant mashed potatoes.

5. Stuff mashed potato mixture into the insides of the split lobster. Add a touch of salt, pepper, and Add a little lime juice, sprinkle with paprika, and spread with butter.

SALT

garlic powder

6. Put lobster in broiler and broil until brown. Serve with cole slaw and native rice and peas. Fit for a King... or Queen!

Captain Ken Young is a native of Ogunquit, Maine. In addition to lobstering, he fishes for Maine Shrimp, Cod, Haddock, and other North Atlantic fish.

The "Ugly Anne", a 40 foot lobster boat with a seating capacity of 30, is moored in Perkins Cove in Ogunquit. From May to October she takes out passengers on scenic cruises demonstrating how lobsters are caught, and explaining the lore of lobstering and the coast of Maine.

Captain Young's recipe for lobster stew can be changed to a hearty lobster chowder by adding a diced onion and four cooked, diced potatoes to the sauté. Both recipes are great.

"Ugly Anne's" Lobster Stew for six.

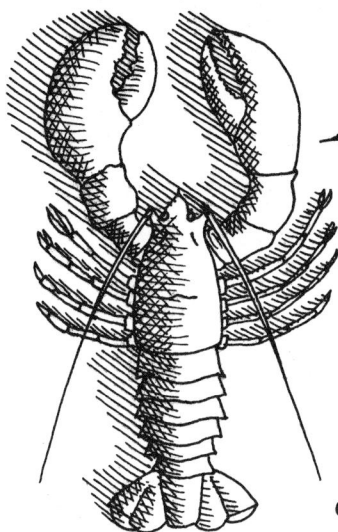

1. Take six 1¼ lb. lobsters or 1½ lbs of clear lobster meat.

2. Place live lobsters in boiling salted water for 15 minutes. Pick out meat, Save the Tomalley (green in body cavity) and the Coral (red in tail on females).

3. In a large Dutch Oven type pan, melt ½ lb. butter and add one tablespoon of white wine, a sprinkling of Chives (to taste) and a dash of lemon juice (to taste)

SALT PEPPER to taste

BUTTER BUTTER

4. Sauté lobster meat, Coral, and Tomalley in the mix for at least ½ hour.

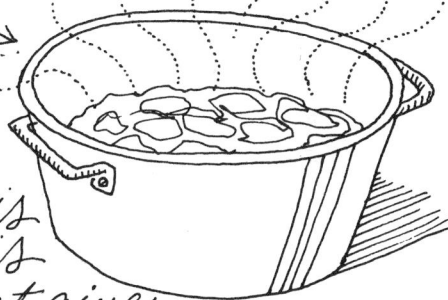

this is what gives the stew a red coloring without the use of paprika.

5. mix 9 cups (1½ cups per lobster) MILK MILK and 3 cups (½ cup per lobster) EVAPORATED MILK and scald in a separate pan and

6. pour into lobster mixture. Heat thoroughly. Do not boil or cover as stew will curdle.

Hint: Stew tastes best if prepared one day ahead and refrigerated overnite.

Author's recipe

Cioppino, because no seafood cookbook should be without a recipe for Cioppino. (This one serves 6 seafood lovers.)

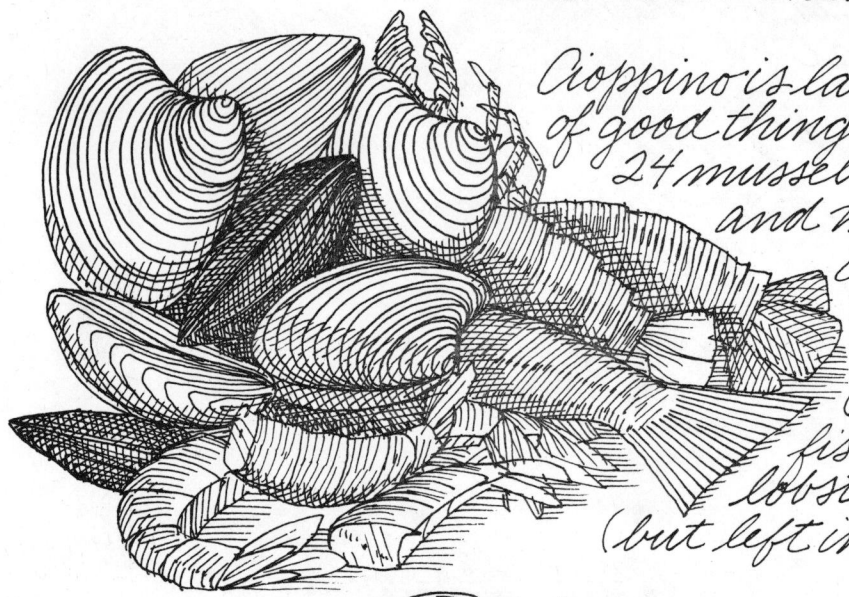

Cioppino is laden with all sorts of good things. You'll need 12 clams, 24 mussels (scrub both clams and mussels well), a pound of shelled and deveined shrimp, 2 pounds of deboned Sea Bass (or other white-meated fish), and 3 1½- to 2-pound lobsters cut up into pieces (but left in the shells).

Cut the fish into 2-inch pieces.

The lobster should be cut in half lengthwise, then cut again in the middle. Break off and crack claws

You'll also need

a green pepper chopped

Some red wine

some parsley (1 cup)

ITALIAN TOMATOES

2 large onions chopped

a 35 oz can of

TOMATO PASTE

a 6 oz. Tomato paste

olive oil

a lemon

6 cloves of garlic minced

BASIL OREGANO

Basil, oregano, salt, and pepper.

and you're ready to start.

1. In ½ cup of oil sauté the 2 chopped onions, the chopped pepper, and the 6 minced cloves of garlic.

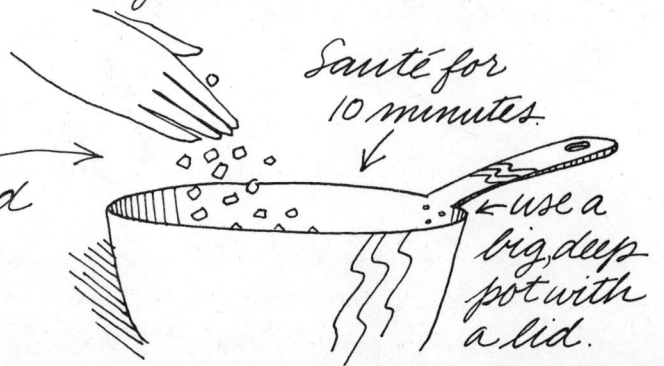

Sauté for 10 minutes.

use a big, deep pot with a lid.

2. Now, add to the pot the following ingredients.

a 35 oz can of Italian tomatoes

ITALIAN TOMATOES

TOMATO PASTE

a 6 oz can of tomato paste

VINO

2 cups

slice lemon thinly.

½ cup parsley

2 teaspoons Basil

1 teaspoon Oregano

1 teaspoon salt and pepper

Bring to a boil, reduce heat, simmer 20 minutes

3. Put into the mix

the 2 pounds of fish

the 3 cut up lobsters

the pound of shelled, deveined shrimp. Cover pot and simmer 20 minutes.

4. Add clams and mussels

Cover and simmer 10 minutes more, or until clams and mussels open.

5. Sprinkle with ½ cup of parsley and serve with chunks of garlic bread. It's fabulously messy and delicious to eat!

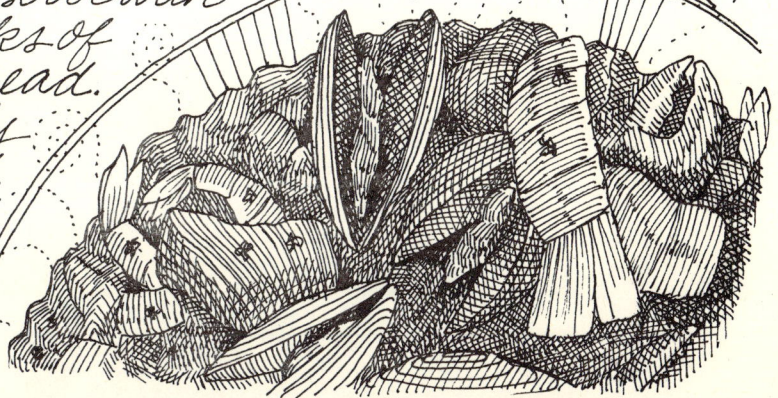

Fish

Whole, filleted, or steaked, they
can be prepared in a countless number
of delicious ways, all of which are
within anyone's capabilities.

The keys to good taste are freshness
and not overcooking. Freshness is
a matter of source. The fresher,
the better. Not overcooking is
as simple as testing with a fork
to see when the flesh is opaque
all the way through.

Do not limit yourself to the species of
fish indicated in these recipes.
If a recipe sounds good to you, it will
inevitably turn out good with
whatever fresh fish you have at hand.

Most of all, don't be afraid
to adjust any of these recipes for
your personal tastes. That's what
this cookbook is all about...
not being afraid.

Basic Cleaning

1. Scale fish.

← run scaler from tail to head.

hold at head

2. Remove entrails.

insert in anus and draw forward to gills in a sawing motion.

pull out entrails and sever here

3. Sever head with a sharp knife.

or lift gill covers and cut around gills ← where they meet body on both sides of fish

connects here cut.

pull out gills

Insert knife and cut on both sides of fins. Pull out fins & bones with a forward motion.

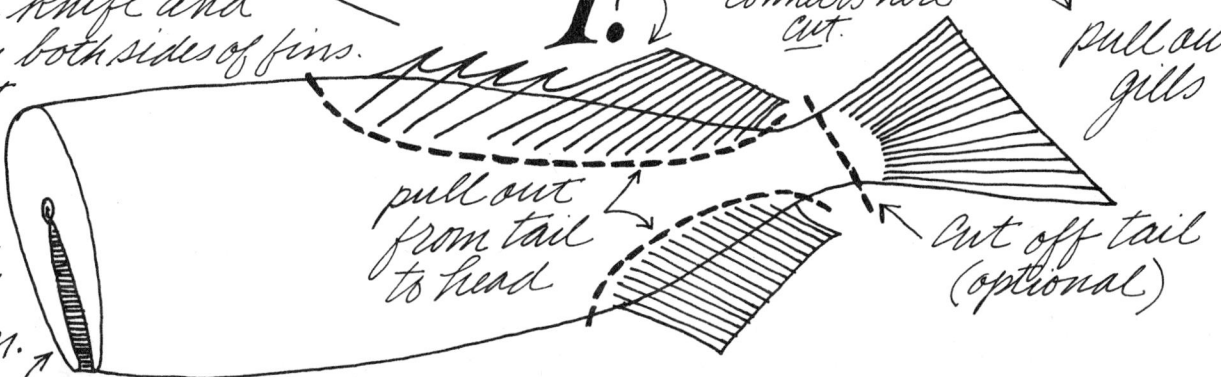

4.

pull out from tail to head

Cut off tail (optional)

clean out blood from stomach cavity.

How to fillet a regular-shaped fish...
(irregular ones come later.)

First and foremost, a sharp fillet knife. I prefer one called a "Rapala" which costs about eight dollars with a sheath.

1. Lay down the fish with its back facing you. Hold head down and insert knife as shown.

Cut through rib cage and intestinal area.

2. Insert blade just behind head. Ride blade down back. Push through rib cage and cut down complete length of fish.

3. Cut across fillet just behind gills and put aside.

4. Turn over and do the same from the back up.

Study the skeletal carcass. It will give you a better understanding of basic fish construction.

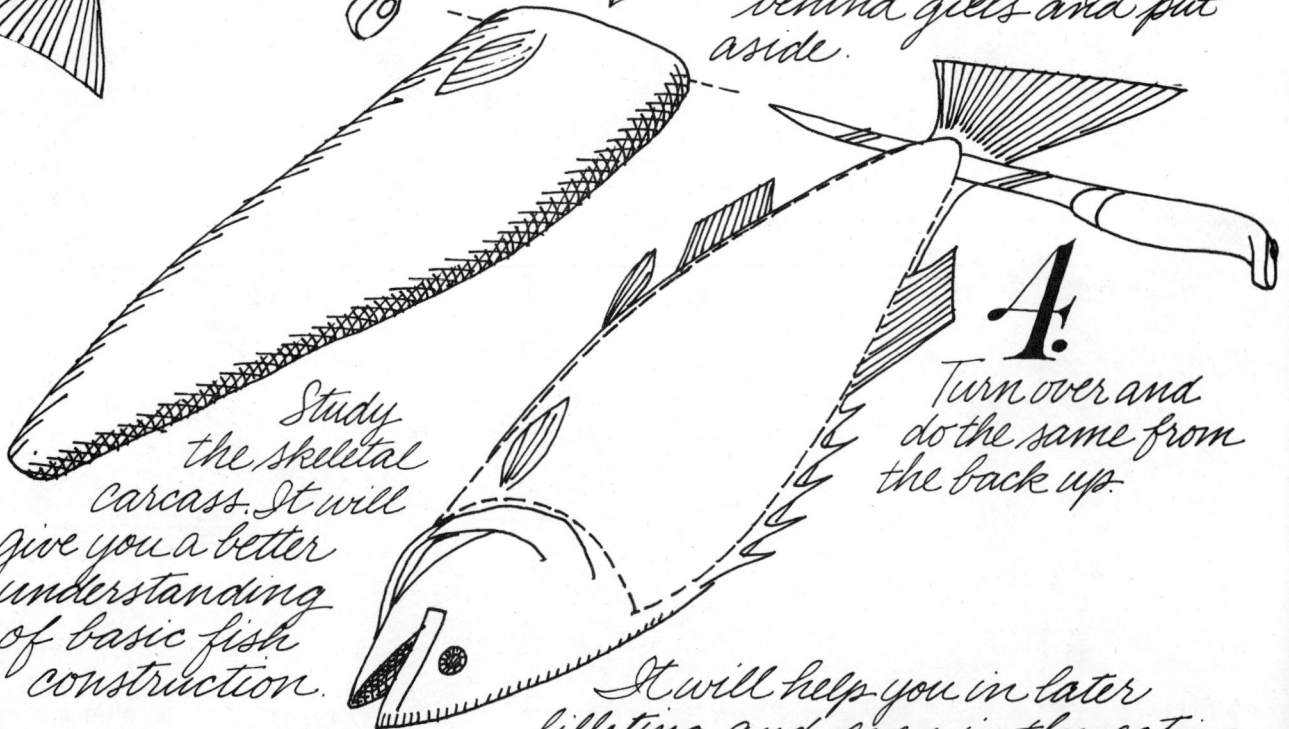

It will help you in later filleting and even in the eating of whole fish.

Now you are ready to skin the two fillets.

Place fillets on a board that is about ½" thick or more (or on a table or counter edge.)

5.

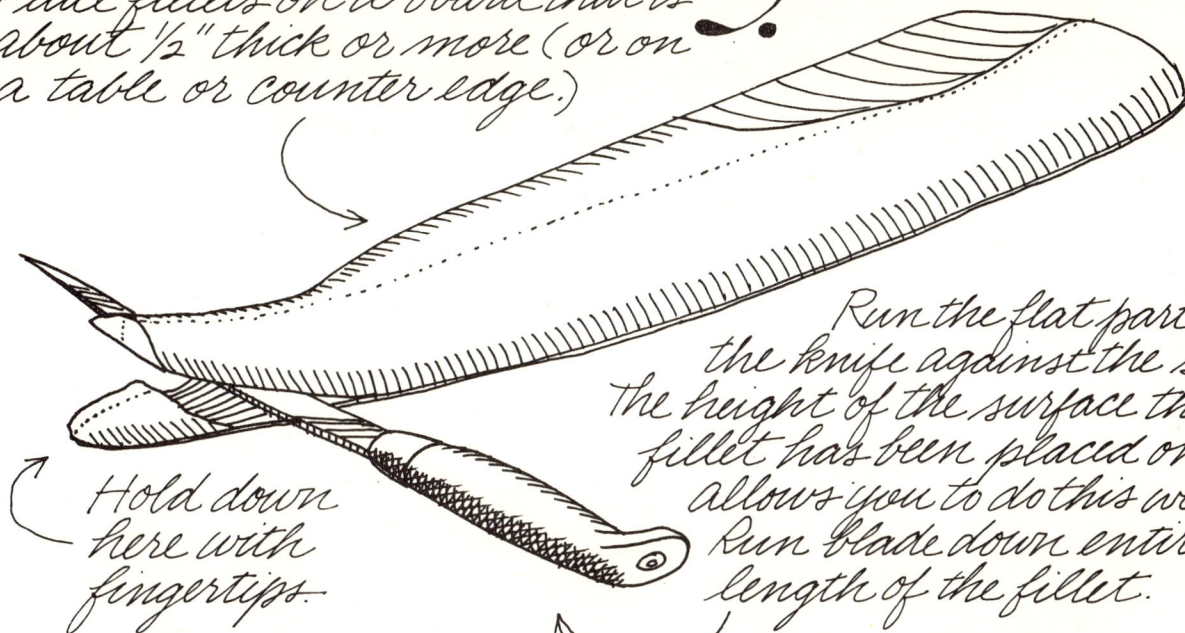

Hold down here with fingertips.

Run the flat part of the knife against the skin. The height of the surface the fillet has been placed on allows you to do this well. Run blade down entire length of the fillet.

6.

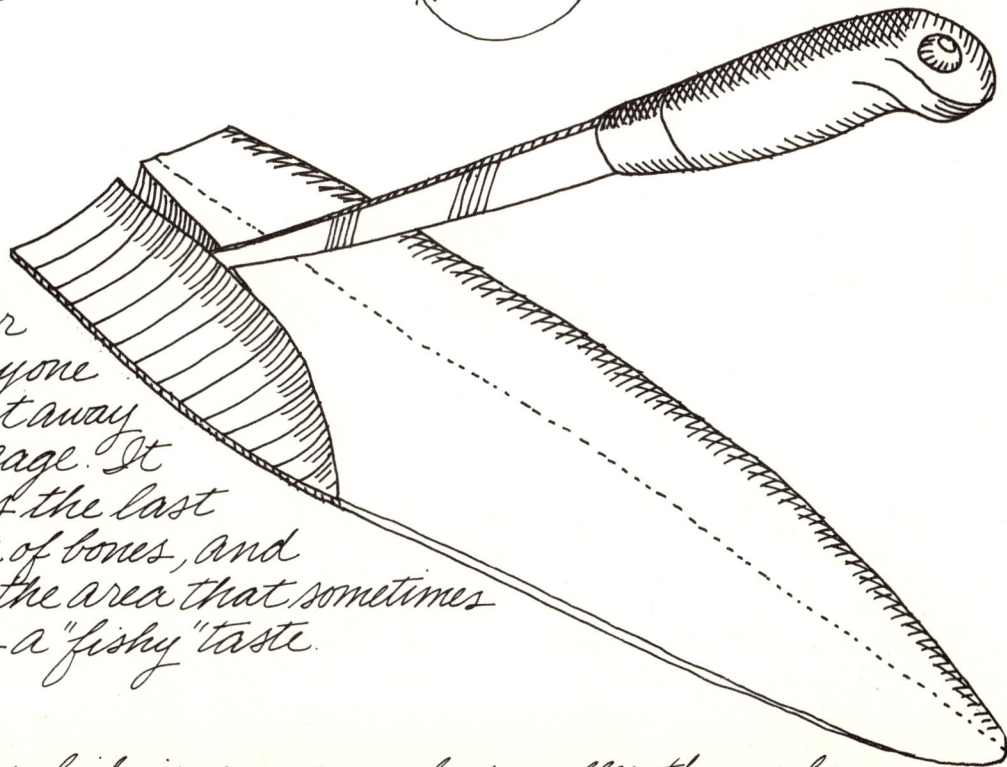

No matter what anyone says, cut away the rib cage. It removes the last vestage of bones, and this is the area that sometimes retains a "fishy" taste.

Your fish is now much smaller than when you started, but it is also now in its best form for any sort of keeping (especially freezing) and eating.

You'll be glad you bothered.

How to love and understand a Flounder, a Fluke, or any other kind of Sole.

Things to remember:

For every fin on the outside of a fish, there is a corresponding fin on the inside that makes it move.

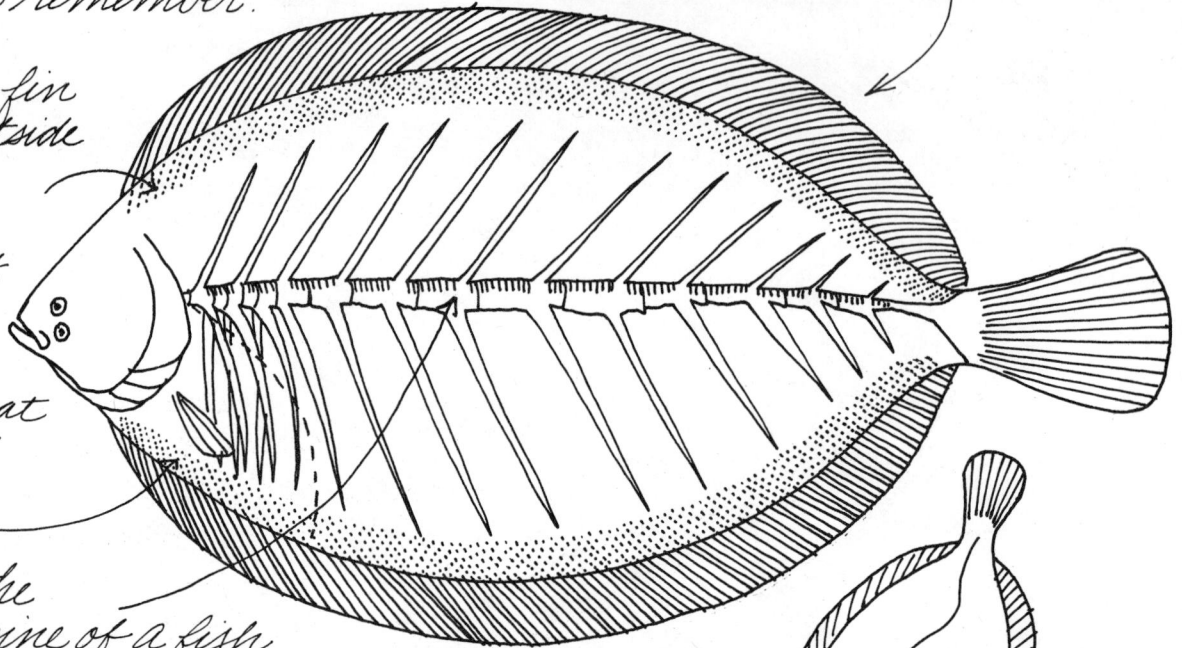

Unlike the basic spine of a fish the intestinal cavity is surrounded by a double set of ribs... a rib cage. This is the area from the anus of the fish to the underside of the head.

The top side of a Flounder-type fish is dark, has thicker meat and heavier scales.

the underside is white, is finer scaled, and has no eyes.

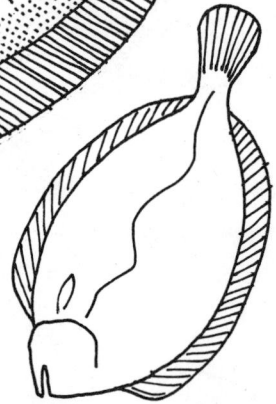

Run knife down center line from head to tail right down to the bone.

1.

Start on the dark side. Cut across head to center line.

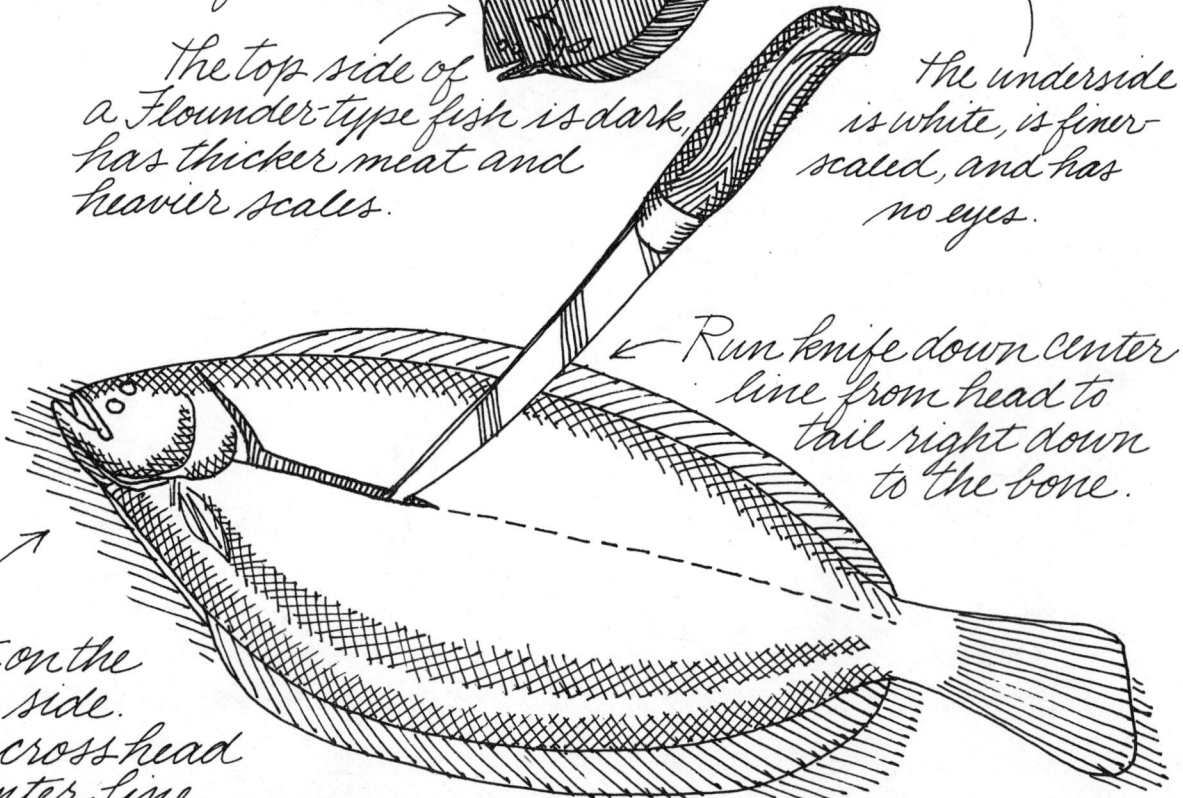

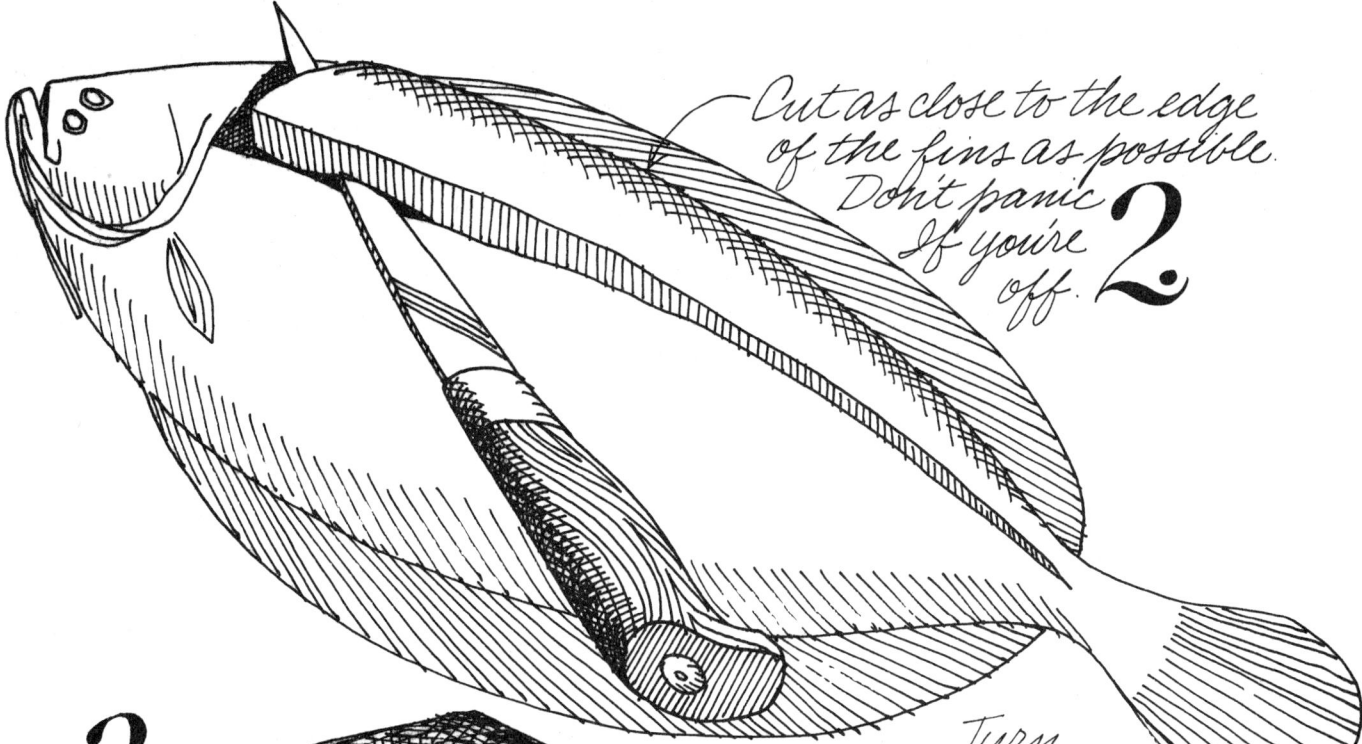

Cut as close to the edge
of the fins as possible.
Don't panic
If you're
off. **2.**

Turn
knife to side
and cut along spine
down entire length of
fish. Do the same on
both halves of top
(dark) side.

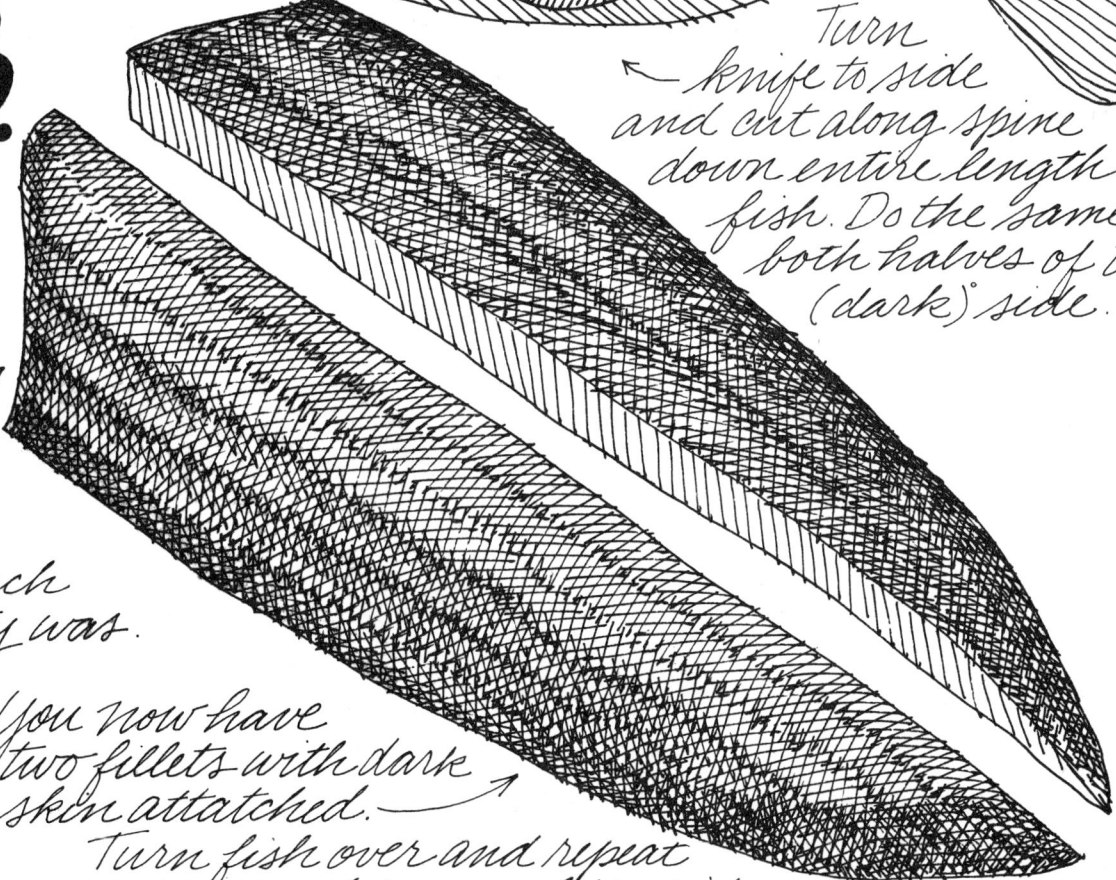

3.

where
stomach
cavity was.

You now have
two fillets with dark
skin attached.
Turn fish over and repeat
procedure on thinner white side.

4. hold
here

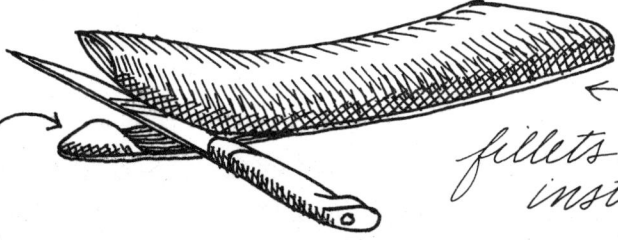

Proceed to skin
fillets as in previous
instructions.

What to remember when buying and keeping fish.

Hard-scaled fish (big flaky scales) last longer than soft-scaled (fine scales) fish, both when refrigerated and when frozen.

The dark meat of the fish and the area around the rib cage are the most perishable and tend to take on a stronger "fishy" taste. Cut away if you intend to keep for a while.

There are local fish, seasonal fish, and fish that are shipped in (frozen or iced) from other places. Don't be afraid to ask about them. You don't want to buy a six-month-old frozen fish.

It is better to fillet and skin a fish if you intend to freeze and keep it awhile.

It is better to wash your fish in salt water rather than fresh, if possible.

If you wish to increase freezer life on whole fish, use a mix of about 1 part vinegar to 2 parts water in the final washing. The surface slime will turn white and can easily be rubbed off with a soft nylon scrub brush.

If fish seems "fishy" smelling or slimy after defrosting (or even when "fresh") rub with flour, let stand for 5 minutes, and wash off.

In many species, the smaller fish are considered to be tastier. That's not necessarily true.

Beware of freezer burn. Pack fish in milk containers of water or glaze and wrap very well.

Save leftover fish and scraps. They are the best possible additions to a chowder.

Author's recipe   A spicy Indian fish dish.
Use any firm-meated fish.

1. Cube fish into pieces about 2" by 2" or smaller.

2. Marinate fish cubes for one hour in a pasty mixture of

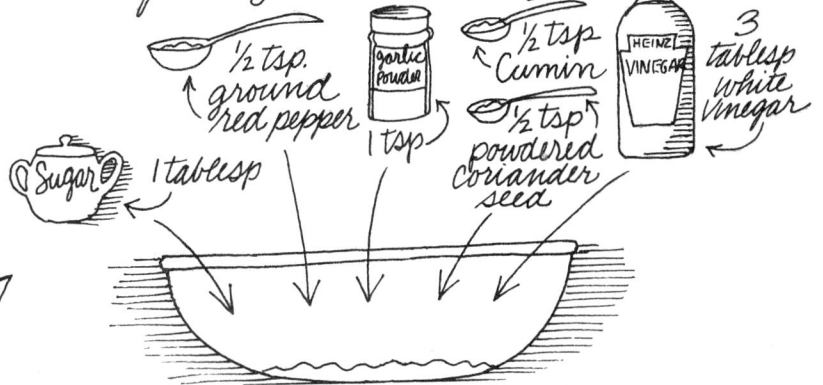

½ tsp. ground red pepper

garlic powder 1 tsp.

½ tsp. Cumin

½ tsp. powdered coriander seed

Sugar 1 tablesp

HEINZ VINEGAR — 3 tablesp white vinegar

3. Chop two medium-sized onions and fry in a quarter cup of Wesson Oil until golden brown, then...

4. In the same pan add one 16 oz. can TOMATO SAUCE

onion and tomato sauce

and simmer for about 10 minutes.

5. Add fish and liquid from marinade. Cook for 10-15 min.

Hint: Reheat the next day. It tastes even better!

Author's recipe   How to bake a whole fish with stuffing.

1. Take a whole fish of 5 to 8 pounds, clean, scale, and remove gills, (you can also remove head if you wish). Lay out on a table or cutting board

Sprinkle inside and out with

SALT   garlic powder

2. Peel a large onion and slice into 1/8 inch thick rings and cut rings in half

Also take a lemon and cut into wedges

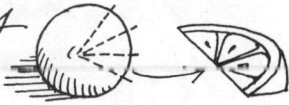

3. Slice fish to the bone on each side in portion-sized sections.

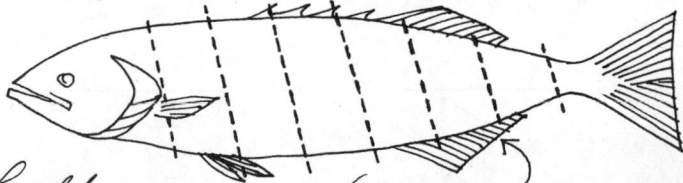

(you can remove top and bottom fins as per earlier cleaning instructions).

4. Insert an onion ring half and a lemon wedge into each slice in fish.

lemon   onion

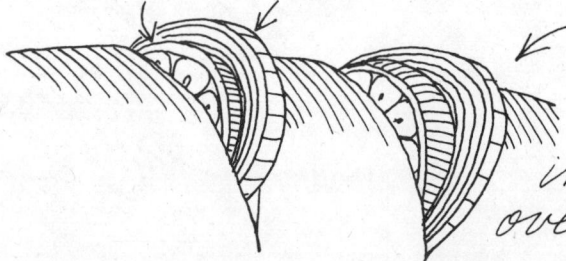

(Make sure to hold in the ingredients when turning fish over, so they don't fall out.)

5. Place fish in a baking pan that fits.

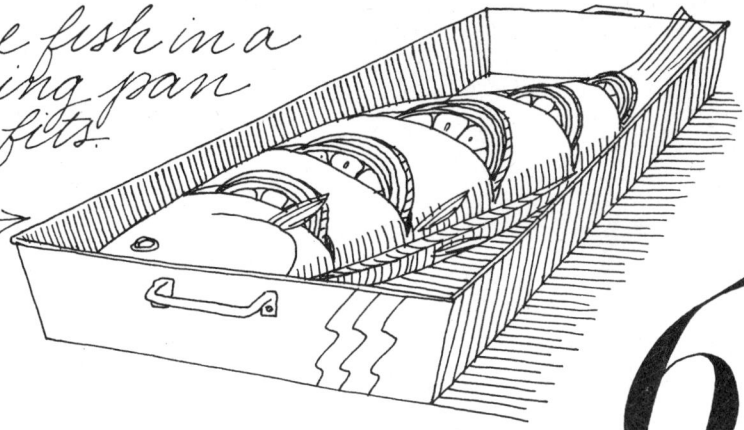

6. Chop up (according to the size of your pan and fish)

tomato   onion   celery   green pepper

mushrooms (canned or fresh)

and mix with some seasoned bread cubes (croutons or bread crumbs). Moisten with white wine (just a bit).

7. Spoon mixture into fish cavity and around fish. Season surface of mixture and fish with

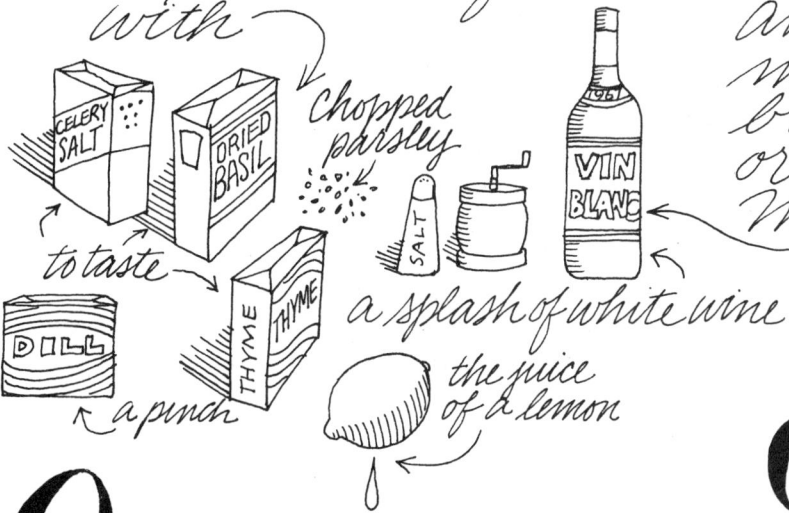

CELERY SALT   DRIED BASIL   Chopped parsley   SALT   VIN BLANC

to taste

DILL   THYME   a splash of white wine

a pinch   the juice of a lemon

8. Cut strips of bacon in half and place one strip on each section.

9. Bake at 350° for 45 minutes to an hour. Baste frequently. Test "doneness" with a fork. Serve with stuffing and remaining liquid.

(Lift each section off whole fish)

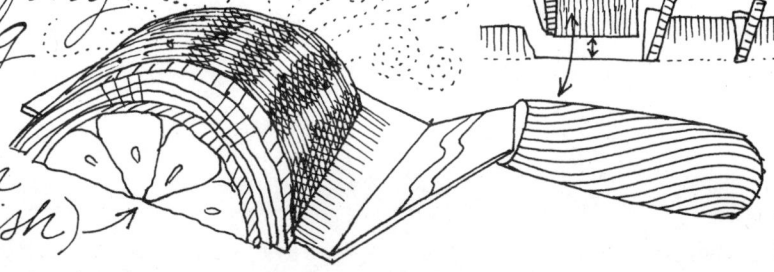

Captain Tom Holliday and his mate Paul Boyer (with rod) stand proudly alongside a beautiful Blue Marlin caught from the 48 foot Sportsfisherman called the "Happy Holliday".

The boat and its crew sail from Battistella's Empire Marina in Empire, Louisiana. They specialize in all types of offshore fishing.

Try their recipe for Barbecued fish. Use any variety. Every one turns out special.

Barbecued Fish Louisiana Style

1. Get as large a folding barbecue rack as you can find.

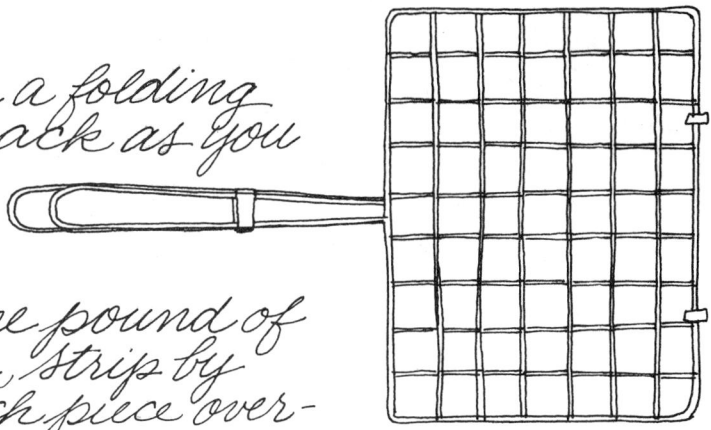

2. Lay one pound of bacon, strip by strip (with each piece over-lapping), over the entire rack.

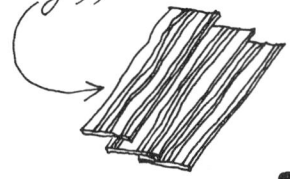

3. Next place a layer of 12 fish fillets, (salted and peppered) over the bacon and repeat with another pound of bacon.

4. Barbecue over an open fire basting with melted butter and lemon juice for approximately 35 minutes or until bacon gets crisp and adheres to fillets.

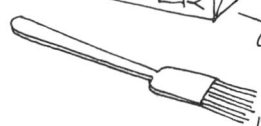

BUTTER

5 To serve, cut in squares.

Captain Gary Harper runs a 60 foot Sportsfishing yacht called the "Zest." It's moored right in front of the home of its owner in Newport Beach, California.

The "Zest" and its Captain and crew roam the Pacific in search of Tuna, Swordfish, and Marlin. They've been pretty successful as they hold the World's record for Big eye Tuna on 30 pound test tackle. A whopping 163 pounds!

Captain Harper's recipe is a "zesty" variation on the popular Ceviche.

"Ceviche" (Mexican) a many-ways spelled and many-ways made dish. Here's another great one to try as an appetizer, cocktail, or even cold soup.

1. Select 1¼ pounds of firm white-meated fish and cube into ½ inch pieces

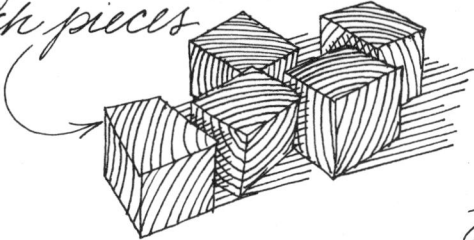

2. Place in a glass or crockery pan or bowl and cover with the juice of 6-8 limes

3. Chop up two small yellow peppers (usually come in jars) and add to dish, also add 2 tablespoons of pepper juice. Marinate all for an hour.

(clean out seeds)

4. Now add to mixture

Stewed tomato/diced tomato — 2 15 oz cans

1 cup chopped celery

1 cup chopped red onions

one Bell pepper chopped

5. Let all ingredients sit for at least 15 minutes before serving to blend flavors.

Serves 8-12 people. Good with beer and chips.

Captain Peter Hoogs, skipper of the Kona Charterboat, "Pamela," has been a commercial fisherman, professional captain, professional diver, and an internationally acclaimed photographer of underwater subjects.

For the last nine years, he has operated his 40 foot haole Sampan, "Pamela", out of Kona, Hawaii.

Try his Fish Stew Hawaii and you'll call him a professional cook.

Fish Stew Hawaii. Make it with any kind.

1. Take 1/4 pound of Bacon and cut into small pieces.

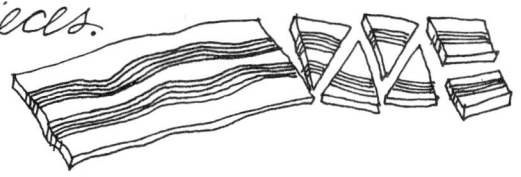

2. Fry gently in a large pan. After 3 or 4 minutes, add one large onion chopped and one green pepper chopped, and fry 3 or 4 minutes

3. Cut fish (one pound of Snapper, Wahoo, Tuna, Grouper, Bass, whatever) into 1" cubes.

and toss a small amount at a time in a plastic bag with flour.

add salt, and pepper to taste

4. Add fish to vegetables and fry 3 or 4 minutes

5. now add

1 to 2 tablespoons Dry Sherry

1 15 oz can

1 Bay leaf

Salt

pepper

2 teaspoons sugar

Simmer for 10 minutes or so, until vegetables are cooked. Serve with rice. Feeds 3-4.

Sprinkle with chopped parsley before serving

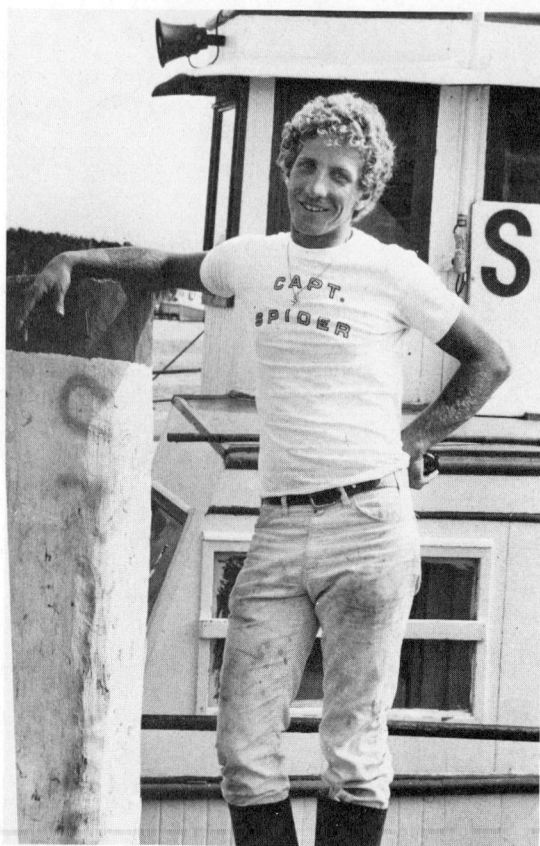

Captain Ernie Libasci runs the 47 foot partyboat Called the "Captain Spider" out of Montauk, Long Island, New York. His craft can take up to 40 fishermen and specializes in bottom fishing the waters off Montauk and Block Island. There they catch Cod, Pollack, Flounder, Fluke, Sea Bass, Porgy, Bluefish, and many other varieties of fish.

Captain Ernie's recipe for a special fish soup utilizes many of them and makes the catch doubly rewarding.

Ernie Libasci's Special Fish Soup

1. Preheat your oven to 375°. You will need a heavy iron roaster or a large casserole with a tight cover →

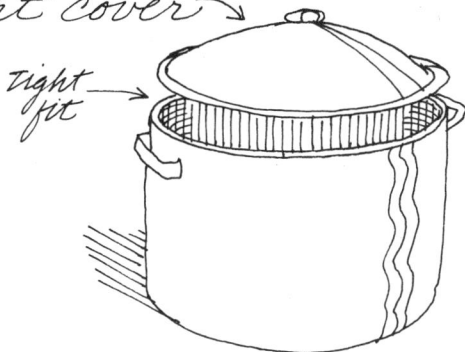

tight fit →

2. Clean and wash all fish, removing scales. Leave heads on at least two fish; you can fillet or steak the others. Scrub the shellfish well.

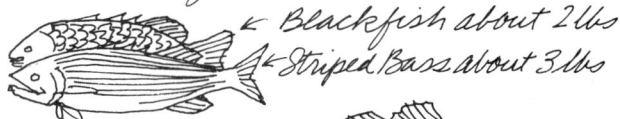

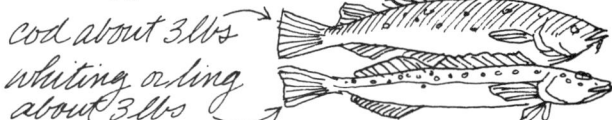

← Blackfish about 2 lbs
← Striped Bass about 3 lbs

cod about 3 lbs
whiting or ling about 3 lbs

twelve mussels

eight cherrystone clams

two Blue Claw crabs or one small lobster

3. Place fish in pan. Sprinkle on one chopped onion, ¼ cup of olive oil, 12 → whole peppercorns, 3 Bay leaves, one teaspoon salt 3 whole cloves garlic, 2 bouillon cubes chopped → fresh parsley and ← ½ bottle of dry white wine (Soave)

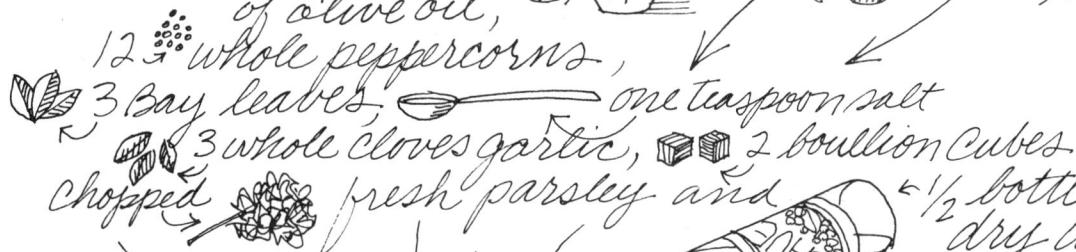

Note: put crabs, clams, and mussels in last →

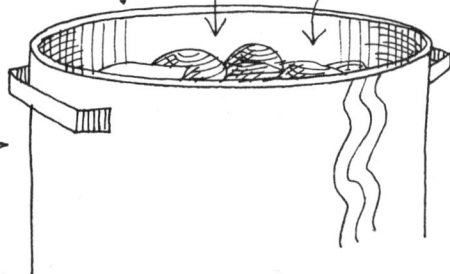

4. Put cover on and shake vigorously for several seconds so oil and wine touch all ingredients! Do not add water

5. Place in preheated 375° oven for 70 minutes. Should feed 6 to 8 hungry people. Serve with French or Italian bread.

Captain Al Ristori is the Director of Field Testing for the Garcia Tackle Corporation, and has fished our continent from east to west, and north to south.

Fishing with him on his fully rigged 22 foot Mako can get you anything from Fluke fillets to Bluefin Tuna Steaks.

Al's flexible and favorite recipe lets you make a delicious treat of either.

A recipe that Al Ristori uses to cook any kind of fillets and turn them into gourmet treats.

1. Melt a generous hunk of butter and a good dose of lemon juice in a moderate-sized skillet. the melted mixture should cover the bottom.

2. Chop half a large onion, a nice fresh tomato and a couple of peppers

and put in skillet to brown.

3. After the vegetables have browned, it's time to add the fillets to the pan.

don't be afraid to add more of your favorite vegetable, butter, or lemon.

4. the fillets should be turned once during the cooking process and may be broken up into smaller chunks to absorb even more of the juices. Don't overcook.

use a fork to check if fish is done. Once it's opaque, it's done.

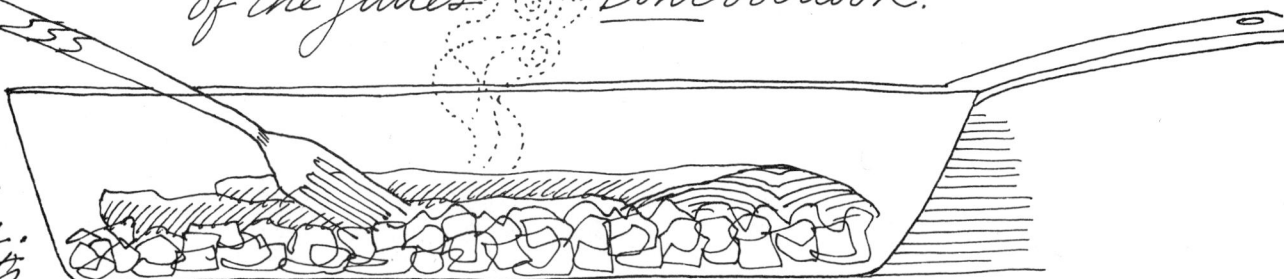

5. Serve with a generous topping of vegetables and sauce and enjoy! (You can easily enlarge or reduce this recipe for your needs.)

Captain Charles Sebastian and his son Captain Tim Sebastian of Grand Isle, Louisiana, own and operate the custom-built, twin diesel-powered aluminum Sportsfisherman called the "Sea Hawk".

They run the broad range of offshore drilling structures in the Gulf of Mexico.

Their motto, "Catch in the A.M., eat in the P.M."
Here's a Louisiana-brand recipe for fried fish that makes it crisp, tasty, and different. It's really good!

Quick 'N Easy Fish Fry 'Cajun Style

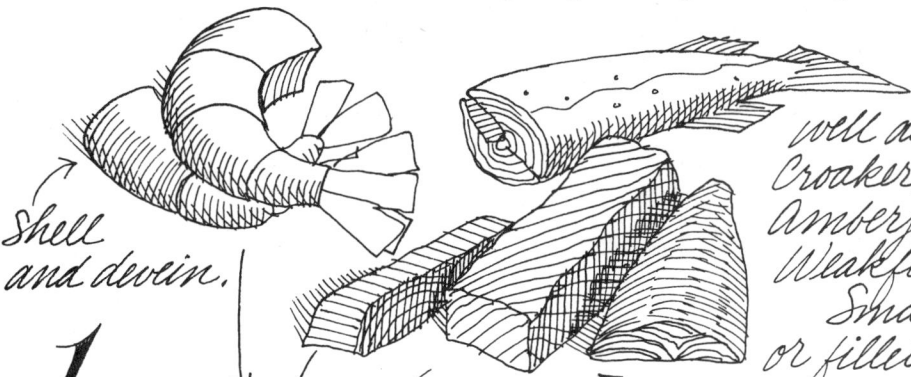

This recipe is splendid for frying shrimp as well as such fish as Bull Croaker, Red Snapper, Cobia, Amberjack, Grouper, Weakfish or Flounder.

Small fish can be whole, or filleted. Larger ones filleted and cut into "fingers".

Shell and devein.

1. Soak pieces in buttermilk for at least five minutes.

BUTTER MILK

2. Take a large bowl and add

its a finely ground corn meal!

CORN FLOUR

— in New Orleans there is a product known as "Fish Fry" that is marvelous.

MSG   Salt   PAPRIKA   CAYENNE PEPPER

Cajuns like it hot!

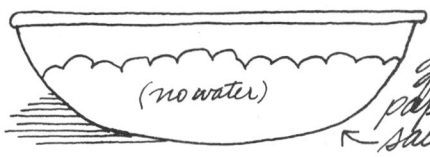

3. Heat oil in skillet.

375°

cooking oil

} enough to cover fish adequately

Season well. It should be quite red with paprika and salty to taste.

(no water)

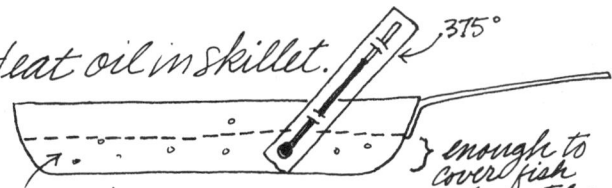

4. dip well in flour and fry to a golden brown on one side, and then the other.

5. Remove from oil and drain on absorbent towels.

Serve hot and crispy with your favorite tartar sauce, garlic French bread and a good green salad.

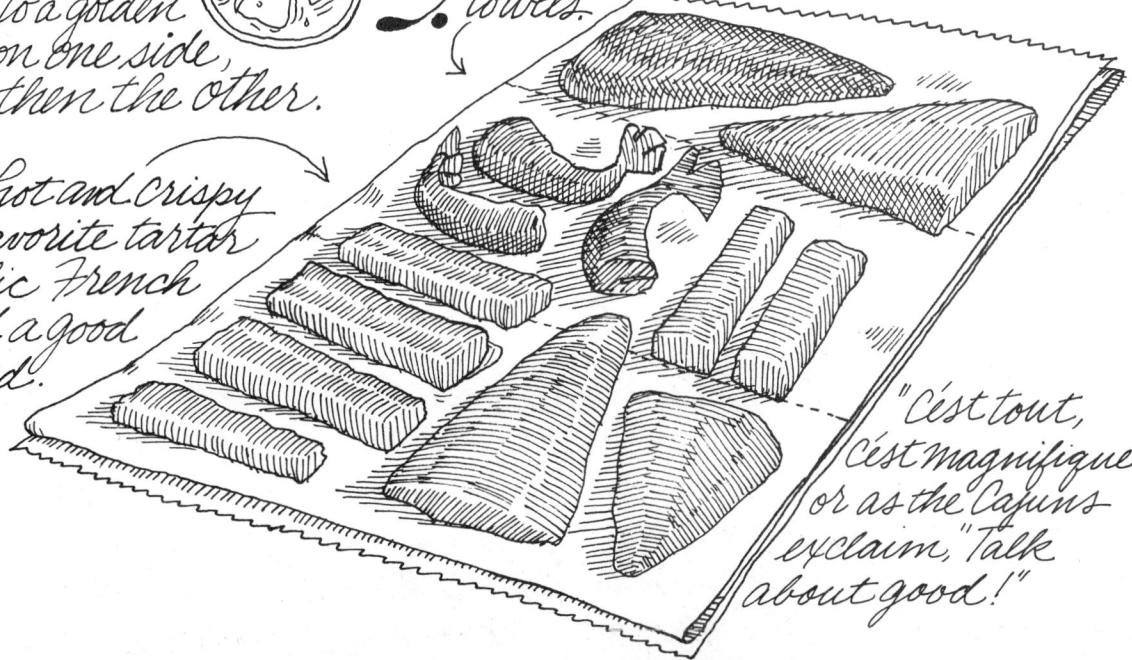

"C'est tout, c'est magnifique," or as the Cajuns exclaim, "Talk about good!"

Captain Philip Clock is a professional fisherman in many respects. He owns and runs a 45 foot Sportsfisherman called the "Tick Tock" out of the Long Beach Yacht Club in Long Beach, California.

He also is the President of the Fenwick Tackle Corporation, a director of the American League of Anglers, the Sports Fishing Institute, and the National Coalition for Marine Conservation.

His recipe for Albacore is a real winner not only for fresh Albacore, but also for fish that has been frozen for over a year. No kidding!

Baked Albacore (Fish Stew)

1. Place Albacore fillets in a roasting pan or casserole. 2 fillets will feed 6 people.

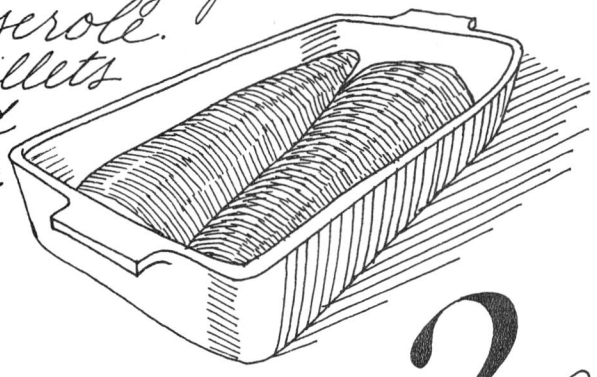

2. Pour the following ingredients over the fillets.

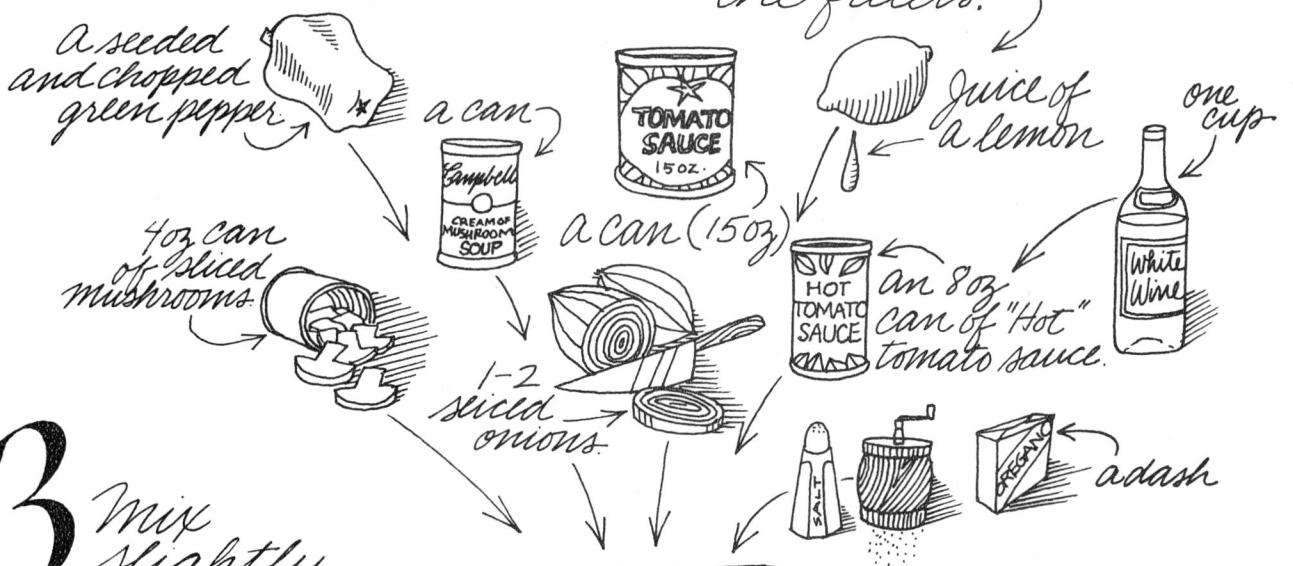

A seeded and chopped green pepper

a can — Campbell's CREAM OF MUSHROOM SOUP

TOMATO SAUCE 15 OZ — a can (15 oz)

Juice of a lemon

one cup — White Wine

4 oz can of sliced mushrooms

1-2 sliced onions

HOT TOMATO SAUCE — an 8 oz can of "Hot" tomato sauce.

SALT — OREGANO — a dash

3. Mix slightly and sprinkle top with sliced green olives (with juice) and Parmesan Cheese.

PARMESAN

4. Bake uncovered at 350° for one hour and serve. Smells great and tastes even greater!

Captain David Labruzzi has been
fishing since he was 10. Now at age 33
he goes to sea on his 42 foot charter
boat the "Fugitive" with the
help of all those years of experience.

He searches the waters of California
for all the Pacific species of fish, leaving
from and returning to San Diego's Point
Loma Sportsfishing Association Marina.

One of the popular Pacific fish is
the Albacore. Here's a way to make
it even more popular.

Baked and broiled Albacore from California

1. Fillet the Albacore into four separate "loins."

One loin will usually feed 3-4

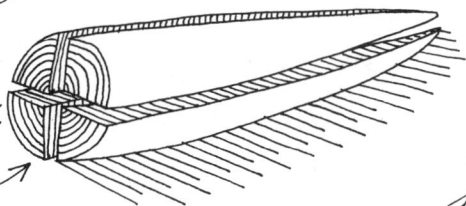

2. Take one or two "loins," wash thoroughly, and place on aluminum foil.

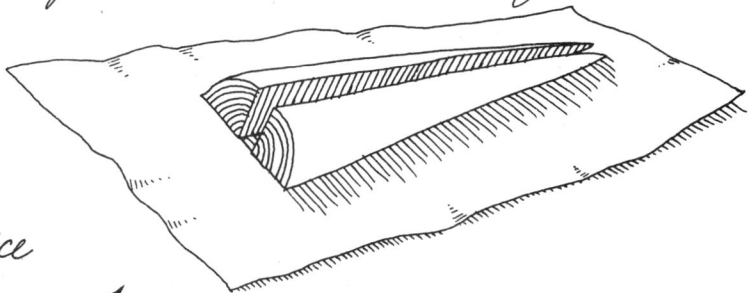

3. Sprinkle with

SALT PEPPER ONION SALT

lemon juice

and a bit of oregano

OREGANO

4. Dot with BUTTER and a clove of garlic sliced

5. Seal aluminum foil and bake at 400° for 10 to 15 minutes per pound (depending on thickness).

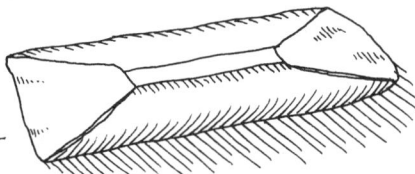

6. Approximately 5 to 7 minutes before "loins" are done, remove from oven, open top of foil and place under broiler to brown top of fillets.

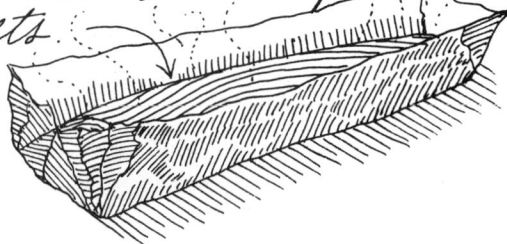

7. Pour out the liquid and add a splash on each serving. A glass of Pinot Chardonnay and you have a perfect meal!

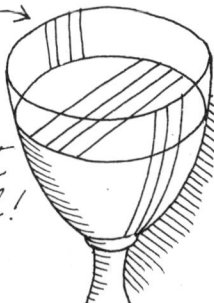

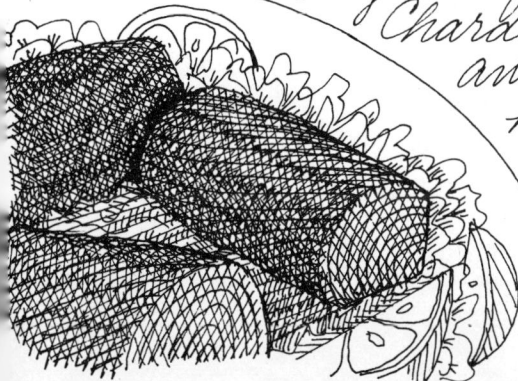

Captain Sy Karlin has been running
party boats for over fifteen years. He specializes
in bay and offshore fishing out of Freeport, N.Y.
His 45 foot boat called the "Blue Fin"
has a capacity of 38 eager fishermen,
and it's Sy's job to keep them happy and busy.

Captain Karlin's recipe is for Blowfish
a delicious morsel often referred to as
"Chicken of the Sea."

Blowfish Scampi - In northern waters the lowly Blowfish is a treat called "Sea Squab" by many restaurants. (Do not use tropical varieties for cooking).

1. Hold by head and cut where head and body meet. Cut only halfway through.

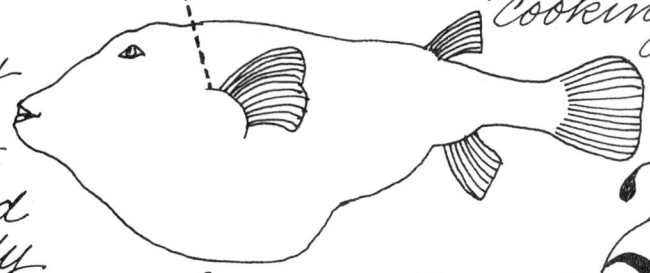

2. "Break" fish. Push fingers into body, turn body inside out and pull out the drumstick-like morsel.

3. Make crumbs out of fresh bread. You can put two slices at a time in a blender.

4. Put crumbs and Blowfish tails in a paper bag and shake.

5. Place on a broiler tray without touching each other.

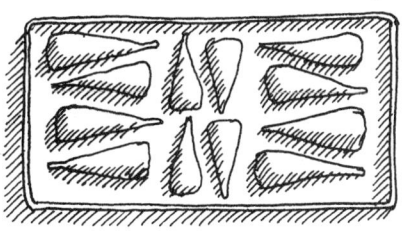

6. Crush two or three cloves of garlic and add to 1/4 pound of melted butter.

7. Sprinkle melted garlic butter on fish and broil to a golden brown; then turn over and do the same on other side.

The most tender, un-fishlike tasting morsel you've ever had.

Captain Steve Bales is well known
as a Bass fishing skipper in the San Francisco
area. He runs a boat called the
"Fisherman II" out of the Emeryville Marina
in Emeryville, California.

Steve loves to eat fish dishes
and sends us his favorite recipe for
a fish fry that uses lots of beer.

If you think that sounds good,
wait till you taste it!

Captain Steve's Special California Fish Fry

1. Fillet one Rock Cod or Striped Bass or any rock fish. Cut into serving-sized pieces

2. Beat two eggs and gradually add beer

enough to cover fillets

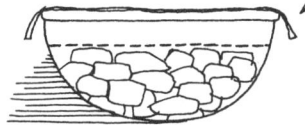

3. Cover dish and refrigerate for 24 to 48 hours. The longer the better.

4. Remove fish, shake off excess moisture and roll (or shake in a bag) in flour, meal, or crumbs into which salt, garlic powder, dried parsley have been added.

5. Deep fry in oil or Crisco until golden crusted brown

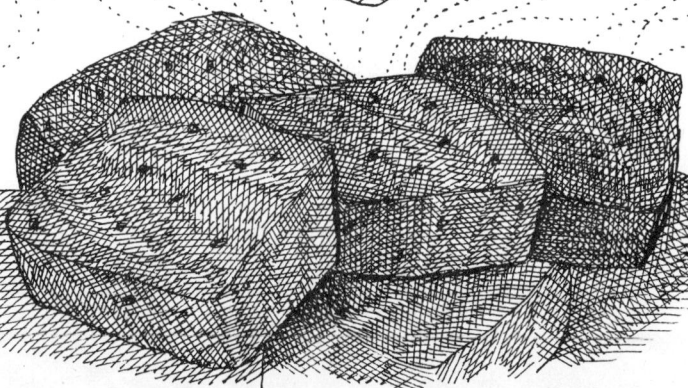

Fantastic!

Bill Dickerson works at what might
be considered the ultimate in Northwest fishing.
Operating out of the Manitou Lodge in
Forks, Washington, Bill fishes offshore
in the Pacific for Salmon from June through
September. From December through April
he fishes Steelhead in the rivers.

The lodge is unique as it caters to
sportsmen who fish real, light tackle
and want the very best.

Bill is used to good food at the
lodge. This recipe will verify that.

Baked Creamed Fish made with Ling Cod, Whiting, or any white-meated bottom fish.

1. Wash 3 pounds of fillets in cold running water and pat dry.

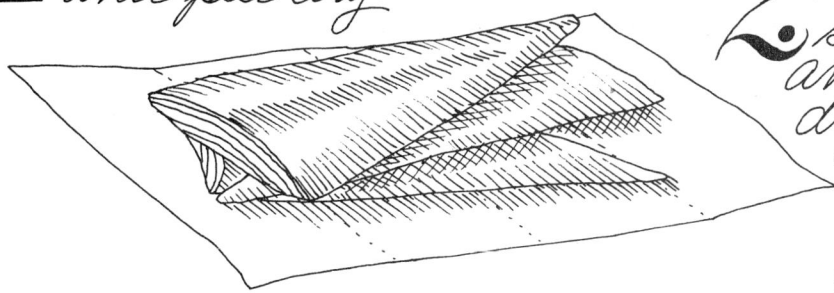

2. Place fillets in shallow dish and cover with dry sherry and marinate for two hours.

3. Remove fillets and pat dry again. Put them in a shallow oven-proof casserole or baking dish and sprinkle with fresh ground pepper

4. In a separate dish mix two cups one cup mayonnaise and one onion chopped fine

5. Cover fish with mixture

6. Bake uncovered for 45 minutes at 345 degrees. Serve directly from casserole with lemon wedges. Serves six.

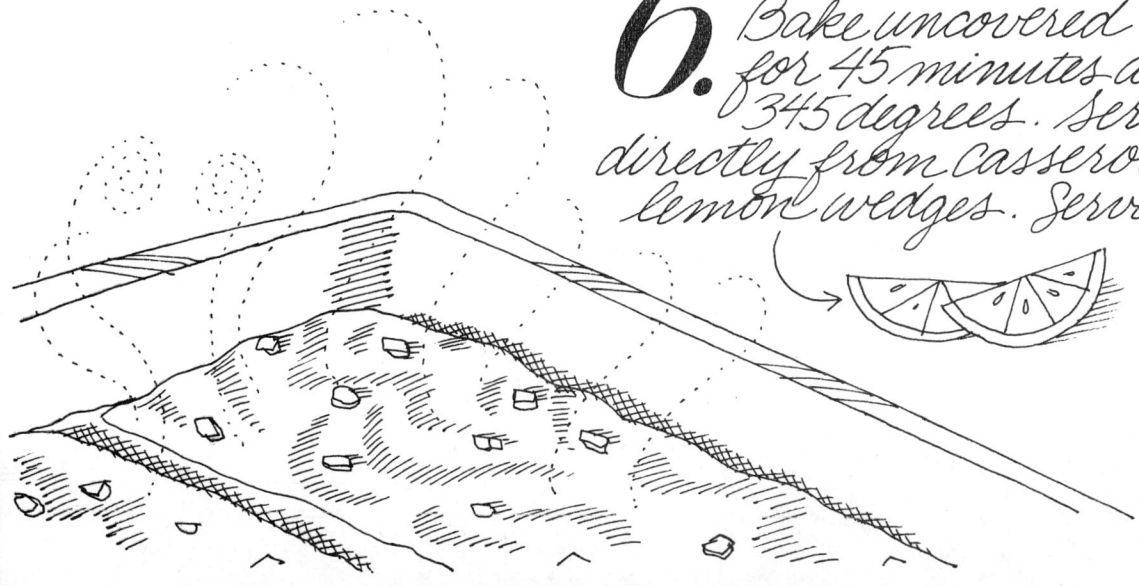

Author's friend's recipe — Codfish fillets the way Suren Ermoyan made them the night we ran my boat back from Montauk.

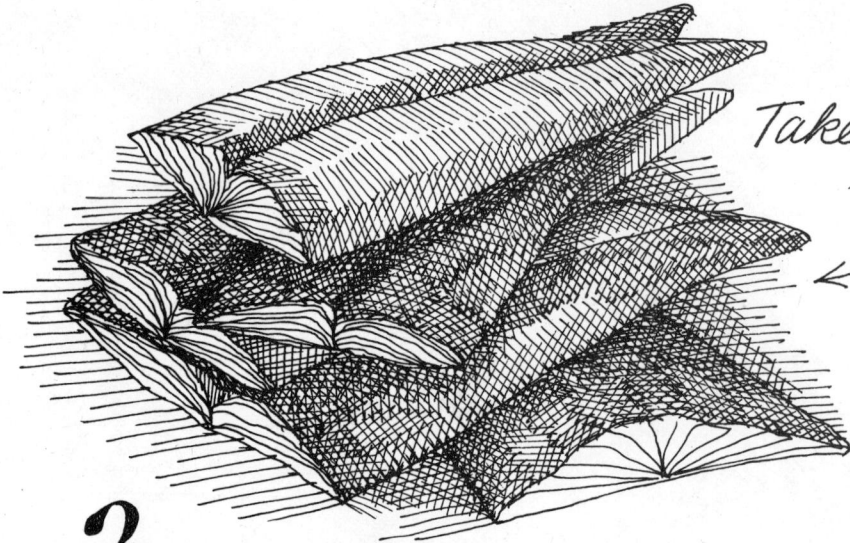

1. Take five or six boneless fillets.

2. Sprinkle with salt and pepper.

3. Place fillets in a shallow pan for which you have a top.

4. Add a quarter pound of butter in pieces on fish.

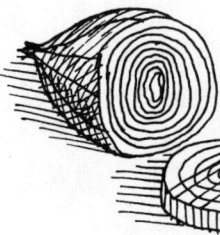

5. One medium onion sliced

half a lemon sliced and placed on fillets

a liberal sprinkling of dill over everything

DILL

6. At this point, get a container of sweet cream (light) or milk, and

pour into pan containing all the ingredients.

Fill to a level where the fillets, onions, and butter are semi-submerged.

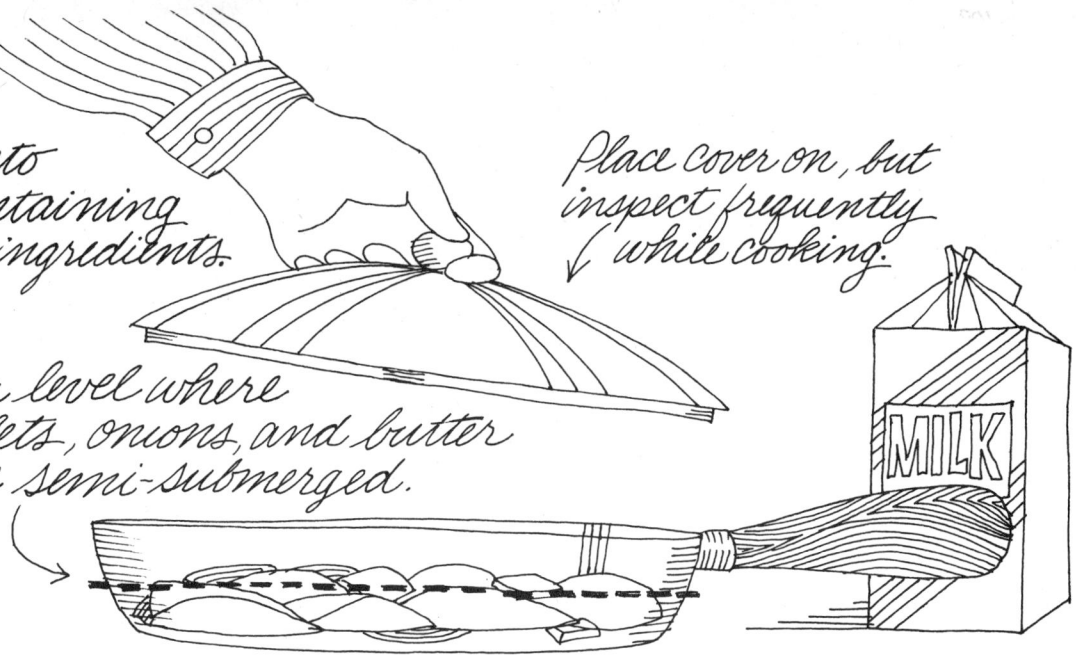

Place cover on, but inspect frequently while cooking.

MILK

7. After putting on cover, place pan over a medium low flame. The butter will melt, the milk or cream will begin to curdle, and the fillets will turn from translucent to opaque.

When that happens, sprinkle liberally with Paprika. →

Remove fillets with a serving spoon and serve in a deep dish with cooking liquid, parsley, potatoes and a glass of white wine. →

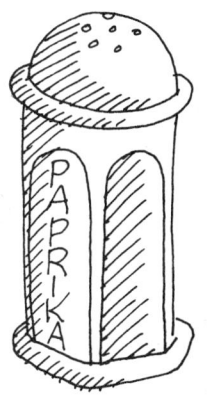

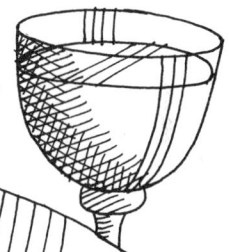

PAPRIKA

1959

Cha

Captain Artie Gerstmann doesn't like
to call it quits when the cold winter months
come. He seems to be just as at home
taking Codfish in December as he is catching
Mako Shark in August.

Artie sails his boat, the "Bumble Bee",
out of the Star Island Yacht Club in
Montauk Point, New York.

His recipe is for his favorite winter
bottom fish, the tasty Cod.

Codfish Creole from the East end of Long Island

1. Thoroughly dry 4 Cod fillets. Dip in flour on both sides.

FLOUR

2. After dipping in flour, dip in a mixture of one cup of milk and one egg beaten together

milk   1 CUP

3. Place fillets on bread crumbs. Press firmly so as to make sure Cod is completely covered with crumbs on both sides.

BREAD CRUMBS

Hint: ground cornflakes make a terrific substitute.

4. Deep fry nice and brown

5. Sauté ½ cup chopped Celery and ½ cup chopped onion or margarine till soft. in butter

6. Add a medium-sized green pepper diced and a large can of Tomato sauce

TOMATO SAUCE

7. Simmer until pepper is soft, then season with salt and pepper to taste

8. Serve sauce over fish and eat hearty

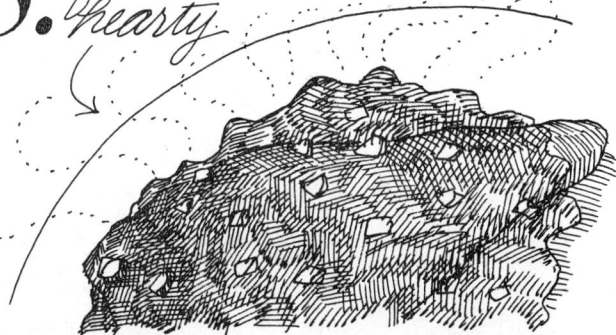

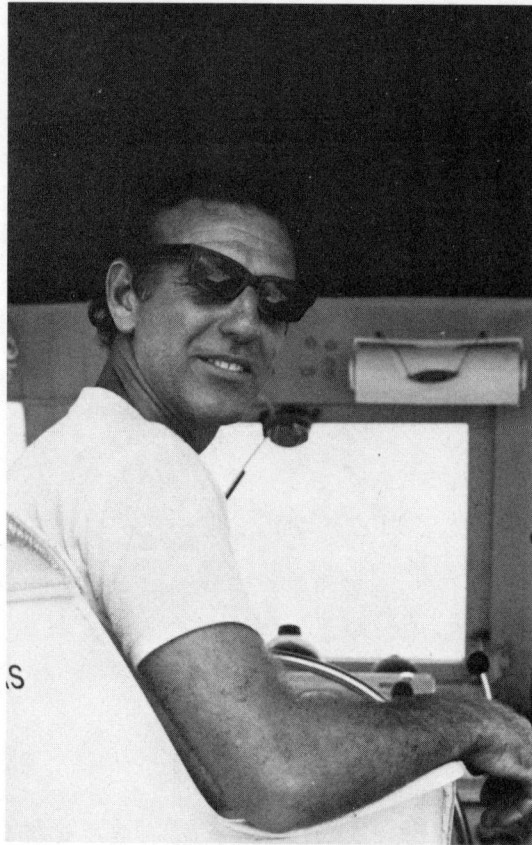

Captain Louis Ramm has been
fishing for over 20 years. By his own
count he's run over 3000 trips on his big
46 foot all-steel sportfishing
boat called the "Early Bird".

He runs his boat from Batistella's Empire
Marina in Empire, Louisiana,
and fishes for almost every species of
food and game fish. His favorite eating
fish is the Bull Croaker. His biggest
catch was a Blue Marlin of 435 pounds.

His favorite dish is one developed by his
deck hand Chuck Hammonds and himself.
It tastes like they're quite a team!

The "Early Bird Special" from New Orleans
(make it with boneless fillets of Croaker,
Sea Trout, or any tender white fish).

1. In a saucepan, simmer one large onion diced, one bell pepper diced and ½ cup of chopped celery in ¼ cup of dry Vermouth or your favorite wine until tender.

2. Add to the saucepan, one 15 oz. can of Tomato sauce and one 4 oz. can of chopped mushrooms. Remove from heat and cover.

3. In a skillet, line bottom generously with fish. Season with Salt and pepper and add another ¼ cup of wine

4. Place in preheated hot oven of 400 degrees for 3 min. turn fish and replace in oven for another 3 min. (or until fish turns milk white and starts to flake).

5. Pour sauce over fish. Top with sliced tomatoes and grated cheese. Replace in oven for 5 minutes more.

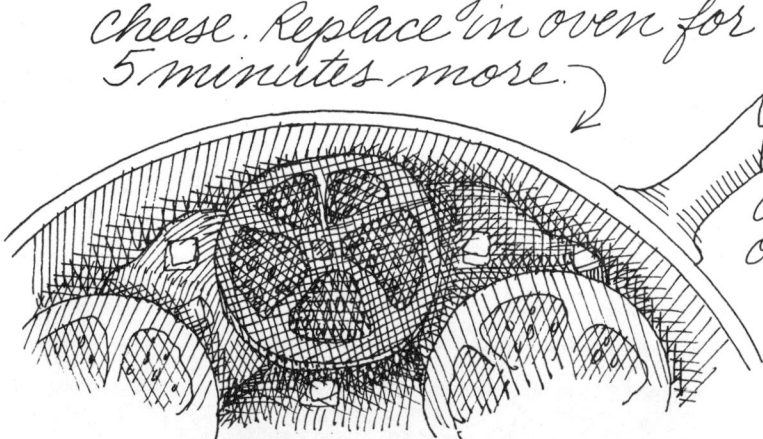

Spoon over noodles or rice for a quick, easy one-dish meal. Serves 4 to 6.

Captain Ken Benson runs the "Marla"
in the exciting and productive waters off
Rhode Island from Point Judith.

The crew and anglers of the "Marla" boated
over 8000 pounds of fish during the
1974 fishing season, many of which were
tagged and released to fight another day.

Swordfish, Marlin, Tuna, Bonito, Shark,
Bass and Bluefish are the "Marla's" favorites.

This recipe for Bluefish is one of
Captain Benson's favorites.

Rhode Island-style Bluefish and Pepper

1. Place one 2 pound Bluefish fillet (skinless) on a sheet of heavy-duty aluminum foil

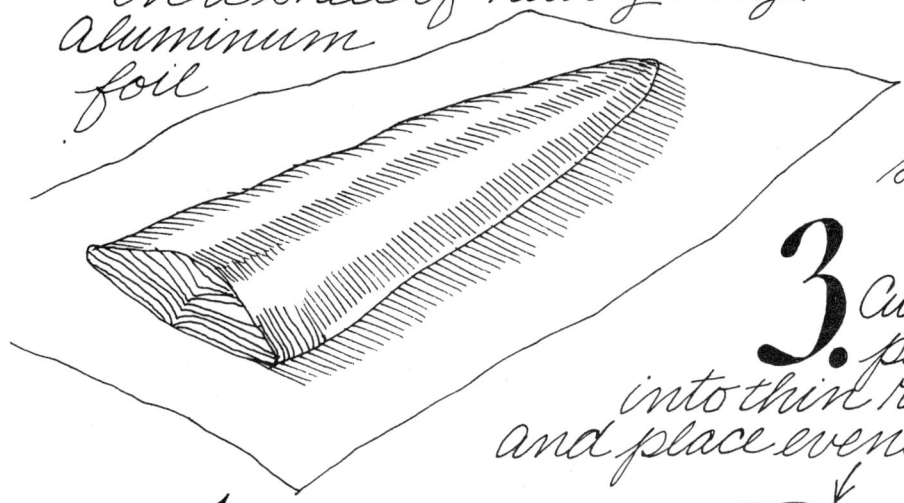

2. Sprinkle with 1/4 teaspoon of salt

3. Cut one small pepper into thin rings and place evenly on fillets

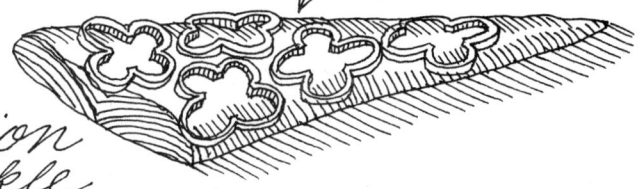

4. Dice one small onion and sprinkle lightly over fillet

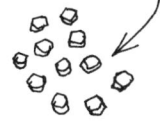

5. Evenly place 2 tablespoons of butter or margarine on fillet

6. Seal all edges of foil tightly on top of fillet

side views

7. Bake at 350° for 30 to 40 minutes. Open and savor the beautiful aroma and taste

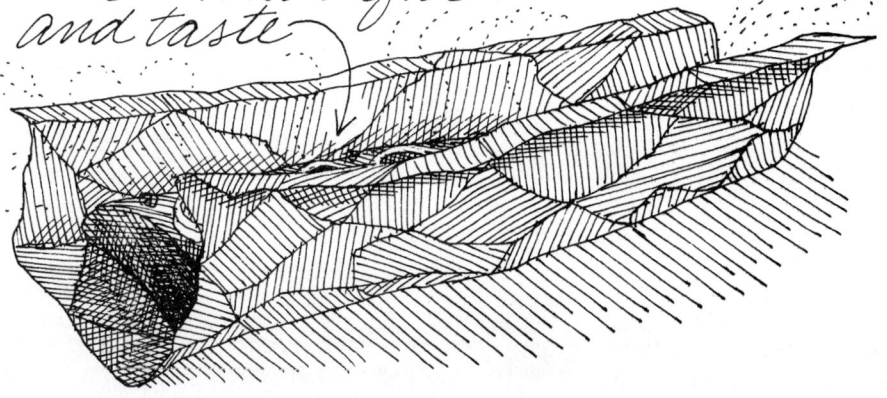

Captain G. B. Elsey is the
skipper of the "Shypoke", a 50 foot
Sportfisherman based at the Belmar
Marine Basin in Belmar, New Jersey.

A World War II Royal Navy veteran
and 20 year charter boat captain,
Captain Elsey has spent much of
his life on the waters of the world.

When given his choice, he prefers
fishing for Giant Tuna and
Shark over other species.

"Shypoke" style Bluefish

1. Fillet and skin fish. Soak in salted water for as long as 1-2 hours. Do _not_ rinse in fresh water. Cut up into smallish chunks.

2. Put as many chunks as you wish to make in a pan or dish. Marinate for 1 to 3 hours in your favorite salad dressing

French   ITALIAN DRESSING   Russian Dressing   BLUE CHEESE DRESSING

3. Roll fish in bread crumbs

BREAD CRUMBS

4. Fry or bake as you prefer. On an outdoor grill wrap fish in foil and get ready for a treat.

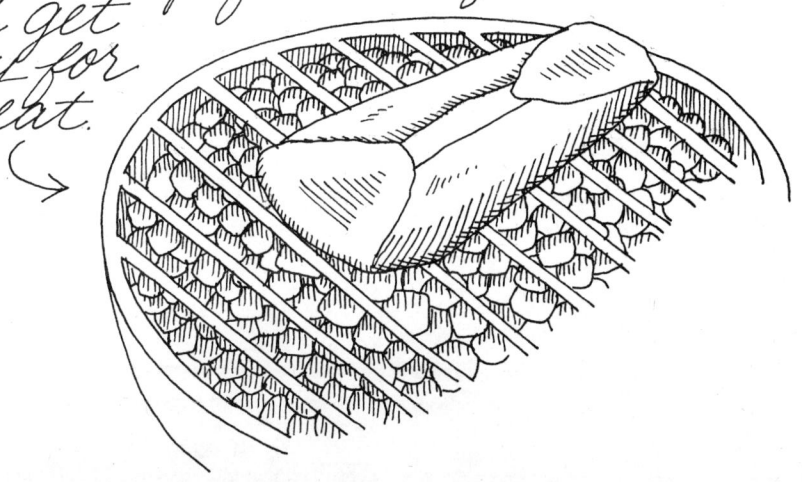

Captain Bob Francis runs his 26 foot McKenzie
Out of Nantucket Island, Massachusetts.
The boat, named the "Possessor," is ideal for
the Captain's specialty, casting for Striped
Bass and Bluefish as the photo shows.

The recipe Bob calls his favorite is really
a winner. Try it with other fish
besides Bluefish and Striped Bass.

Deep-Fried Bluefish done in a way that even people who don't like Bluefish will take second helpings.

1. Skin your Bluefish fillet and then cut into bite-sized chunks.

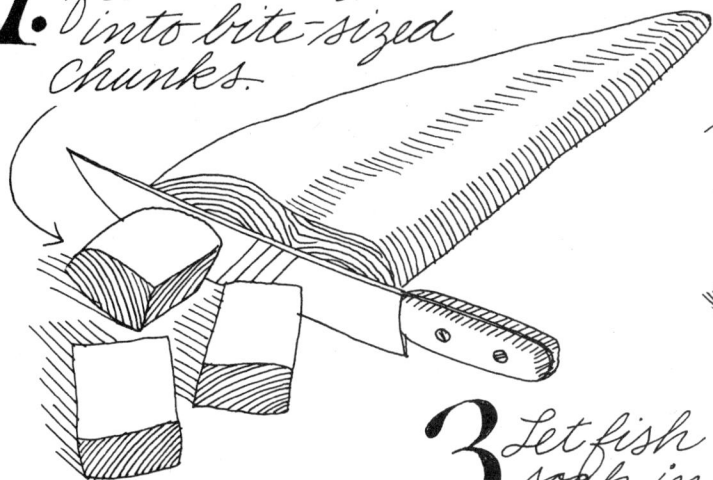

2. For one pound of fillets make a marinade of

a dash

GARLIC POWDER   NUTMEG   MSG

1½ tablespoons

SOY SAUCE

Dry Sherry

one egg

4-5 tablespoons

3. Let fish soak in marinade for at least three hours turn occasionally

4. Cover each individual piece well with a mixture of

⅓ BREAD CRUMBS   ⅓ GRATED PARMESAN   ⅓ CORN STARCH

5. Deep fry in corn oil at 375° for about 4 minutes

6. Serve nice and hot. Try it with Striped Bass and other fish, too.

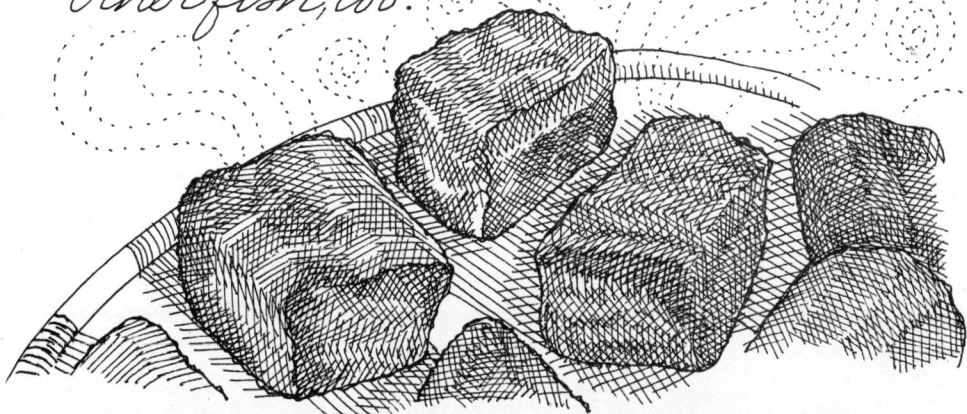

Captain George Glas owns the first steel catamaran in the party-boat business. It's called the "Hel-cat" and it runs out of Groton, Connecticut.

This stable craft fishes "the Race" where Long Island, Block Island, and Fisher's Island Sounds meet. This area abounds with giant Bluefish during the summer months.

Pay special attention to the washing and rinsing part of his recipe as it can make a good-tasting fish a great-tasting fish.

Bluefish à-la-Claire from Groton, Connecticut

1. Fillet, skin, and remove dark meat that runs down length of fillet on skin side.

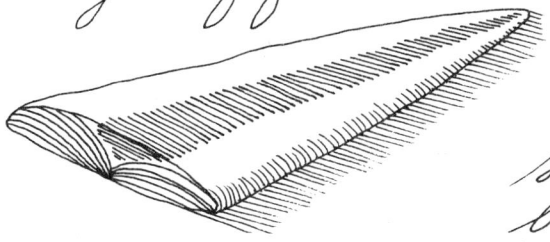

2. Important... soak fillets in a solution of cold salted water to get all the blood out, then rinse in running water until water runs clean.

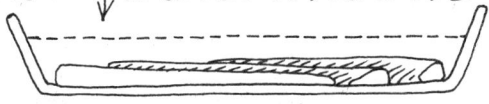

3. Place fish in broiler pan. Salt and pepper and sprinkle with lemon juice.

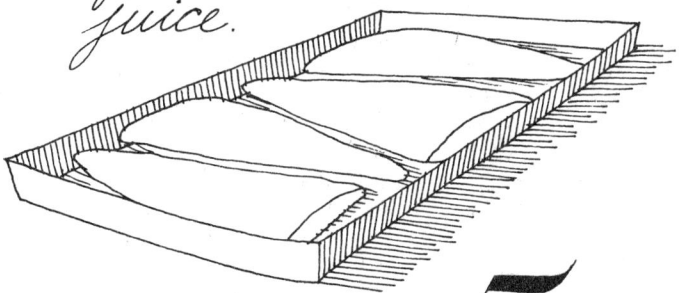

4. Put one-inch strips of bacon on fish, then sliced Bermuda onions, then sliced fresh green peppers.

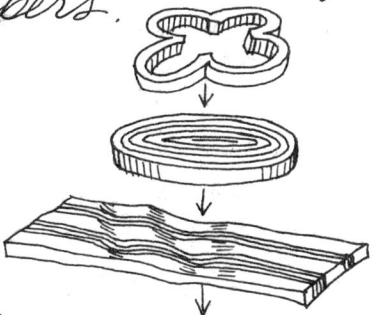

5. Broil until done. Test with a fork. Don't overcook.

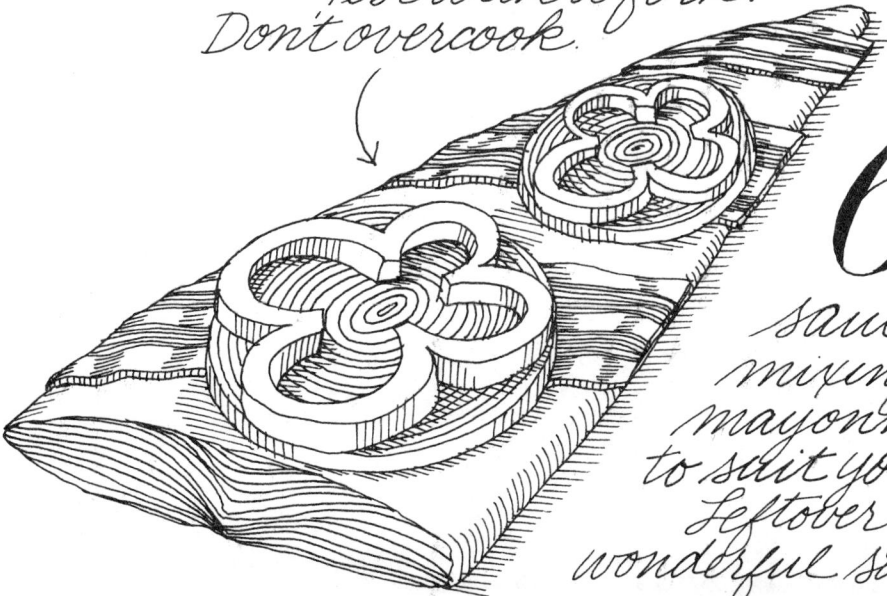

6. Fish can be served plain or with a simple sauce made by mixing horseradish and mayonnaise in proportions to suit your own taste. Leftover fish makes a wonderful salad.

Captain Paul A. Huch and his
beautiful 42 foot Norseman named
the "Excalibur" are based at the Belmar
Marine Basin in Belmar, New Jersey.

Captain Huch has been a charterboat
captain for 18 years. His is a family operated
business, as his 3 sons work with him.

Bluefish run the entire Atlantic
coast and are often a charter captain's
mainstay. Here's another simple,
quick, and tasty way to make it.

Quick and Simple Bluefish Bits
(or any other kind of fish bits).

1. Always soak your fillets in salted water for 15 minutes. Pat dry, cut away dark meat and cut in chunks

2. Mix up a batch of your favorite pancake batter. Make it thick as it will coat better. Now add one teaspoonful and

SEASONED GARLIC SALT

PARSLEY FLAKES

3. Preheat oil in deep pot or electric deep-fry cooker. Do not use until oil begins to smoke.

4. Dip pieces in batter and then into fryer. Do 4 or 5 bits at a time.

5. Fry to a golden brown on both sides. Remove and drain on paper toweling

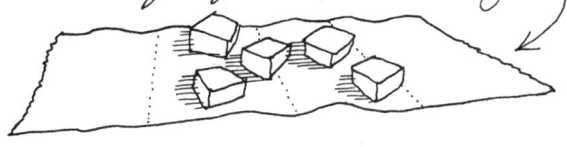

6. Place on a platter with french fries.

Serve with Tartar sauce or red cocktail sauce or sprinkled with wine vinegar

126.

Captain Roger Jarvis and his 29 foot boat
the "Misty" ply Massachusetts waters out
of Brant Rock in search of big Striped
Bass, Bluefish, Tuna, and Shark.

He names this dish after his boat,
and, like the craft, it's a beautiful,
solid, and dependable
recipe for good fish.

"Misty" Bluefish. Super simple; Super good.
(Use a 1 or 2 pound fillet)

1. Combine these ingredients in a bowl.

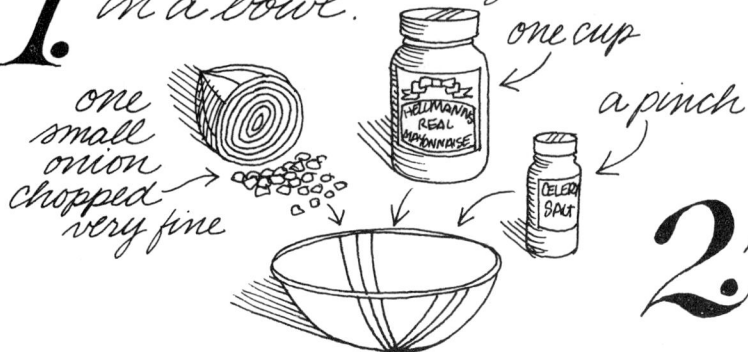

one small onion chopped very fine →

one cup

HELLMANN'S REAL MAYONNAISE

a pinch

CELERY SALT

2. Place fillet on broiler tray.

3. Spread half of mixture over fillet (cover completely).

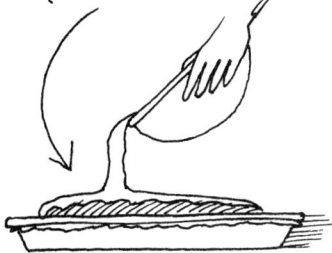

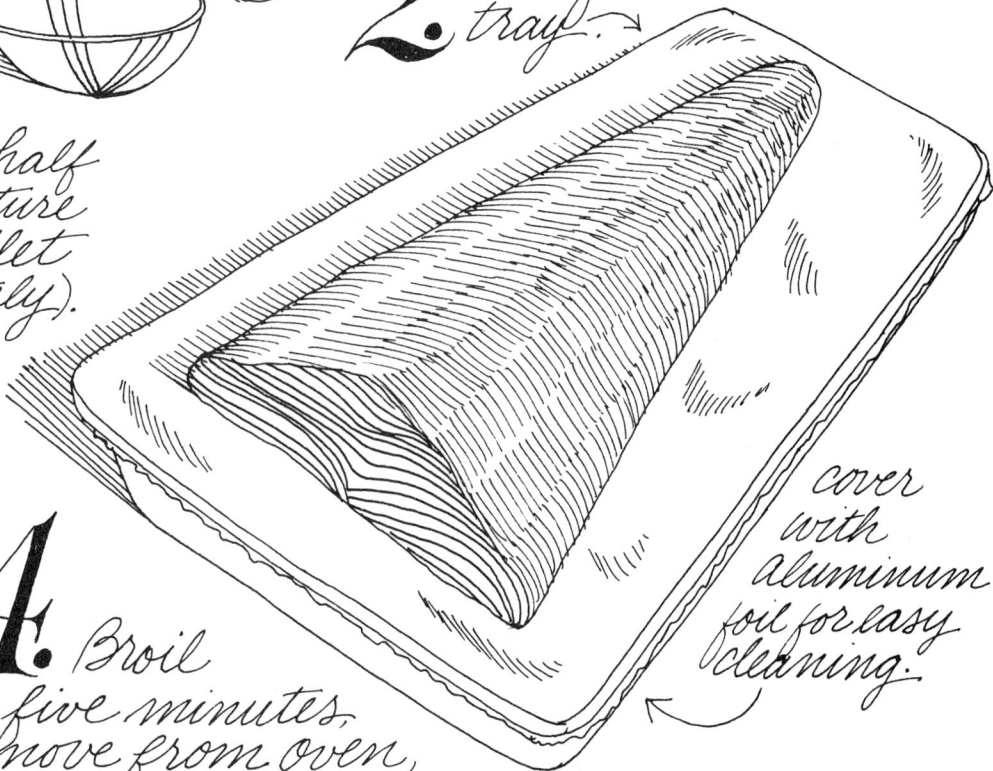

cover with aluminum foil for easy cleaning.

4. Broil for five minutes, remove from oven, turn over with a spatula, and spread other half of mixture on other side.

5. Broil for five to eight minutes more and serve. Note: A fresh Bluefish fillet is grey and red in color. This sometimes turns the Cook from purchasing it. When cooked properly, the meat turns a beautiful white and looks much like Cod or Haddock.

Molly Lockwood went out on one of the Author's Charters. After a successful day on the water, we exchanged Bluefish recipes. I thought hers sounded rather strange, and told her so. She said if I tried it, I'd eat my words. I did, and not only ate my words, but an awful lot of Bluefish too!

It's an absolutely wonderful way to turn Bluefish fillets into golden-brown gourmet delights in minutes.

An incredible recipe for Bluefish that has to be tried to be believed. It takes just a few minutes.

take

1.

HELLMANN'S REAL MAYONNAISE

HORSERADISH

and mix in equal parts in a bowl and mix together to a consistent blend

Don't be afraid that it will be too "hot". Something wonderful happens to it while cooking.

2. Squeeze a lemon on the fillet

3. After lemon juice cover completely with mixture and then sprinkle with paprika.

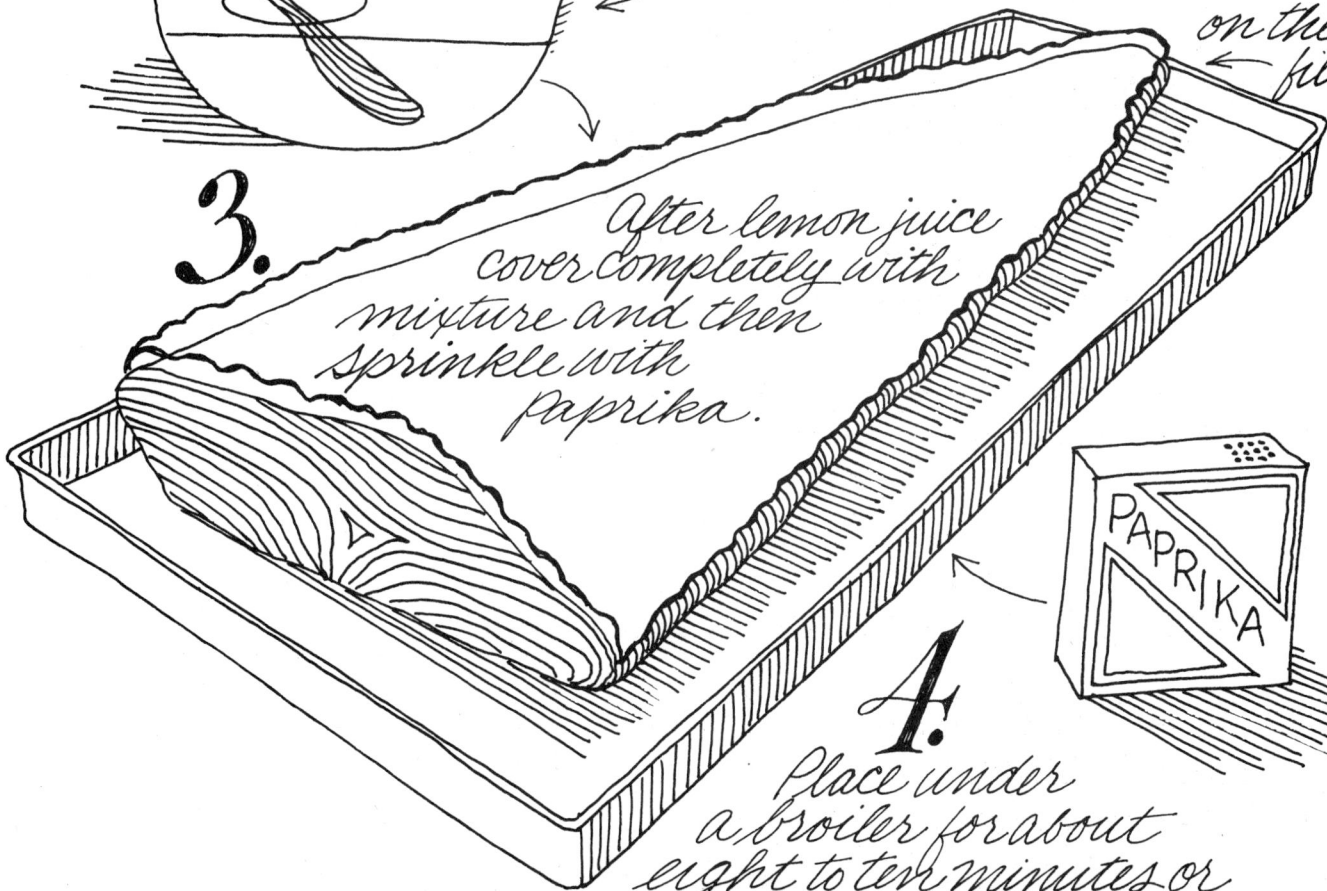

PAPRIKA

4. Place under a broiler for about eight to ten minutes or until the surface turns to a bubbly golden brown. Test with a fork and then start eating!

Captain Zander Budge holds up a big, beautiful Mahi-Mahi (Dolphin) caught on his 31 foot Bertram Charterboat called the "Spooky Luki". It sails out of Kawaihae, Hawaii, in search of light-tackle World records for Marlin, Tuna, and Dolphin.

In fact, Captain Budge is a former World record holder for Blue Marlin caught on 80 pound test line.

His recipe for Sweet and Sour Mahi-Mahi is marvelous!

Sweet and Sour Mahi-Mahi (Dolphin)
If you can't get Dolphin, use another kind of fish.

1. Skin fillets and cut away dark center meat and discard

Dark meat runs length of fillet on skin side.

← skin

2. The white meat is then sliced diagonally so each piece of fish is 1/2" thick. Put aside and prepare sauce.

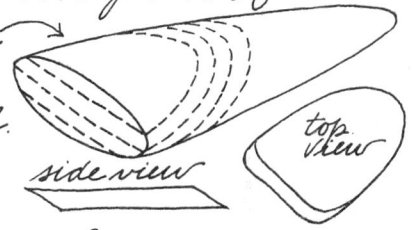

side view

top view

3. Take one tablespoon of oil and two or more green onions, chopped and put in a pan with medium flame

4. In a separate bowl, add dry ingredients. Then add:

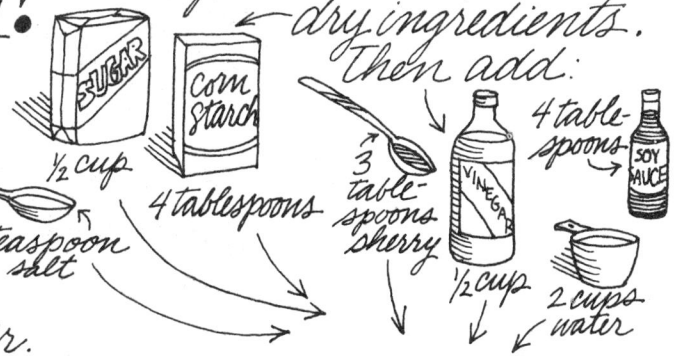

SUGAR 1/2 cup

corn starch 4 tablespoons

1 teaspoon salt

3 tablespoons sherry

VINEGAR 1/2 cup

4 tablespoons → SOY SAUCE

2 cups water

mix all well

5. Add mixture to pan with onions. Stir. When it becomes translucent, it's done.

6. Dip fillet slices in batter (your favorite) and sauté each side in butter, oil, or margarine. Be sure to remove fish before it is cooked through (like an egg it will continue to cook when removed from pan).

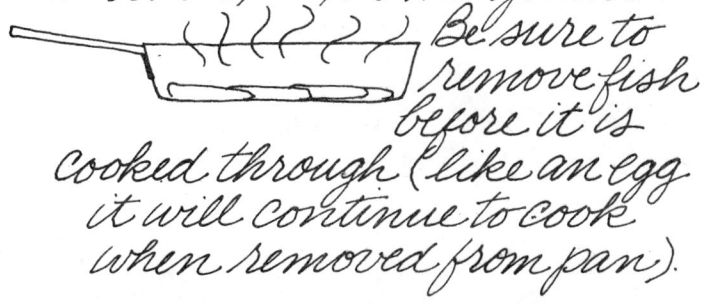

7. Place on warm platter, cover with sauce and sprinkle with

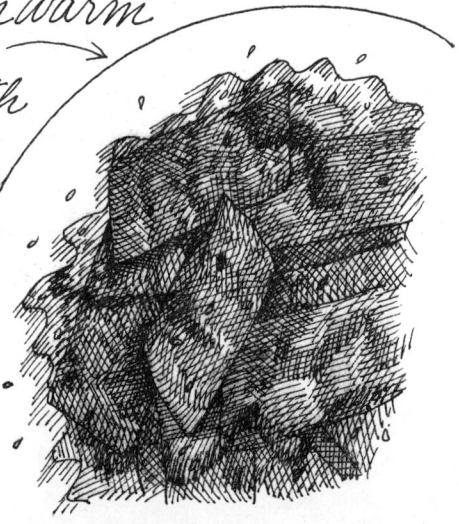

SESAME SEEDS

Delicious!

Captain Emory Dillon, Jr. is based in
Hatteras, North Carolina. His 43 foot boat
the "Early Bird" is moored at Oden's
Docks and is a perfect boat for fishing
offshore for Marlin and Dolphin.

The Dolphin has been long reputed
to be one of the finest eating fish around.
Here's Captain Dillon's contribution
to keeping that reputation going.

Charcoal-Broiled Dolphin Carolina

1. Use Dolphin fillets that are only 3/4 to 1 inch thick they should be small enough so there will be 2 per serving.

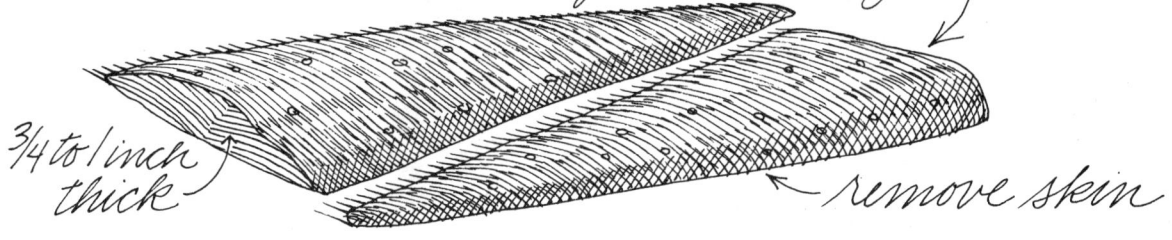

3/4 to 1 inch thick

remove skin

3. Let fish get to room temperature Pat with paper towel to remove any water, then dip fillets into a pan of melted butter to coat.

2. The charcoal should burn to a slow, even heat As fish will burn if it's too hot.

4. Place fillets on grill skin side down. Baste well to keep from sticking. the length of time will depend on thickness of fish. Cook almost all the way.

more butter

5. Turn fish and Cook for only 3 minutes and serve. Season to your own taste. Beautiful!

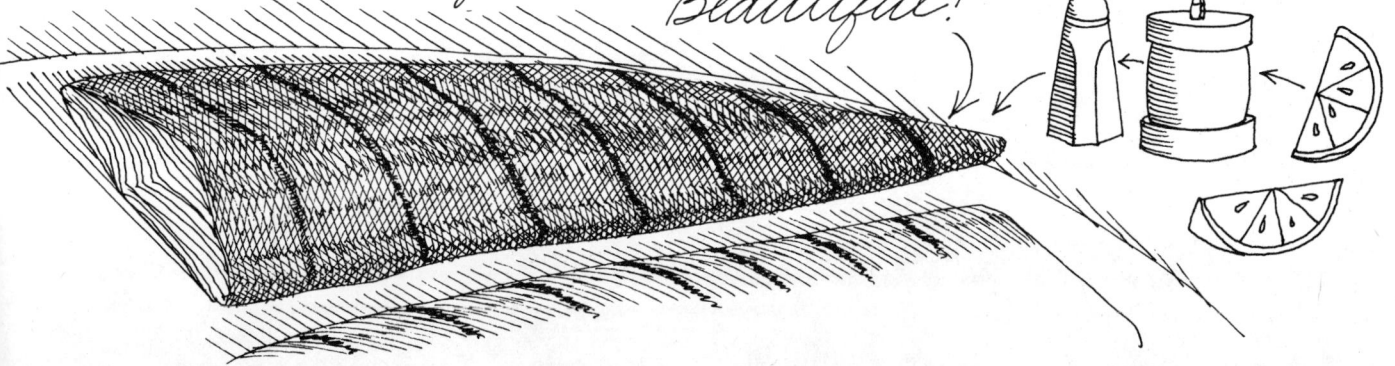

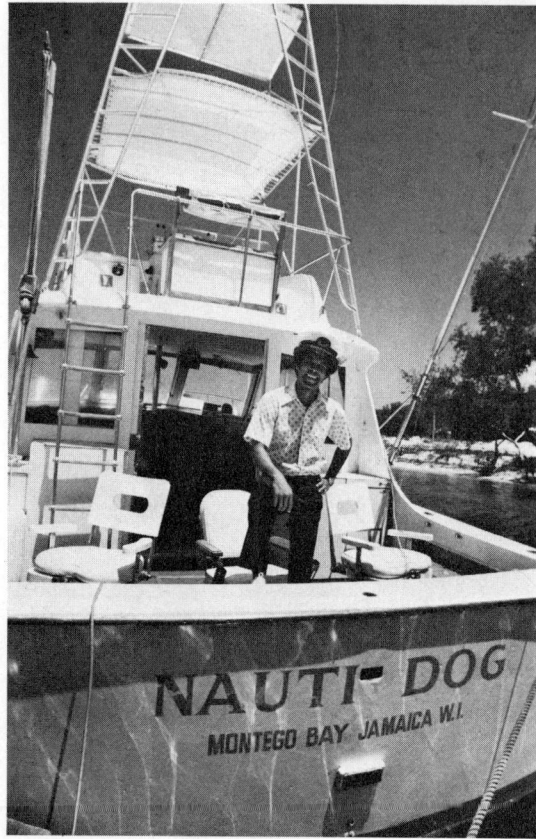

Captain Hudson Hooshing stands on the stern of the "Nauti-Dog", a 41 foot Hatteras Sports fisherman that charters from the Esso Marina outside of Montego Bay, Jamaica, West Indies.

Captain Hudson has been fishing these blue waters for 14 years now, and has taken Marlin, Kingfish, Wahoo, Bonito, Tuna, Shark, Barracuda, and many other species.

This is his recipe for his favorite eating fish, the multi-colored, high-jumping Dolphin which is so popular and so plentiful in the Caribbean.

Dolphin Fillets Montego Bay style, by Captain Hooshing. A tasty recipe that can be used on other fillets, too.

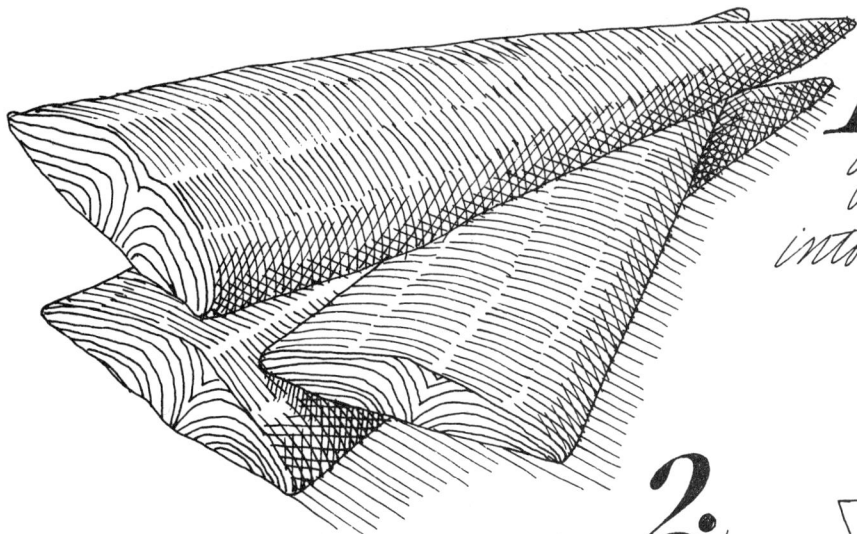

1. Prepare about half a pound of fish per person. Put fillets into a frying pan.

2. add to the pan

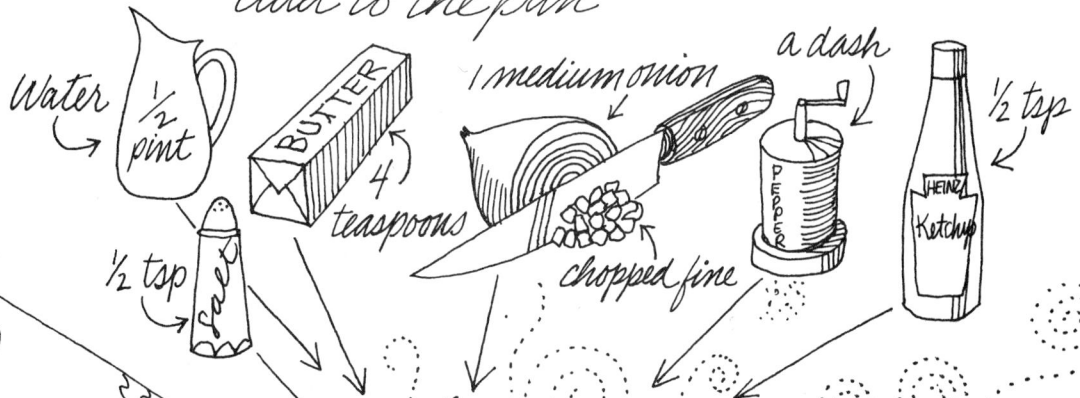

Water — ½ pint

½ tsp (salt)

BUTTER — 4 teaspoons

1 medium onion — chopped fine

a dash (PEPPER)

½ tsp (Heinz Ketchup)

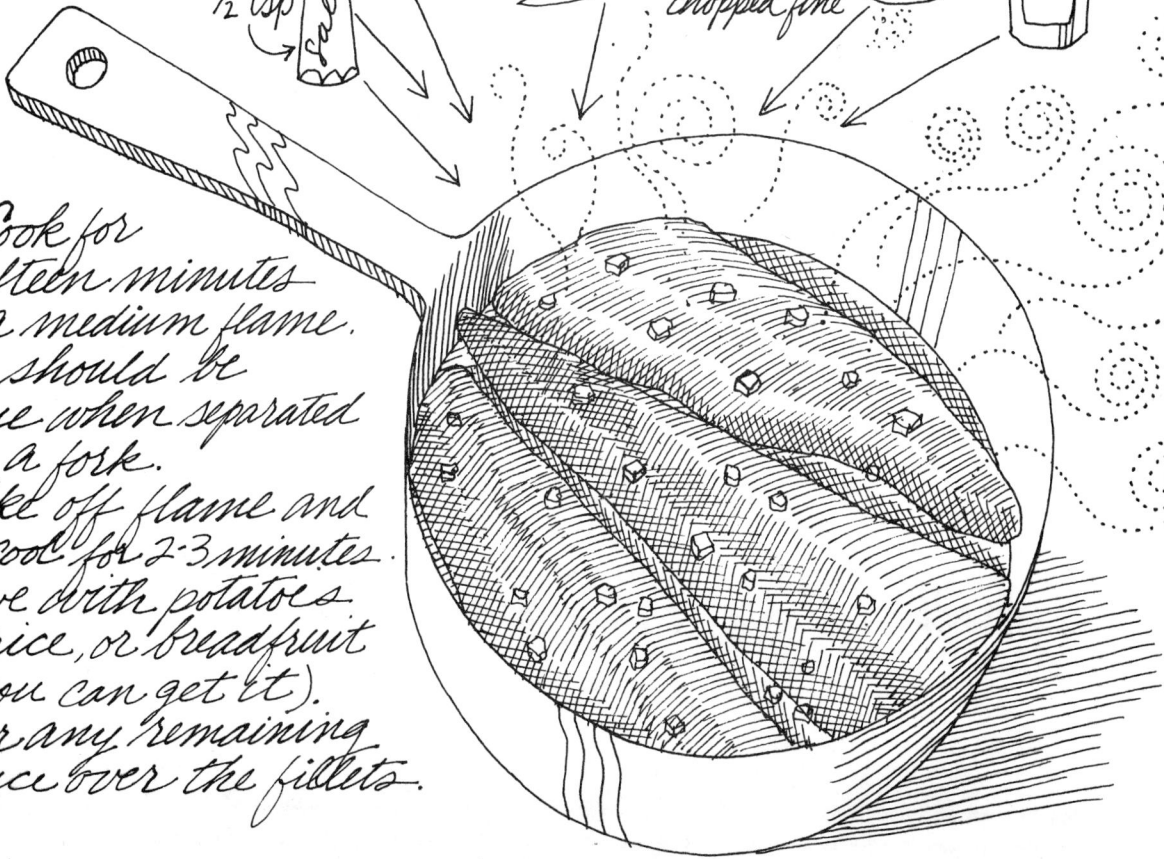

3. Cook for fifteen minutes over a medium flame. Fish should be opaque when separated with a fork.

Take off flame and let cool for 2-3 minutes. Serve with potatoes or rice, or breadfruit (if you can get it). Pour any remaining sauce over the fillets.

Captain Bill Poole has been in sports-fishing for 28 years. His 113 foot custom-made "Royal Polaris" was built by his own new company, the Poole Boat Company.

The "Royal Polaris" sails from San Diego's Fisherman's Landing on exciting 6-7-10 day trips to catch Wahoo, Tuna, Yellowtail, Amberjack, Sea Bass, Dolphin, and Marlin.

What a way to spend a week!

"Savichi" as its made and served on the "Royal Polaris".

1. Fillet a Dolphin (the "Mahi-Mahi" of the islands) and cut into small cubes. Cut up as much as you feel you'll need.

2. Place in a Pyrex dish and squeeze fresh lime juice over fish to "cook" it. Use enough to keep mixture quite wet.

3. As it marinates add tomatoes (chopped), green onions (chopped), peas (frozen, or fresh shelled but not cooked), and parsley.

4. Season to taste: Salt, pepper, and tabasco sauce (not too much). TABASCO

5. It will be ready to eat in about 30 minutes. Spoon into small dishes and eat with spoons or forks. (If it sits too long the lime juice may make the fish rubbery. It rarely sits long.)

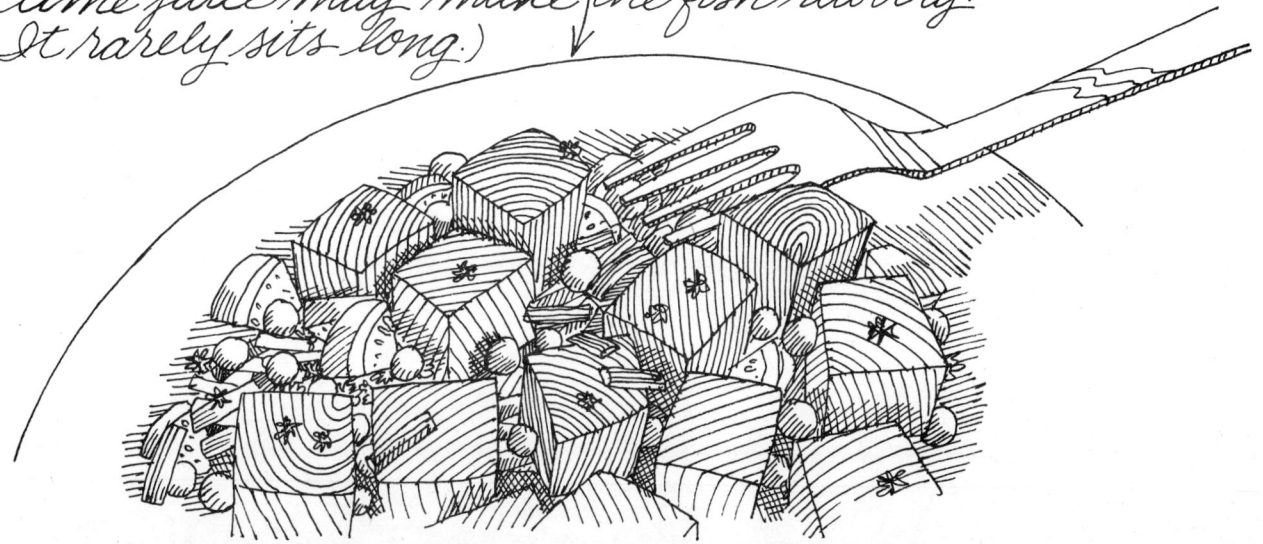

Captain Mike Verges runs the 40 foot
custom-built sportsfisherman called the
"Sea Witch" out of the Shark River,
Neptune, New Jersey.

Mike has run charter boats out of
many ports and has interesting
recipes from all of them.

This one for the colorful and
tasty Dolphin of tropical waters is
different, delicious and quite
a surprise to make.

Photo by James Allen

"Feché" Dolphin. An amazing tropical recipe that's easy to make and delicious to eat.

1. Fillet a Dolphin.
If fish is large, split fillet lengthwise so as to keep it from being too thick

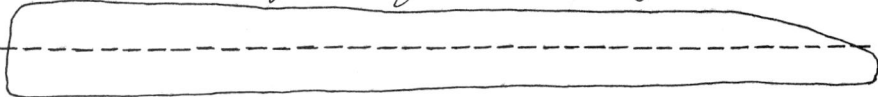

2. Lay fillets in a Pyrex or crockery pan. Do not use any kind of metal.

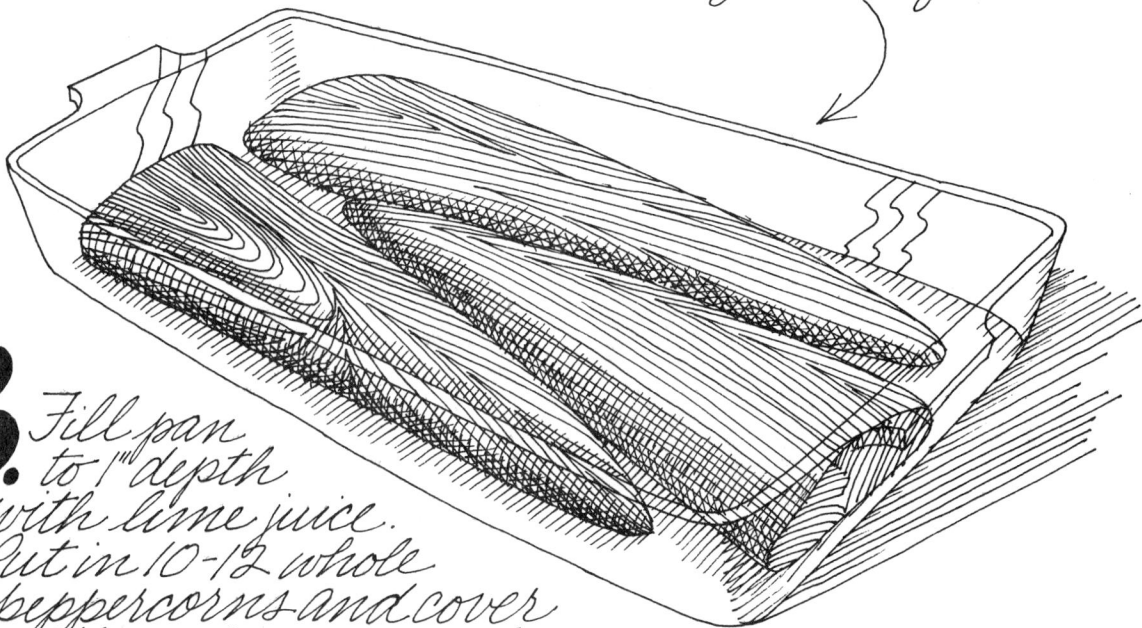

3. Fill pan to 1" depth with lime juice. Put in 10-12 whole peppercorns and cover with a damp towel.

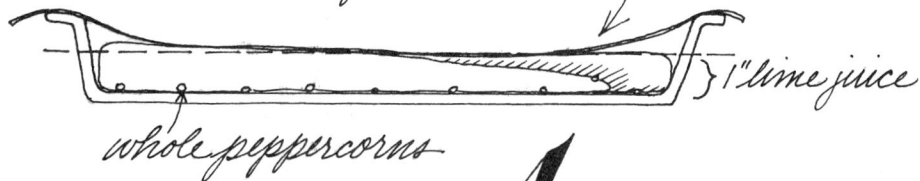

1" lime juice

whole peppercorns

4. Place pan in vegetable compartment in your refrigerator overnite. The meat will have "cooked" in the lime juice and can now be eaten and enjoyed just as if it had been made the conventional way. Its terrific!

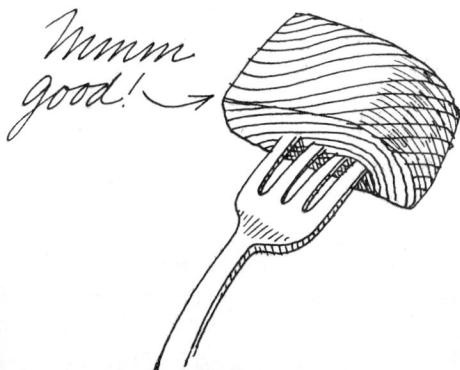

Mmm good! →

Captain Edward "Spider" Andresen runs
the "Stormy Petrel" out of Menemsha on
Martha's Vineyard.

Though most often found fishing for
big Stripers among the rocks of the Vineyard,
it would not be unusual to spot him
stalking the Key West Tarpon flats
in the month of May.

Once you've tried his recipe on some fillets
it won't be unusual finding yourself
making it again and again.

A broiling sauce for Flounder or Sole
(It's good for any non-oily fish.)

1. In a saucepan, melt half a stick of butter.

2. Squeeze into the pan the juice of half a lemon picking out the seeds.

3. Add a good dollop of mayonnaise and half a shot of Dry Vermouth and stir with a whisk or fork.

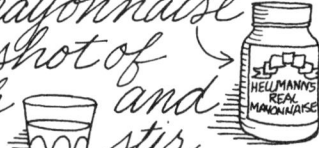

4. Lay out fillets on foil on a broiler pan.

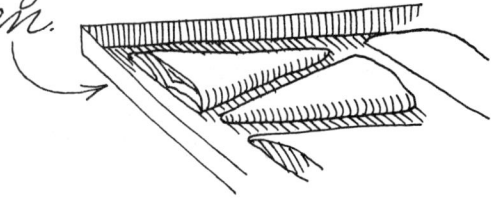

5. Pour and spread evenly the mixture from the saucepan over the fillets and let sit for fifteen minutes or so.

6. Sprinkle with a little paprika and broil close to the flame.

7. It will come out brown and bubbly. As with all fish, try not to overcook. Test with a fork.

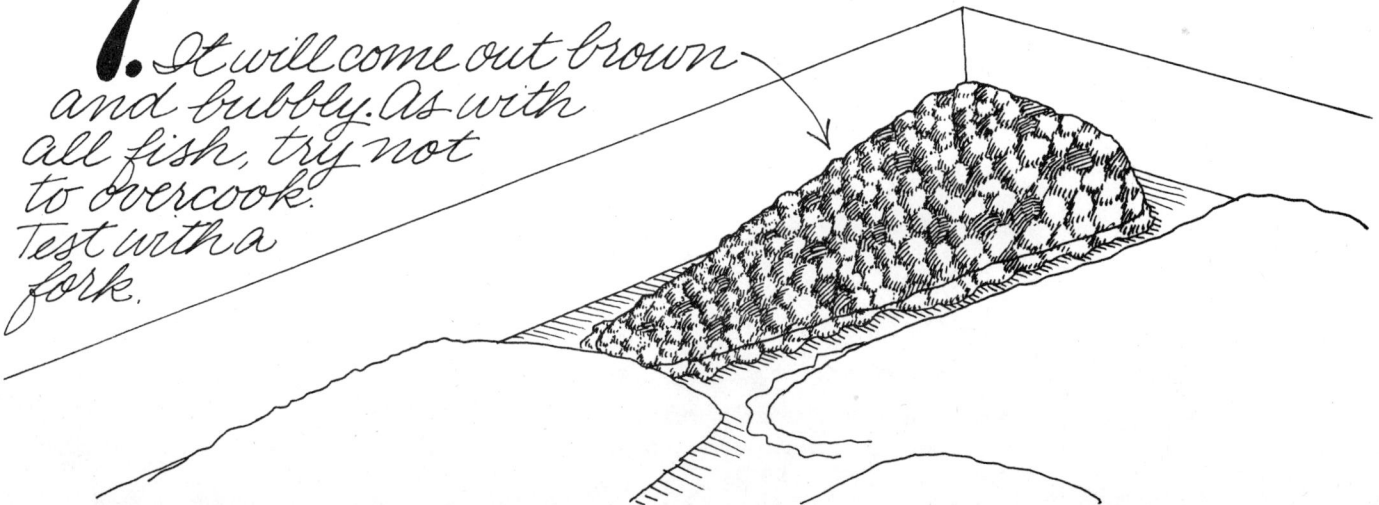

Captain Jerry Veronikis and his boat
the "Chalet" can be found at the Belmar
Marine Basin on the Shark
River in Belmar, New Jersey.

He takes his well-rigged 36 foot Egg
Harbor Sportsfisherman out onto South
Jersey waters to troll, chum, and
bottom fish for the many species
that are found in the area.

His versatile stuffing for Flounder
can be used for almost any fish dish.
One taste and you'll have a new
favorite to rave about.

Baked Flounder Stuffed with Crabmeat Imperial

1. To mix the Crabmeat Imperial, combine the following ingredients in a bowl:

WHITE PEPPER 2 teaspoons

WORCESTERSHIRE SAUCE 1½ oz Worcestershire

2 raw eggs

BUTTER 4 oz melted, but not browned

1 tablespoon salt

2 teaspoons Coleman's Dry Mustard

REAL MAYONNAISE ← 3 tablespoons Mayonnaise

And mix well with a whisk

2. Add to the mix six slices of white bread without the crust and mix well by hand till it becomes a paste.

3. Chop up one sweet pimento pepper and add to mix for color

4. Fold in one pound of fresh picked Crabmeat. Mix gently so as not to break up Crab- meat too much.

5. With this mix you can stuff shrimp, Flounder, make Crab Cakes, etc. For stuffed Flounder, take two fillets and put Crabmeat mixture between.

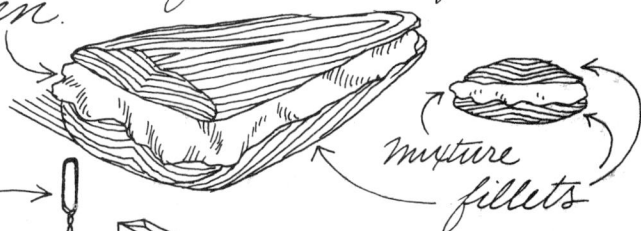

mixture fillets

6. Brush with melted butter, sprinkle with paprika and bake for 20 minutes PAPRIKA in a greased pan at 350 degrees. A gourmet treat!

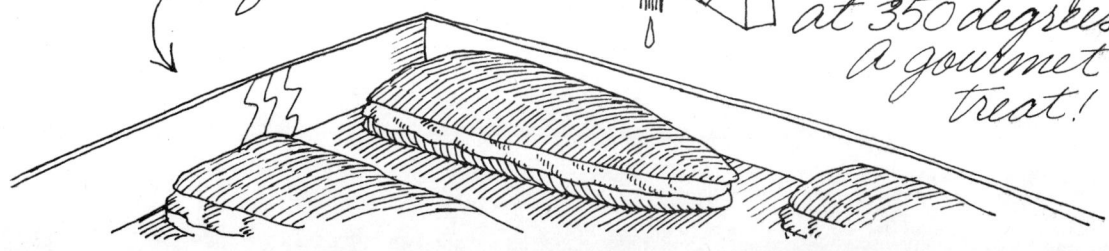

Captain Frank Buchanan runs the private boat called the "Peggy" on alternate weeks fishing inshore for Striped Bass and offshore for Swordfish, Giant Tuna, and Shark. The rest of the time he spends working a tugboat on the waters of Connecticut, Long Island, and New Jersey.

He's shown here with the author and a 21 pound School Tuna they took offshore.

Frank's recipe for Fluke fillets and Eggplant is not only delicious, but also flexible. Use it with almost any fish.

Fluke (or any other kind of Sole) and Eggplant

1. take one medium Eggplant and slice crosswise into circles about 3/4" thick.

2. Sauté Eggplant in butter or oil until they get a bit soft on both sides.

3. Next Place Eggplant rings in greased baking pan.

4. Now sauté a sliced onion chopped and a green pepper in butter with a dash of garlic powder till soft, and put aside.

5. Put fillets on the Eggplant slices. Put thin lemon rings on fillets. Sprinkle lightly with seasoned bread crumbs

6. Place sautéed sliced onion and pepper over bread-crumbed fillets. Dot with lots of butter and put in 375° oven until fish is opaque. then chop up a large fresh tomato and some parsley and top each serving. Its great!

Captain John Pinder runs the 48 foot Wheeler craft called the "Mageor" on the clear blue waters of the Bahamas.

Based at the Nassau Yacht Haven, he searches the ocean for Tuna, Sailfish, Marlin, Wahoo, and Dolphin.

One of the warm water area's tasty treats is the bottom feeding Grouper. Captain John's recipe is a delicious way to make them, as well as many other species.

Broiled Bahamian Grouper
A versatile dish for almost any fish

1. You'll need a 2 pound fillet of Grouper and a suitably sized pan or baking dish.

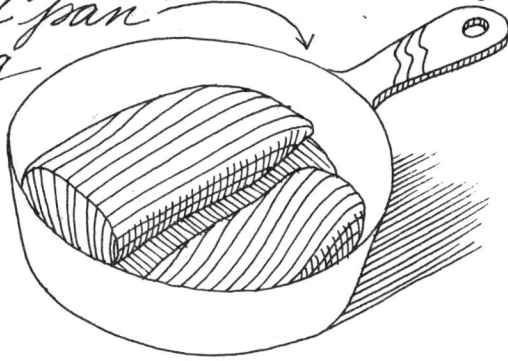

2. Mix the following ingredients in a separate saucepan.

the juice of 2 native limes

¼ pound of butter (melted)

garlic salt — A dash

SALT

2 teaspoons

3. Spread the seasonings on the fillet in the pan and place in oven at 350°.

2 tablespoons cooking Sherry

a dash of Seasonall (Seasoned Salt)

stir

4. Baste fish at intervals of about 5 minutes to prevent fish from drying out.

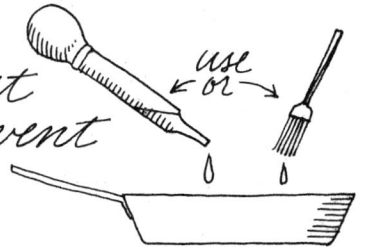

use or

5. Cook for approximately 25-30 minutes and serve with lime wedges and your favorite vegetable.

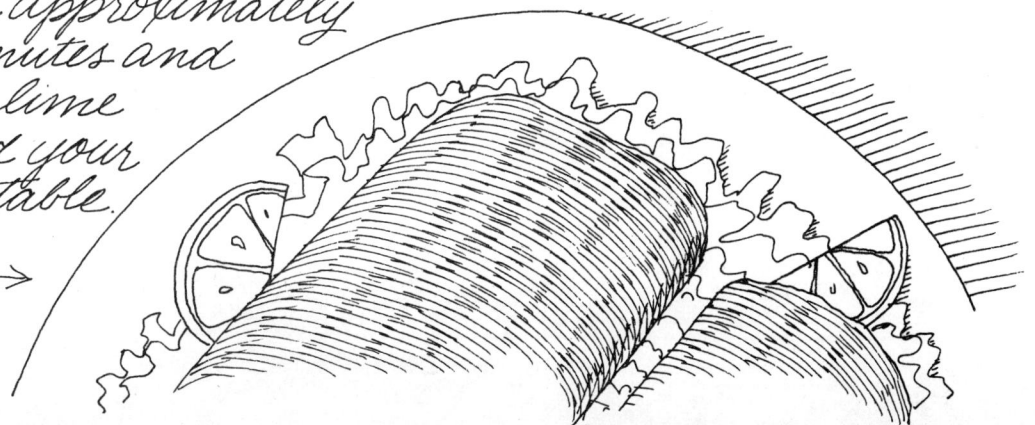

Captain Bob Brister is not a Charterboat Captain, but an editor of Field and Stream Magazine based in Texas. He runs his own private boat on the gulf. His unusual way of preparing King Mackerel is different, tasty, and well worth trying.

Boneless King Mackerel done a really different way

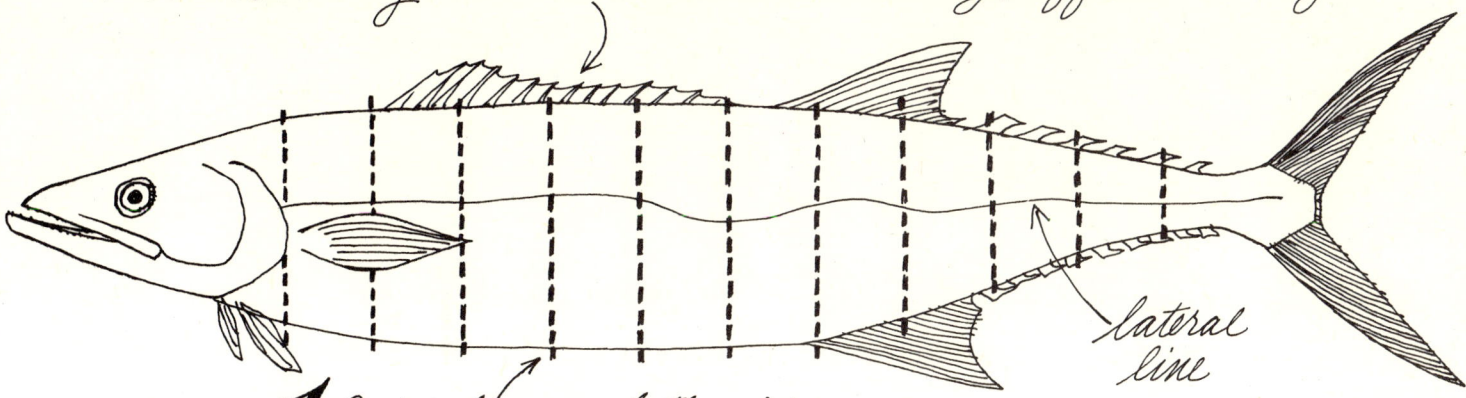

lateral
line

1. Cut to bone on both sides about 2" apart.

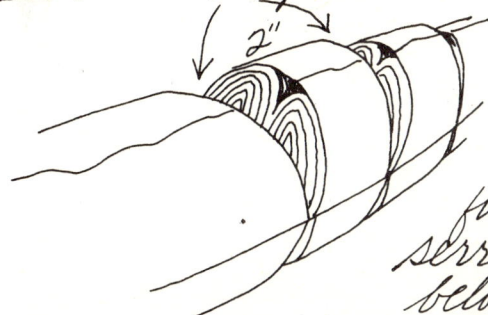

2"

2. Push a finger into each serration above and below the lateral line and push out a "ball" of flesh from each side

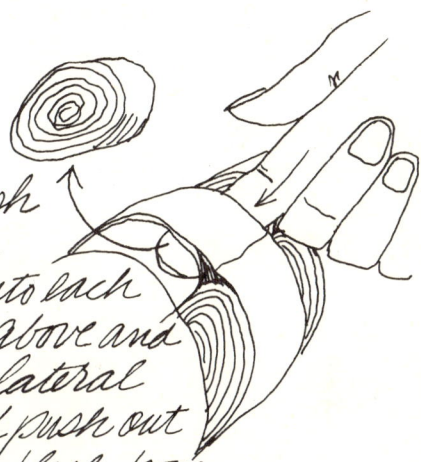

3. place removed flesh in plastic bags and immediately ice

4. Mix up your favorite cornmeal batter

dip in batter

5. Deep fry and enjoy!

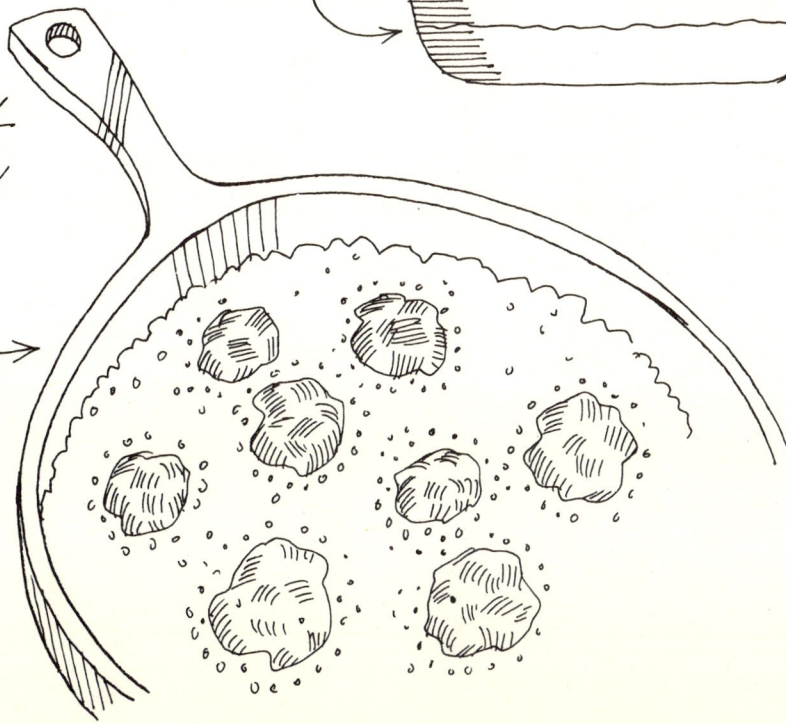

Captain Walter Haab runs the 41 foot
Charterboat "Seacon IV" out of the Montauk
Marine Basin on Eastern Long Island.
A master at both inshore and offshore
fishing and Captain on a few light-tackle
World record fishing trips, Walter and
his son Glenn know the waters
of Montauk inside out.

One of Walter's favorite catching fish
is Marlin. One of his favorite eating
fish is Smoked Marlin. Here's his
recipe for a Smoked Marlin spread
thats really remarkable.

Smoked Marlin Hors d'Oeuvres (they also come out terrific when made with other varieties of Smoked fish).

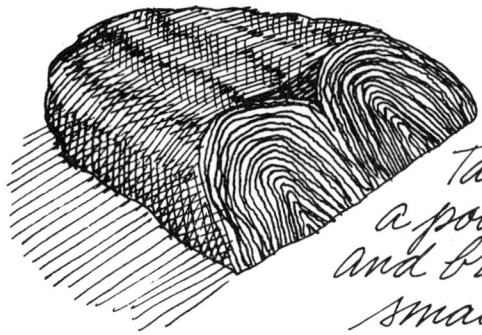

1.
Take about half a pound of Smoked Marlin and break it up into small pieces.

2.
then take two stalks of Celery and half an onion and chop them up finely.

or your favorite brand.

3. Mix Marlin, onion, celery together with enough mayonnaise to enable all the ingredients to stick together.

HELLMANN'S REAL MAYONNAISE

a dash of black pepper.

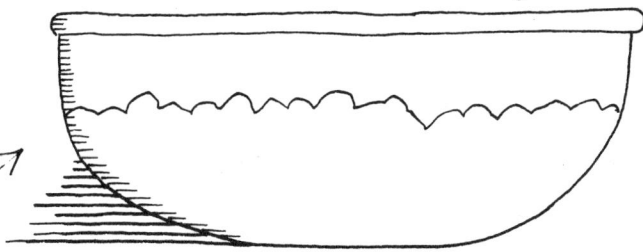

4.
Spread on Specialty crackers and garnish with a sliced olive. Terrific!

Hint:
Make the mixture a day in advance so the mayonnaise will take on the flavor of the Smoked fish. It makes a difference!

152.

Captain Al Petrosky fishes for Blue
Marlin in the crystal clear waters off
St. Thomas in the U.S. Virgin Islands.

His boat, the "Fish Hawk," is moored
at the Fish Hawk Marina in the lagoon
on the east end of the island.

This recipe is a surprise as
up North the only "billfish" eaten
is the Swordfish. Marlin and
Sailfish cooked Al's way
are a real treat!

Baked Sport Fish from the U.S. Virgin Islands

1. Cut Blue Marlin, White Marlin, or Sailfish into 3/4" fillets. Use 3 pounds for this recipe.

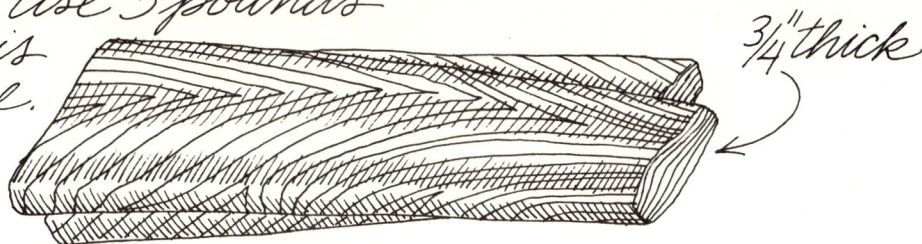

3/4" thick

2. Mix together all of the following ingredients and pour into an 11" by 15" baking pan.

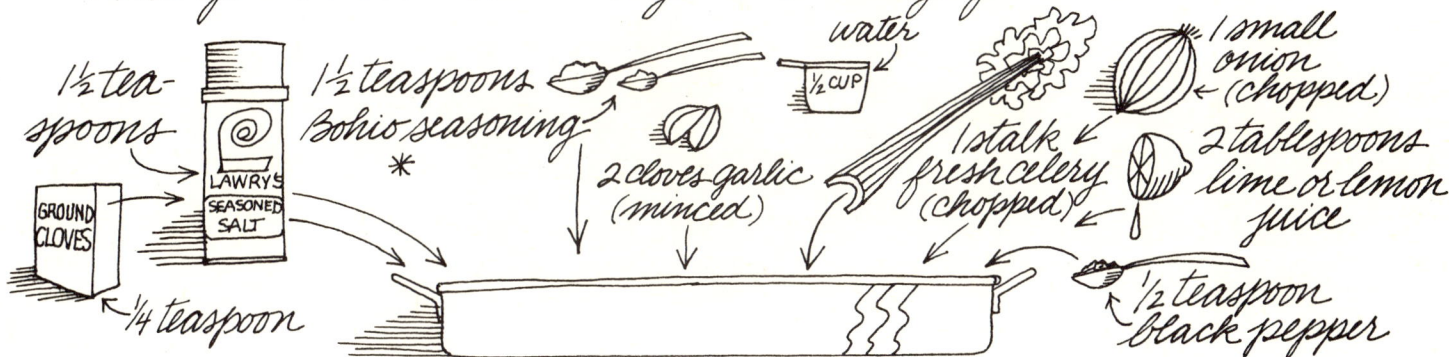

1½ teaspoons — GROUND CLOVES — ¼ teaspoon

LAWRY'S SEASONED SALT — 1½ teaspoons

1½ teaspoons Bohio seasoning *

2 cloves garlic (minced)

water ½ CUP

1 stalk fresh celery (chopped)

1 small onion (chopped)

2 tablespoons lime or lemon juice

½ teaspoon black pepper

3. Place fillets in pan and marinate fifteen minutes on each side.

turn over once.

4. Bake in a preheated oven at 250 degrees for 40 to 45 minutes or until meat flakes easily with a fork. (And they told you those fish weren't good to eat!)

*Bohio is a seasoning by Treiria Co., Puerto Rico. If unavailable, substitute 1¼ teaspoons garlic salt (Durkees preferred) and ¼ teaspoon Oregano.

Captain Jack Ross charters his
42 foot Flybridge Sportsfisherman "Miss
Kona" out of Keauhou Bay on the Kona
(lee side) of the big island of Hawaii.

The area is reputed to have the calmest
water in the world and is known for
its record Pacific Blue Marlin,
Allison and Yellow fin Tuna.

Captain Jack supplied us with much
input and knowledge of the Blue
Marlin. His recipe for Marlin
Pan fry is passed on for you
to someday try and enjoy!

Pacific Blue Marlin Pan Fry from Hawaii

1. Dip steak into a beaten egg with a small amount of lime juice (about one teaspoon per egg).

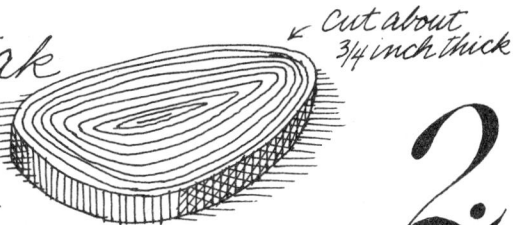

Cut about 3/4 inch thick

2. Place steaks in a strong paper or plastic bag and shake in flour. Use about half a cup for four steaks

3. Preheat electric fry pan to 350°-375.° Pour in 1/8 inch of Wesson or corn oil.

4. Fry steaks until brown on underside and meat starts to turn snow white (2 to 3 minutes).

5. Turn over and sprinkle grated Parmesan cheese on browned side

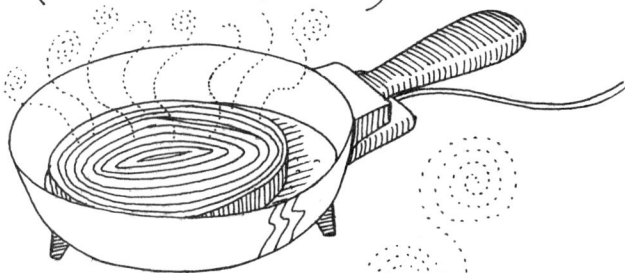

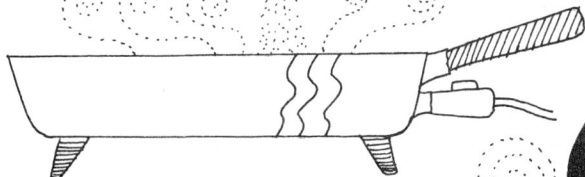

6. Cover pan and cook until meat flakes with a fork. Add salt and pepper and enjoy your feast

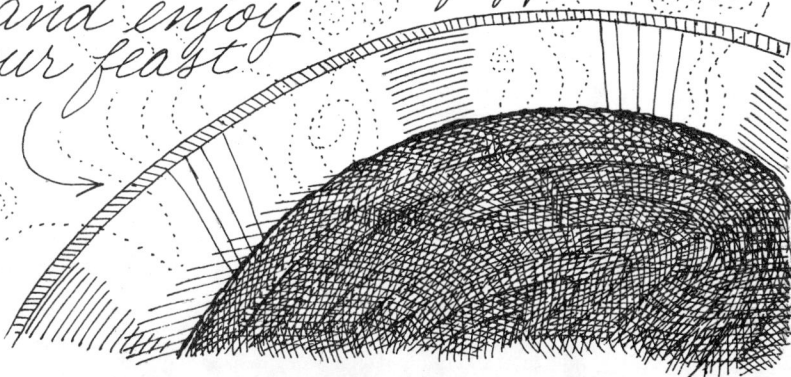

Captain Lester E. Sweet is the oldest
Charter boat Captain in Louisiana. At the
age of 71, he's still actively fishing for all species
of eating fish. The 28 pounder shown
above attests to that fact.

His boat is a 38 foot cabin cruiser called
the "General A" and runs out of the
Empire Marina in Empire, Louisiana.

Captain Sweet's recipe is for Redfish
(Channel Bass) but is equally excellent
with other white-meated fillets.

Captain Sweet's Redfish Court Bouillon

1. Start with 3 tablespoons of cooking oil and the following ingredients, and bring to a simmer in a large deep skillet or pan.

one cup green onions or shallots chopped fine

one cup celery chopped fine

8 fresh Tomatoes chopped fine

one lemon sliced in rings

one sweet green pepper sliced lengthwise

2. Add
2 Bay leaves
2 sprigs thyme
one teaspoon parsley
Salt to taste and simmer for 10 minutes.

3. Now add a dash of, the tip of a fresh red pepper chopped fine, and 3 cloves of garlic sliced.

4. Add fillets from a 5 or 6 pound Redfish (Channel Bass).

And simmer for 30 minutes. Serves 6 people deliciously!

Captain Stanley Wormuth's 34 foot
all-steel, twin diesel-powered Sportsfisherman
is named the "Playboy" and is moored at
Battistella's Marina in Empire, Louisiana.

Captain Wormuth specializes in King
Mackerel and Grouper fishing. His recipe
for Redfish Courtbouillon can be made
with Channel Bass (also called Red Drum
and Redfish), Grouper, Striped Bass, or
any other white-meated fish.

Captain Wormuth's Redfish Courtbouillon
(You can use Channel Bass, Grouper, or Striper)

1. Heat a small amount of oil and brown two large sliced onions until golden brown

2. Add 4 cans of Tomato sauce (8 oz.) (with seasoning) Cover, stir occasionally at first then, as it cooks down, lower heat and stir more often

3. Cook until you have about 1/4 of what you began with and it's brownish in color. Add 1½ quarts of and bring to a boil. Set aside on a low flame.

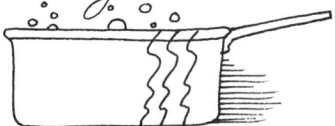

4. Make what is called a "Roux." In a seasoned cast-iron pot or pan, add enough cooking oil to cover bottom. Heat and add 3 tablespoons of flour and cook (stirring) until quite brown. Do not burn.

5. Add hot "Roux" to the tomato mixture that has been on low heat. Stir and now add a bay leaf, 2 cups (crushed) chopped parsley, 2 lemons sliced, a bunch of green onions and tops minced, 1/4 stalk of Celery chopped and a pinch each of BASIL OREGANO ALLSPICE crushed red pepper and salt to taste.

6. Simmer for about one hour.

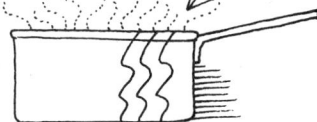

7. Lay fish steaks in a baking pan. Pour gravy over and place in a preheated oven at 350° for 15-20 minutes.

8. Baste frequently. Add a cup of red wine 10 minutes before serving over hot rice. Great!

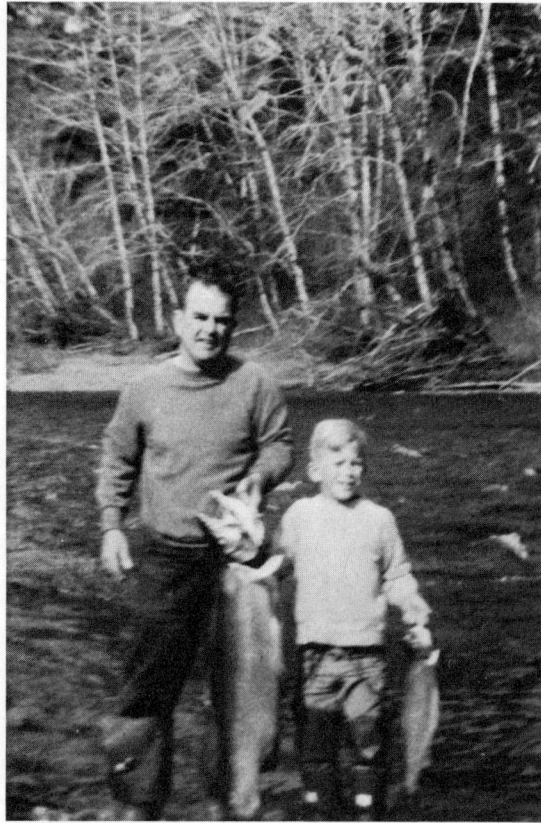

Archie Larson has been a fishing
guide in the Great Northwest for around
twenty years. He has also been
a commercial fisherman.

He guides on the rivers and salt
water with his beautifully kept
McKenzie river boat.

He's shown above with his son
Archie, Junior, who of course caught
the bigger of the fish.

Archie Larson's Seasoned Salmon and Steelhead

1. Fillet and skin a Salmon or Steelhead Trout

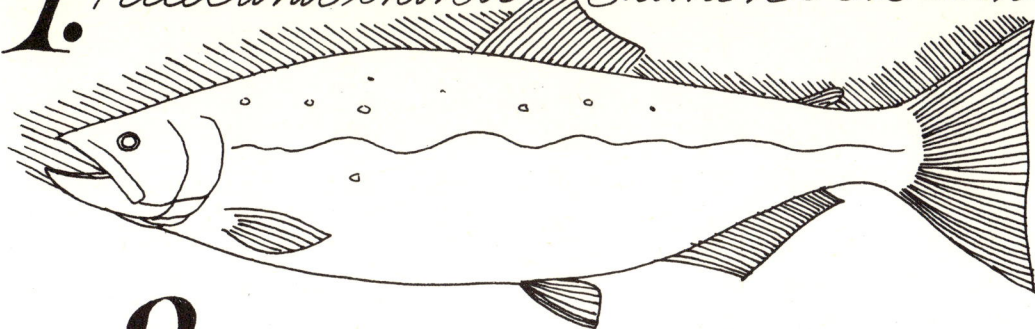

2. Cut in portion-sized pieces and sprinkle liberally with seasoned salt. (Archie recommends a local brand called "Johnny's").

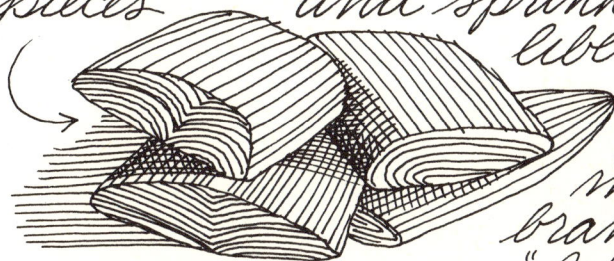

3. Let stand for fifteen minutes, then→ **4.** Roll fillets in flour

FLOUR

5. And fry in butter or oil at a medium temperature until done

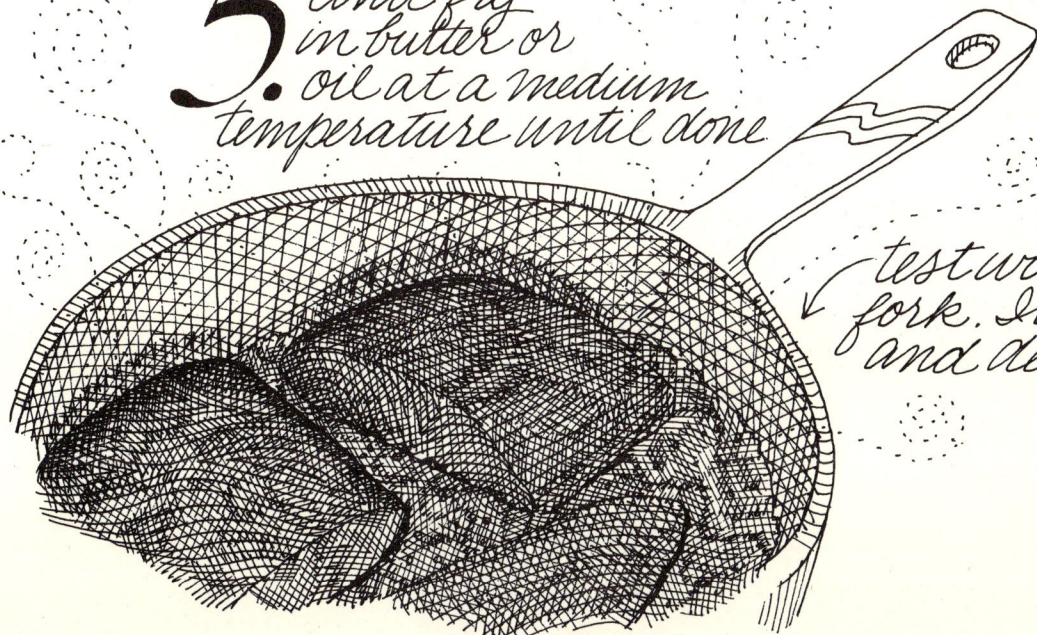

test with a fork. It's tender and delicious.

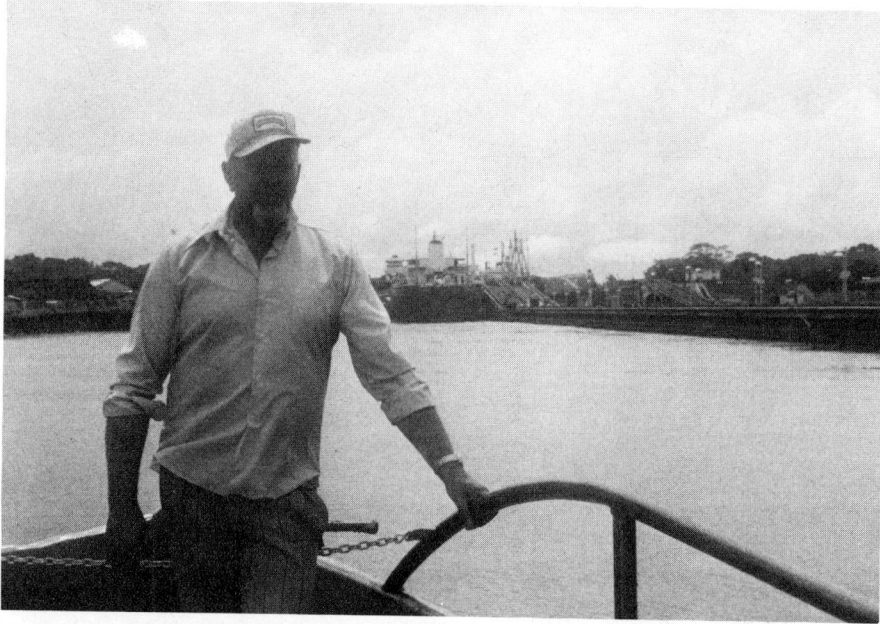

Captain Ron Hornlein runs the
"Rock Cod Queen", an 85 foot, twin-screw
boat that specializes in Rock Cod
fishing at the Farallon Islands.

Home port for Ron is Fisherman's Wharf
in San Francisco, California.

His recipe for pickled Salmon was
learned in Europe and makes up a
delectable quart jar of fish.
Be ready to double, triple, and
quadruple the formula.

Captain Ron's Pickled Salmon Swedish Style
(Recipe makes one quart jar)

1. Clean fish. Do not wash under tap water. Skin and fillet.

2. Pack fillets in medium rock salt alternating layers of fish and one-inch thick salt. Leave fish in rock salt 10 to 18 hours.

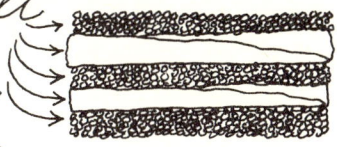

3. Brush off salt and cut fish into ½ to one inch chunks.

4. Bring to a boil the following ingredients.

water ½ cup · ¾ cup · SUGAR · HEINZ CIDER VINEGAR ⅔ cup · 3 tablespoons white wine

5. Cool the just boiled mixture. Pack Salmon chunks in a quart jar, alternating layers with a mixture of red onion slices, whole black peppercorns a couple of Bay leaves, Cloves, and Allspice.

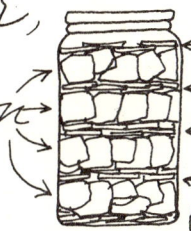

Salmon

6. Fill jar with cooled vinegar mixture. Tap bottom to make sure all air escapes.

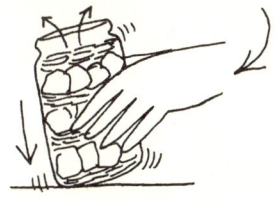

7. Add any necessary liquid to cover Salmon and onions. Keep refrigerated. After 2 to 5 days you will enjoy a delicacy you won't forget!

Captain Fred Lyman steams out
of San Francisco Bay daily in search
of tasty Salmon and Rock Cod.

"The boat he runs is the 55 foot
"Sunfish" out of Emeryville Marina
in Emeryville, California

If you like the flavor of fresh
Salmon, you're going to like it
even more after you've tried
it made this way!

A recipe for delicious "Charcoaled Salmon"

1. Clean and scale one 4 to 6 pound Salmon. Place on a large sheet of aluminum foil.

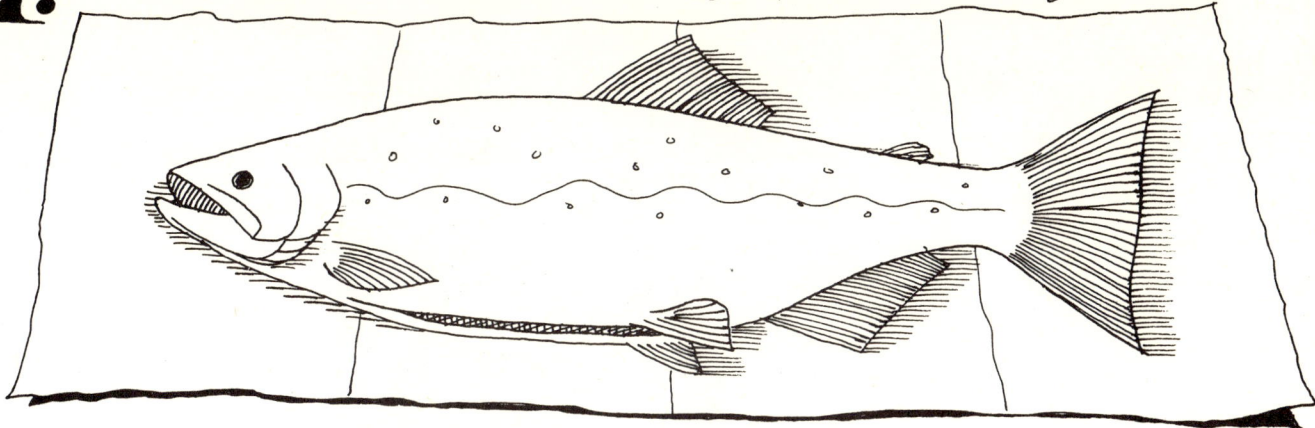

2. Take one lemon (sliced) 3 garlic cloves (chopped) and 1/2 cup of butter or margarine and place all ingredients inside fish cavity.

3. Wrap fish tightly in foil

Punch a few holes so smoke flavor can creep in.

4. Place fish on charcoal grill about 3 inches from coals for 20 minutes on each side. Discard skin and cooked lemon. Garnish with lemon slices.

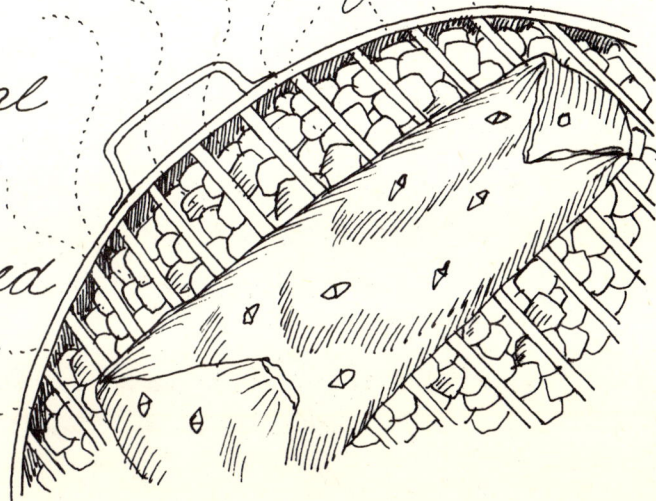

Captain Arlin Leiby is a native of the middle Keys and has been a sportsfishing guide for over 17 years. He is an official field tester for the Shakespeare Tackle Company. His specialty is light tackle fishing for all types of sport fish.

Captain Leiby fishes out of the Mariner Marina on Big Pine Key or the Duck Key Marina from March to October, depending upon weather and tidal conditions on the flats. Then home to Duck Key for offshore fishing from November to Mid-March.

No matter where you find him, his tackle will be light, and his fish will be heavy.

Baked Mutton Snapper (5 pounds or over)

1. Clean, scale, and remove head. cut here and bones will go with fins.

2. Soak 1½ cups of Pepperidge Farms Cornbread dry stuffing mix with _hot_ water to moisten.

3. Dice ¾ cup celery, one medium onion and put aside.

4. Peel one lemon or two Key limes. Grate one tablespoon of peel and dice lemon (or limes) after peeling. Discard seeds.

5. Toss stuffing mix, celery, onion, peel, and diced lemon. Season to taste.

6. Salt and pepper cavity of fish. Fill lightly with stuffing.

7. Place fish in greased baking pan. Place onion and lime slices on top. Bake at 375 degrees for about 40 minutes, depending on size, until fish meat flakes. Serve with parsley and Key lime wedges.

The pride and joy of Captain Hal Abrams
is his 44 foot Wheeler Deluxe Sportsfisherman
the "Pelican" which is shown above.

Captain Abrams has been fishing from the
same location, across from the Blockade
Runner Hotel in Wrightsville Beach, North
Carolina, for the past seventeen years.

His catches include Marlin, Sailfish,
Wahoo, Dolphin, Mackerel, Tuna, Bonito
Cobia, Bluefish, Jack Crevalle,
Grouper, and Red Snapper.

Here's a way to make Red Snapper
that's unusual, and unusually good.

Baked Red Snapper Fillets with Grapefruit

1. Skin Fillets and place on a double thickness of aluminum foil

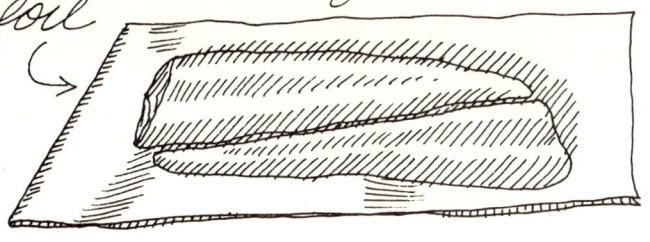

2. Season with salt and sprinkle well with grapefruit juice and grated skin of the fruit.

3. Cover fillets with some grapefruit sections and dot with butter.

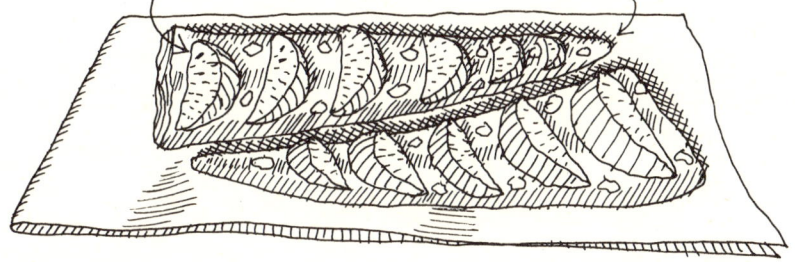

4. Seal foil

or slide into a brown paper bag and seal end with a twist tie.

5. Bake at 400 degrees for about 25 minutes. Test for doneness. Serve with chopped parsley.

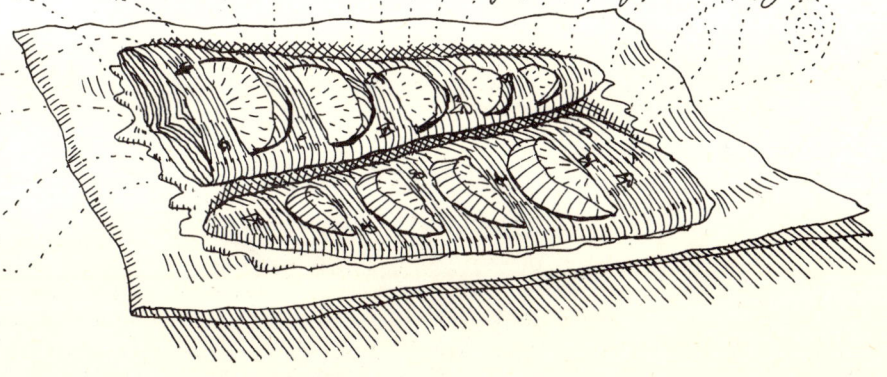

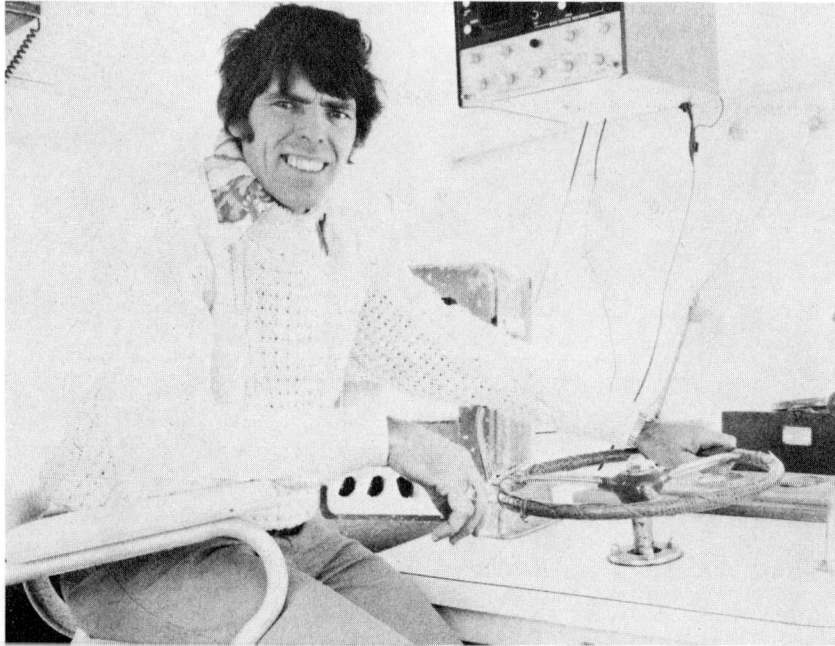

Captain Larry Hatchitt is a Sarasota,
Florida, party boat captain with over 15
years of experience on the waters of
the Gulf coast.

His 60 foot sportsfishing type boat
is one of the largest and fastest around.
It's licensed to take up to 49 fishermen
offshore for a day of bottom fishing
for Grouper, Snapper and Scamp.

It's named the "Sea Trek".

The recipe is named Baked Snapper
"Larry". Enjoy them both!

Baked Snapper "Larry"

1. Grease a large shallow baking pan and line with raw potato slices or lime slices (whichever you prefer).

2. Wash and wipe dry one five to eight pound Red or Mangrove Snapper and place in pan.

3. In a medium bowl, beat two eggs just enough to combine.

4. Add to the eggs

3 tablespoons butter melted

one can (6½ oz) CRABMEAT drained and flaked

one small onion, minced

½ cup diced celery

¼ cup minced parsley

1½ to 2 cups fine soft white bread crumbs

Mix lightly but thoroughly. If stuffing seems dry, add 1 or 2 tablespoons of water.

5. Stuff cavity of fish. Close opening with skewers and lace closed.

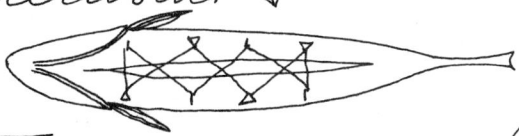

6. Melt a bit more butter. Add two teaspoons liquid gravy seasoning and browning sauce. Brush on fish.

7. Sprinkle with paprika. Bake at 500 degrees for 10 minutes and 400 degrees for 40 more.

Captain Hugh "Pudgy" O'Connor runs
the 35 foot Charterboat "Colleen" out of both
Empire, Louisiana, and Port Eads at
the mouth of South Pass.

He's shown here trolling alongside one of the
offshore drilling rigs that have become
popular havens for Red Snapper,
Pompano, Grouper, and many other
varieties of salt water game fish.

His recipe makes a delicious treat
out of the part of a fish we have all probably wasted at one time or another.

Red Snapper "Throats"

the "throat" is the small triangular piece of meat on the under-side of the fish between the gill covers.

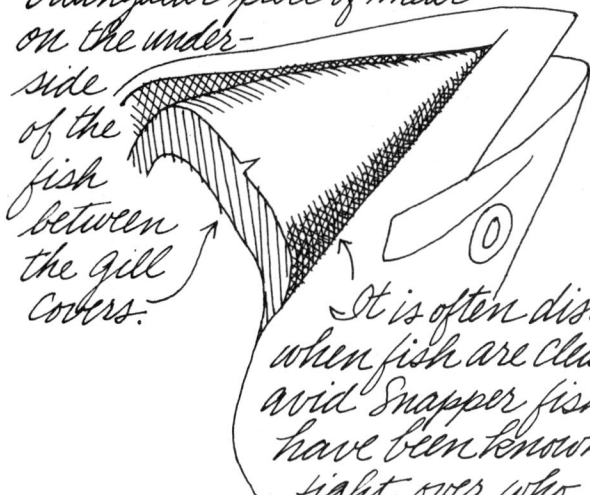

It is often discarded when fish are cleaned, but avid Snapper fishermen have been known to fight over who keeps them.

1. Skin the "throats" to waste as little flesh as possible. the throats from three five pound Snappers will be enough for a very hungry fisherman.

2. Marinate the throats for several hours in the refrigerator in a mixture of:

1 cup white wine

the juice of a lemon or lime

2 tablespoons Worcestershire sauce

½ teaspoon freshly grated black pepper

a few finely chopped shallots

a faint hint of freshly pressed garlic

it should have a tight fitting cover

3. Place fish in shallow baking dish or pan that has a tight-fitting cover.

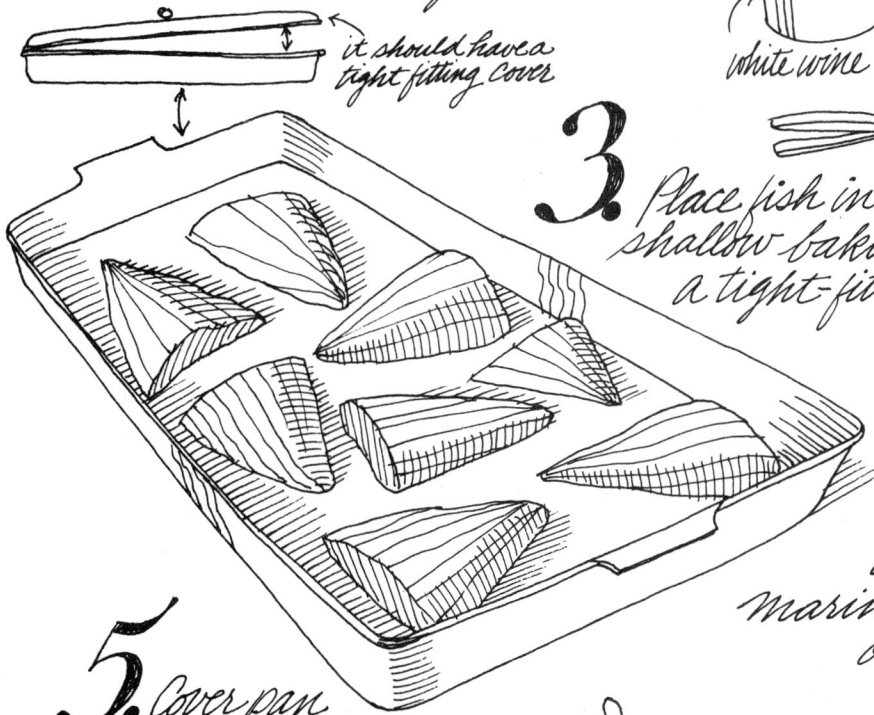

4. Melt ½ pound of lightly salted butter in a saucepan and, along with marinade, pour over the "throats."

melted butter and marinade

5. Cover pan and bake 10 min at 275°, then continue basting every few minutes until done (which should be no more than 25 minutes).

6. Remove cover from the pan for the last five minutes to help brown, at which time some and a dash of may be added.

Spanish Capers

PAPRIKA

It's a treat!

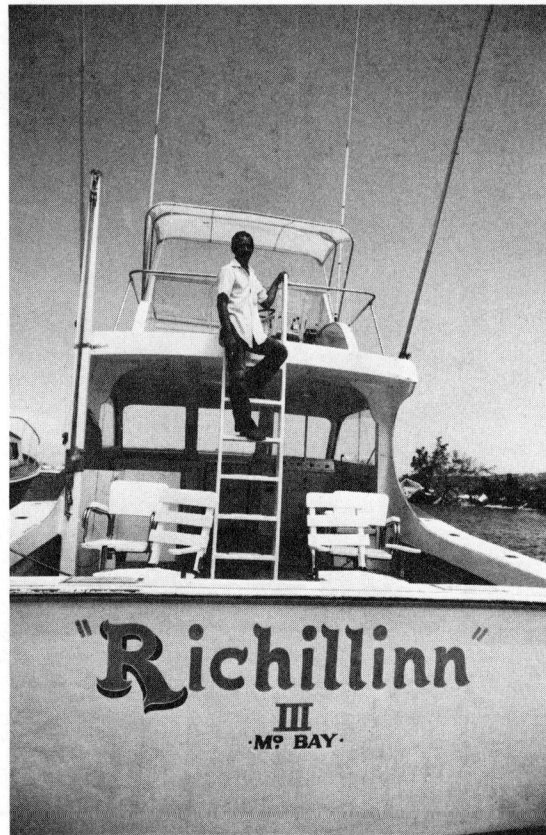

Desmond Sang stands on his spotting perch on the ladder of the 40 foot Willis Sportsfisherman called the "Richillinn III."

He's a professional Mate and Marlin hunter, and works out of Montego Bay, Jamaica's Esso Marine Center.

His recipe for Red Snapper fillets is very simple and very versatile. It can be used with almost any kind of fish.

Fried Red Snapper - simple, quick, and tasty
(Try it with most any other fish, too.)

1. Salt and pepper fillets.

one egg to 1 tablespoon flour

2. Make an egg and flour mixture (as much as you think you'll need).

3. Dip fillets in mixture. Use about a half pound per serving.

4. Heat cooking oil in a frying pan 'till its good and hot but not burning.

about 375°F.

5. Deep fry until golden brown. The fish will cook quickly, so don't let it get too golden brown unless you like it that way.

6. Serve on a bed of lettuce with fresh sliced tomatoes and wedges of lime. Super simple and super delicious!

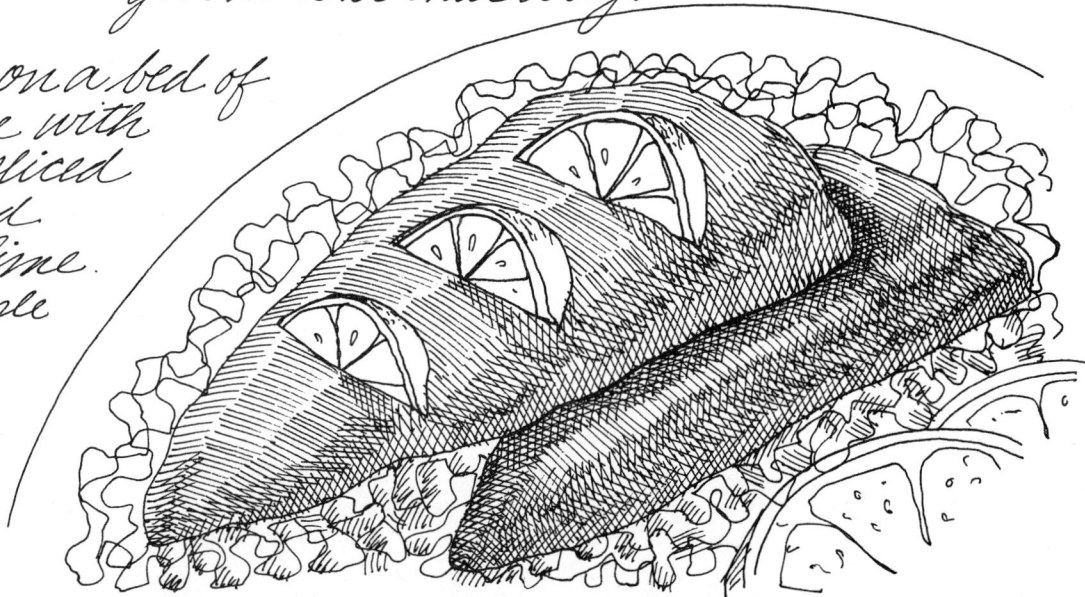

Captain Bob Baron fishes Florida's
10,000 islands out of Marco Island.
He can usually be found on board
his 24 foot custom-built Sportsfisherman
the "Lil Cracker III" catching jumbo Snook
and high-jumping Tarpon.

Captain Bob contributes his favorite
recipe for Snook that makes the pleasure
of catching them even greater. The
recipe is, as he puts it, "Simple,
and special".

A recipe for Snook (Robalo) fillets that's called, and really is, an "Angler's Delight."

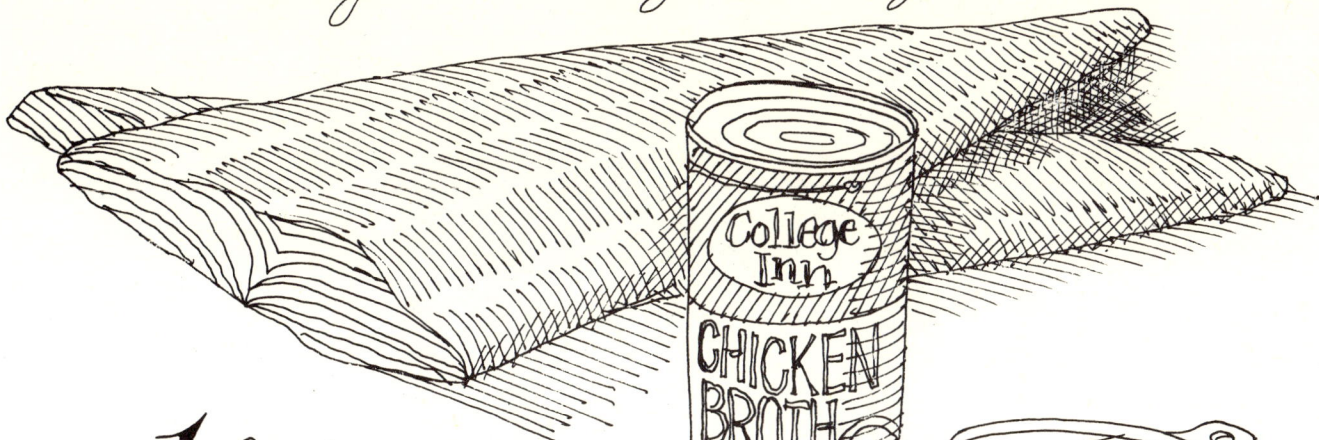

1. Combine one can of chicken broth and one half cup of Wesson oil in a pan and insert fish fillets.

2. Bake fillets in liquid until about ⅔ cooked. Remove from oven and pour juices into a bowl. (Bake at 325°)

3. add

2 tablespoons of Brown sugar

one stick oleo

juice of a lemon (add last to your own taste for tartness).

¼ bottle (2 oz)

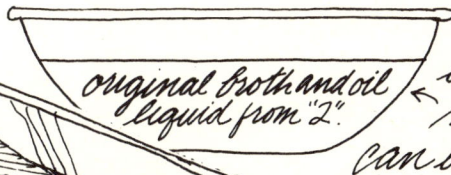

original broth and oil liquid from "2". extra mixture can be used at table to taste

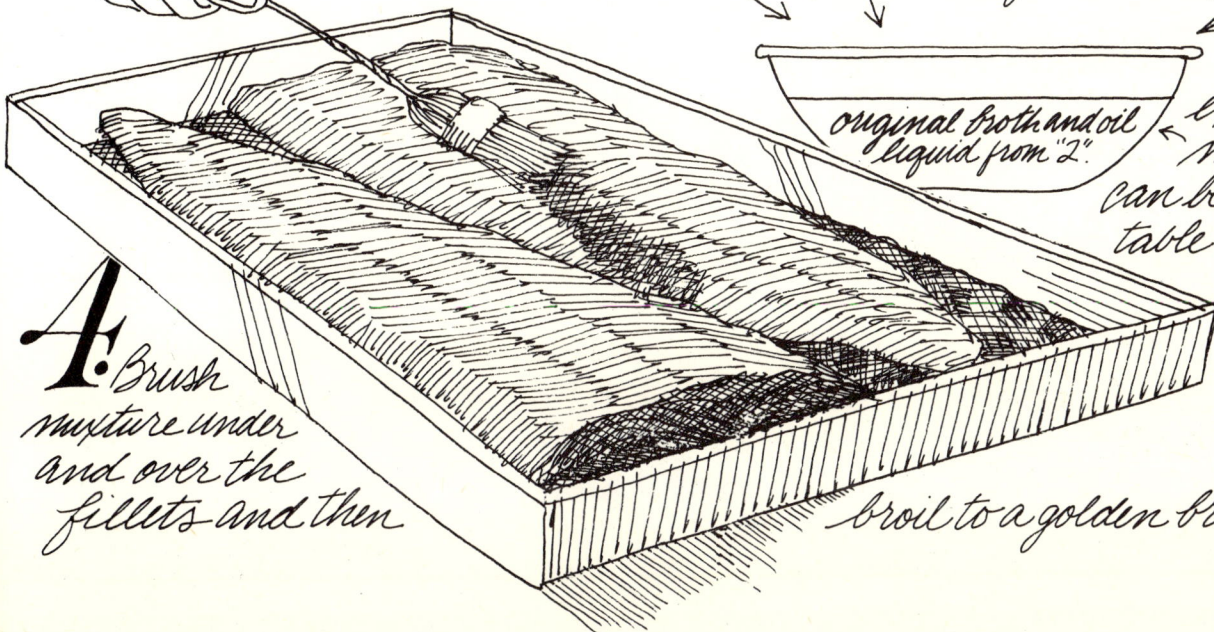

4. Brush mixture under and over the fillets and then broil to a golden brown!

Captain Al Urban fishes for Bonefish out of Islamorada, Florida, on his 17 foot Aquasport skiff and for Striped Bass on his 30 foot open boat on the Eastern end of Long Island, N.Y.

Al's customers are a special breed of fishermen who like to cast for their fish with light tackle. It's real sport.

His recipe works equally well with fish from down South, up north or out West, as long as it's a white-meat fish.

Steamed Fish with Subgum Ginger
(You can use snook, Striped Bass or any other white fillets).

1. Wash and dry one and a half pounds of fish fillets

2. Place fillets on a raised rack over one inch of water. Cover and steam for 15 minutes.

then sprinkle with salt

3. Mince 4 tablespoons of Subgum Ginger* (also called Stem Ginger). Also mince a piece of smoked ham or Smithfield ham. Use enough to make one tablespoon. Split two scallion stalks into 4 or 5 long strips, then crosswise into two inch sections.

4. Sprinkle all the ingredients over steamed fish

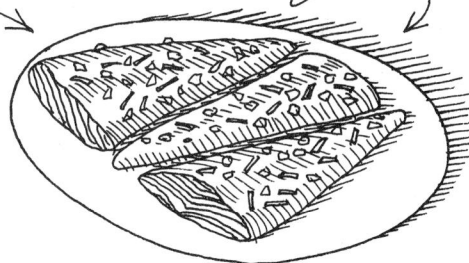

5. Crush one clove of garlic and place in a pan with 2-3 tablespoons of Peanut Oil.

Heat until oil begins to smoke.

* Can be purchased at any Chinese grocery or gourmet department.

6. Remove from heat and let stand for one minute. Discard garlic and pour oil over fish. Serve at once. Fabulous!

Captain Bob Bauer has spent most
of his adult life chasing the elusive
Striped Bass.

He fishes the waters of Cuttyhunk and
Martha's Vineyard from mid-May
to November both day and night
and in all kinds of weather.

His boat is a 23 footer named the
"Linda B" and is made specifically to
meet the needs of a Bass fisherman.

the Chowder Bob recommends
is especially welcome after a cold
night out on the water.

Hearty Cuttyhunk Striped Bass Chowder
(Serves 4-6.)

1. In a heavy iron skillet, fry ¼ cup of diced salt pork until brown, then remove and set aside.

2. In the pork fat, sauté one chopped onion until tender.

3. Lower heat. Add two pounds of Striped Bass fillets and one large raw potato, cubed or sliced.

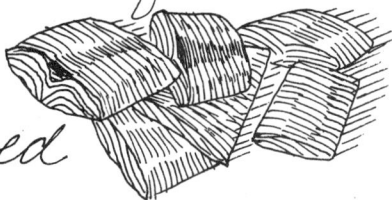

4. Cover fish and potatoes with water and salt and simmer 'till potatoes are tender.

5. Slowly add one quart of milk while slowly raising heat. Season with salt and pepper to taste.

6. Stir in browned pork bits and top with a tablespoon of butter.

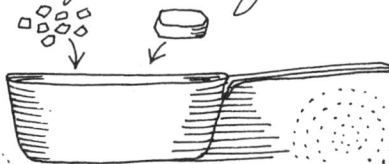

7. Cool, then reheat and serve.

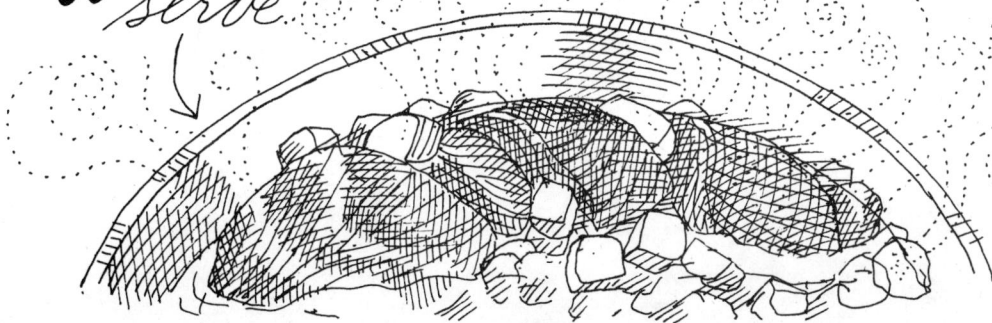

Captain Henry Colombi owns and operates the
Star Island Yacht Club in Montauk,
Long Island, New York.

Henry's Marina has grown so much
in the past three years that it now can
hold up to 200 boats of all sizes

You can usually find him running
from boat to boat giving advice, making
repairs, weighing in fish, pumping gas,
and securing lines...always with a smile.

If you make his recipe for Star Island
Fish loaf, you'll smile too!

Star Island Fish Loaf
(Serves 4 to 6)

You'll need one 4-5 pound striped Bass

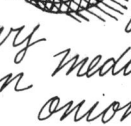

six hard-boiled eggs chopped fine

heavy cream

a medium onion

1/4 lb butter or margarine

BREAD CRUMBS

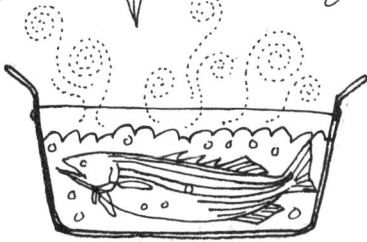

1. Boil fish in slightly salted water. When fish falls away from bone, drain off water, let cool, then flake.

2. Sauté thinly sliced onion in butter or margarine until golden brown.

3. thoroughly blend eggs, flaked fish, sliced onion-butter mixture, heavy sweet cream, and salt and pepper to taste.

4. Lightly grease a loaf pan or fish mold and sprinkle bread crumbs in and around sides

Shortening

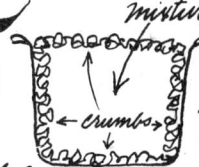

5. Pack fish mixture into mold. Spread crumbs on top, then dot with butter or margarine.

mixture

crumbs

6. Place mold in a larger baking dish containing water 1/3 the way up pan.

water

7. Bake one hour in a 375° oven. Turn over, remove mold, garnish as you wish, and enjoy!

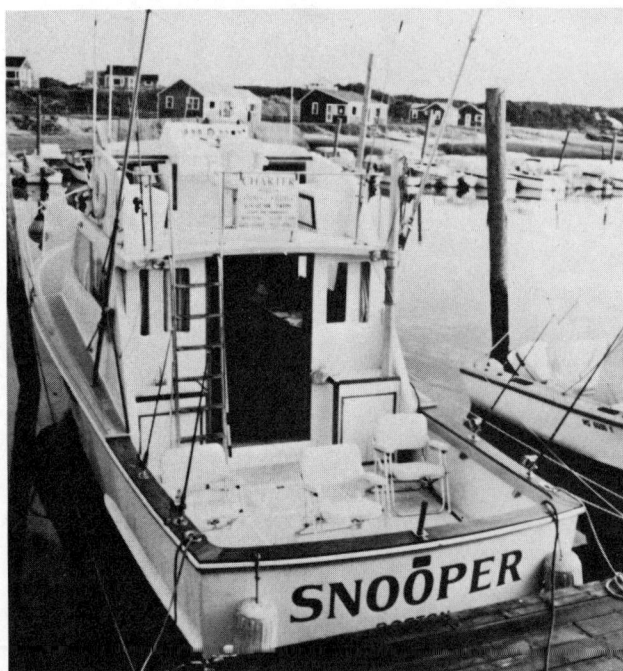

The "Snooper" is a 36 foot fiberglass
Sportsfisherman run by Captain Joe Domenico.
It specializes in Giant Tuna, Bluefish,
and Striped Bass fishing, and is
moored at the Wellfleet Marina in Cape
Cod, and the Cape Ann Marina in Gloucester, Mass.

Captain Domenico and his beautiful
boat have caught many a giant fish
while working Massachusetts waters,
and, in fact, caught the largest Giant
Tuna in the Cape Cod Charter Boat Association's
1974 and 1975 awards competitions.

Here's his recipe for Stuffed Striped Bass.
Try it with other whole fish too.

Baked Stuffed Striped Bass Massachusetts Style
(Serves 3-4)

1. Take a whole 2½ to 3 pound Striped Bass. Wash inside and out. Pat dry with paper towels.

Fins and head may be removed (optional).

2. Chop up ½ cup of onion and ½ cup of celery, then sauté in ¼ cup of BUTTER or margarine until tender (5 min).

3. Add 2 teaspoons of chopped parsley, ½ teaspoon salt, ½ teaspoon thyme leaves, and one cup of dried bread cubes.

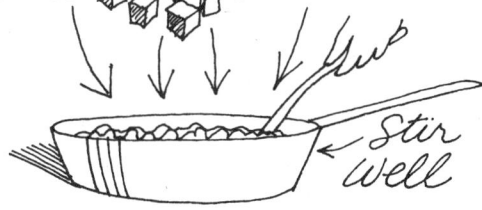

Stir well

4. Spoon stuffing into cavity of fish, and close opening with skewers or wooden picks, and/or string.

5. place fish in large greased roasting pan. Arrange three bacon slices diagonally on fish. Don't overlap. Sprinkle with pepper.

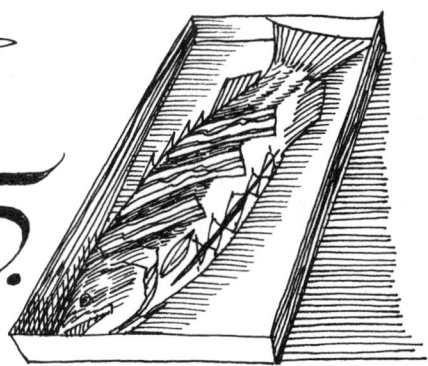

6. Bake for 35-40 minutes or until fish flakes easily when tested with a fork.

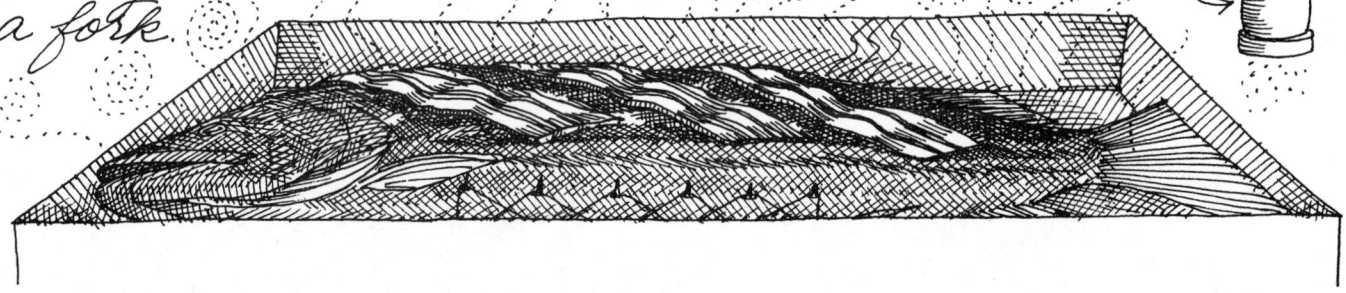

Captain Bob Glas, along with his father, runs the bright red catamaran that is known in eastern waters as the "Hel-cat".

This boat is especially suited to bottom fishing although the skippers have fished for every inshore and offshore species the area has to offer.

His recipe is for Striped Bass, but it can be used with almost any species of white-meated fish.

Striped Bass Patrician (can be made with Cod, too.)

1. Take fillets from two small Stripers or from one large one. split lengthwise

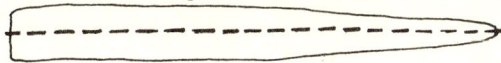

2. Soak fillets in cold salted water. Rinse in running water and drain

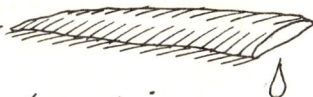

3. In a skillet, sauté in butter or margarine until thoroughly heated, one large onion chopped

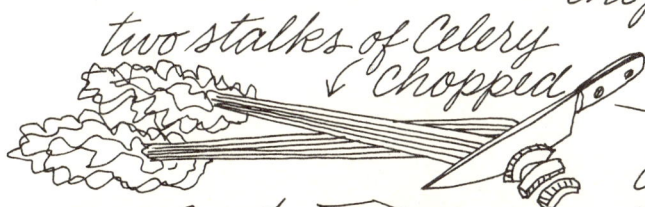

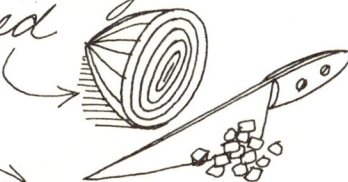

two stalks of Celery chopped

one 6 oz can of Crabmeat

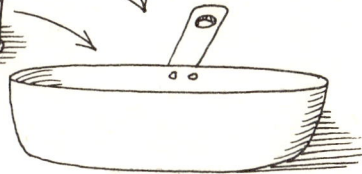

and enough to make mix stick together like dough. BREAD CRUMBS (add more butter or margarine if necessary).

4. Place half the fillets in a baking dish. Dot with butter or margarine. Place stuffing on fillets and cover with remaining fillets.

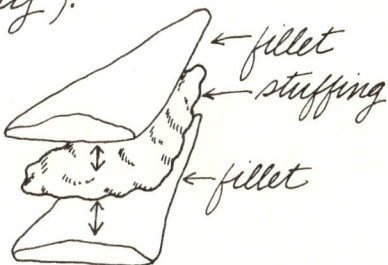

← fillet
← stuffing
← fillet

5. Bake for 20 to 30 minutes at 350° until fish is just beginning to flake.

6. Prepare a cream sauce by mixing some flour with some heavy cream or evaporated milk until it becomes a thick sauce. Add Sherry or white wine to thin to a creamy consistency.

CREAM CREAM   FLOUR

7. Pour cream sauce over fish and return to oven for 10 minutes. Serve and enjoy.

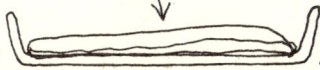

Captain Larry Keller runs the Charterboat "Jean III" out of Tuma's Dock on Montauk Point. In the Spring and Fall, Larry fishes the rips and beaches of the area for big Striped Bass and Bluefish. During the Summer months he moves offshore in search of Shark, Giant Tuna, Marlin, and Swordfish.

Larry's recipe for Stuffed Striped Bass uses both Crabmeat and Vermouth. If that combination doesn't tempt you, what will?

Baked Stuffed Striped Bass, Montauk Style
(for a 6-7 pound fish).

1. First prepare the stuffing. Mince one large 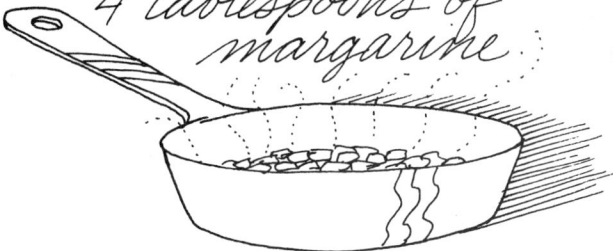 onion and sauté in 4 tablespoons of margarine

2. Add one tablespoon chopped parsley, one tablespoon 2-3 cups chopped 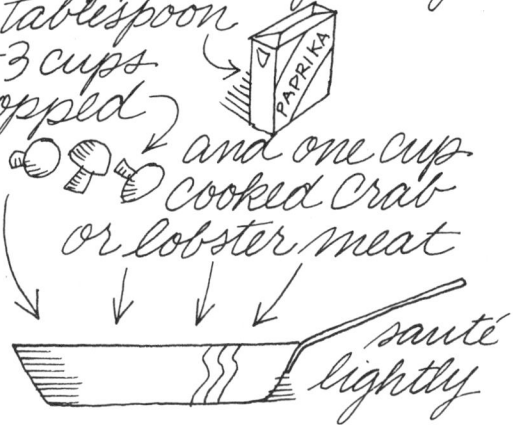 and one cup cooked crab or lobster meat

sauté lightly

3. Remove from heat and mix in soft bread crumbs

 and enough dry Vermouth to moisten (mmmm) 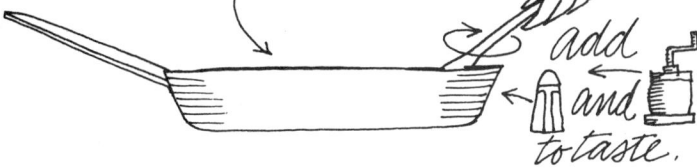 add and to taste.

4. Fill fish with stuffing and secure with skewers

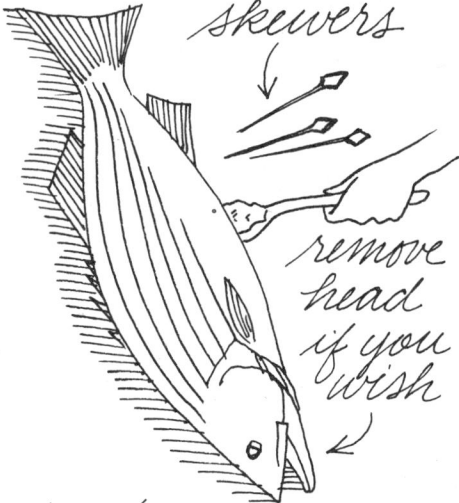

remove head if you wish

5. Place fish in roasting pan and brush with melted butter add 1/3 cup dry Vermouth

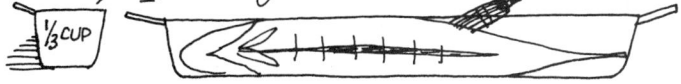

And bake at 350° for about 45 minutes or until fish flakes

6. Serve

During baking add more Vermouth and baste with pan juices

Captain Don Lynch is a Cuttyhunk Massachusetts Striped Bass specialist. He and his 26 foot McGinnis Bass boat work the coast of Cuttyhunk Island in search of this elusive fish.

Captain Lynch and the "Susan J." fish days and nights out of the Cuttyhunk Marina, and his recipe proves that he not only knows how to catch them but also how to cook them.

Cuttyhunk Stuffed Striped Bass
(Should feed 8 very well.)

1. Take one 9-10 pound Striped Bass. Clean, scale, and de-gill. (Remove head if you wish.)

2. Use 2 boxes of Stove Top Stuffing and prepare as directed on package.

Add a bit of oyster juice from item 3 to the water.

3. Chop up one onion and fry in one tablespoon of margarine till clear but not brown. Also chop up the contents of one can of oysters and a can of mushrooms.

OYSTERS   MUSHROOMS

4. Add all chopped ingredients to stuffing mix.

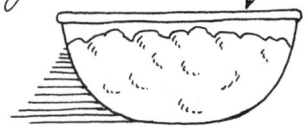

5. Stuff fish with mix and place on a cookie sheet covered with foil.

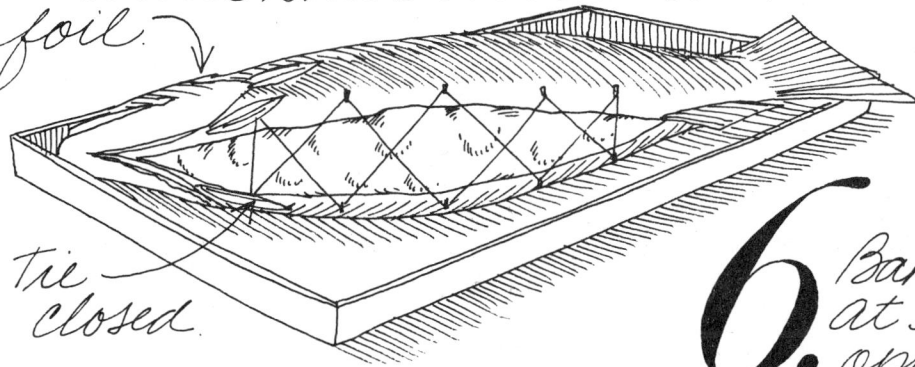

Tie closed.

6. Bake for one hour at 350 degrees. An optional touch is to place whole cranberries on top of stuffing surface.

Captain Davey McMahon (shown above),
and Captain Gus Pitts run the "Marie II" out
of the Star Island Yacht Club on Montauk
Point, Long Island, New York.

Davey and Gus specialize in inshore fishing and
seem to always catch Striped Bass and
Bluefish, even when no one else can find
them. They're a tough team to outfish.

Terrific fishermen and terrific people
to be with, they contribute a recipe
thats hard to believe until you've tried it!

How to make Striped Bass taste like Crabmeat.

1. Fillet and skin a Striped Bass. Remove the dark meat.

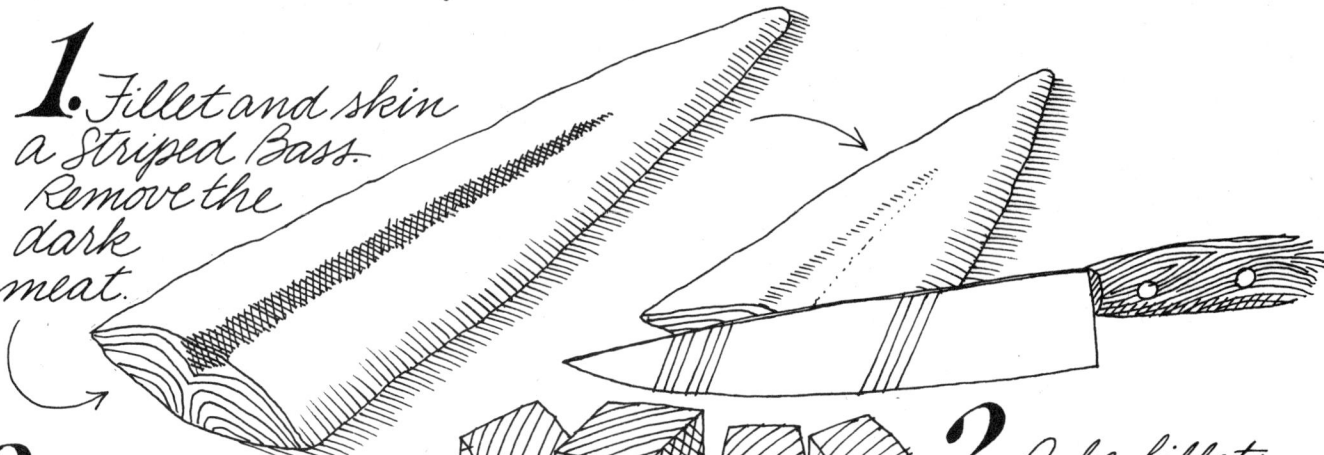

2. Cube fillets into pieces about one inch square.

3. Take 4 Bay leaves, the juice of 2 lemons

Some Salt

one tablespoon olive oil, and pepper

and put into a pot of boiling water for 3-4 minutes.

the pot and the amount of water should be enough to take the fish without overflowing.

4. Add the fish cubes, cover and cook for 10 minutes.

5. Pour contents into a Colander and drain.

6. Arrange fish chunks on a platter and refrigerate until well chilled. Just before serving, add more lemon juice. Great!

Garnish with lettuce

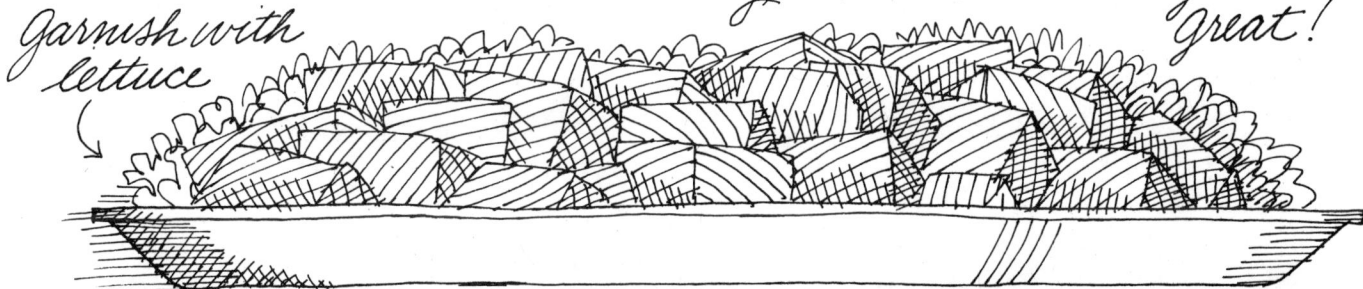

Terrific with a cocktail sauce, too!

Captain Bud Phillips stands on the
bridge of his 40 foot custom sportsfisherman
called the "Surfmaster IV." It runs out
of the Foscle Marina on Sakonnet Pt.,
Rhode Island, in search of
Swordfish, Tuna, and Shark.

Captain Bud's recipe for the East
Coast's popular Striped Bass is a
tasty and flexible one. Try
it with other species of fish
if Striped Bass is not available.

Striped Bass Sakonnet Style

1. Steak or fillet a Striped Bass of about five pounds

2. Melt eight tablespoons of butter in a baking dish, then place fish in the dish.

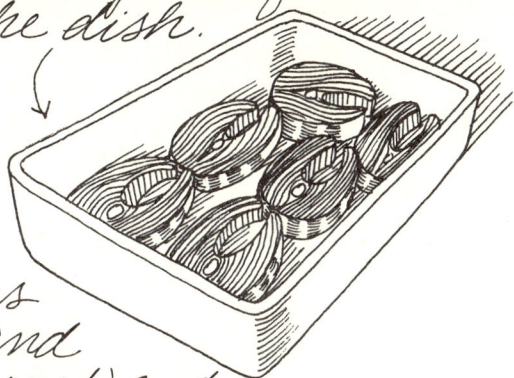

3. Make 2 tablespoons of breadcrumbs by putting onion and garlic croutons in blender. Sprinkle on fish and add a medium onion (chopped) and a 4 ounce can of sliced mushrooms

4. Add a tablespoon of Vinegar, a glass (4oz) of dry Vermouth and two tablespoons of shredded parsley

HEINZ VINEGAR

5. Bake at 350 degrees for 50 minutes and baste frequently

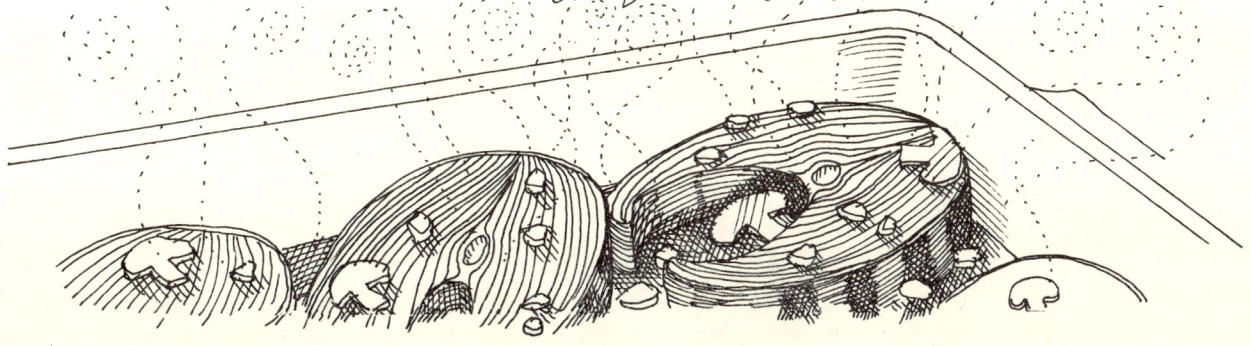

Captain Jim Tactikos has been fishing the waters of Great South Bay and southern Long Island, New York for over 20 years now.

His boat, the "Take Five", is a 28 foot Sportsfisherman that runs out of Massapequa, Long Island, and specializes in fishing for Striped Bass and Bluefish.

Jim's recipe for stuffed Striper can be adapted to many varieties of fish, and should be tried and enjoyed even if Striped Bass is not available.

Barbecued Stuffed Striped Bass.

1. Clean and scale fish. Remove head and tail. Split fish and remove center bone, being careful not to cut through top skin.

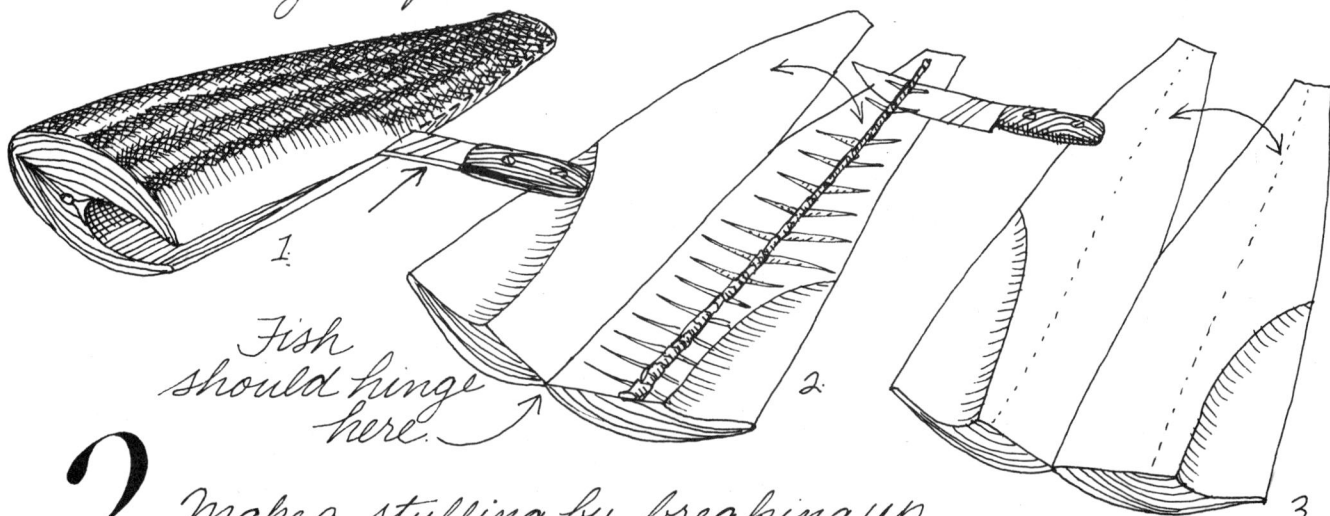

Fish should hinge here.

1

2

3.

2. Make a stuffing by breaking up 1½ cans of Anchovy fillets into small pieces. Add to 5 ounces of bread crumbs and a small can of chopped mushrooms. Also add ½ cup of finely chopped onion, one teaspoon, one teaspoon pepper, a pinch of Dill. Moisten with 2 tablespoons of oil and enough water to moisten crumbs. Mix well.

BREAD CRUMBS

BLACK PEPPER

½ CUP

GARLIC SALT

DILL

3. Place stuffing in fish and place fish on a well-greased fish rack, and place on a hot fire

4. Baste with a sauce of ¼ pound of butter, melted and mixed with the juice of one lemon.

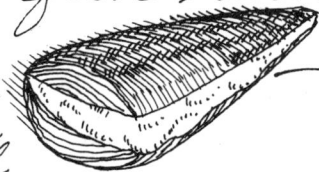

P.S. the rack is important and is well worth the investment.

198.

Captain Frank N. Tuma, Jr. comes from
a long line of charter fishing captains.
His grandfather pioneered sport fishing
on eastern Long Island in the early 1920's,
and was followed by his father and
now by himself.

Frank, Jr. runs the "Gannet III," a custom-
built sportsfisherman, out of Tuma's dock
in Montauk, Long Island, New York.

Specializing in both inshore and offshore
fishing, Frank maintains the family tradition
that calls for big catches of big fish.

Montauk Striped Bass in Gingersnap Sauce

1. Boil 4 pounds of Striped Bass (that has been cut into 2 inch steaks) in a quart of water in which you have put

one carrot
one celery root
2 sliced onions
2 Bay leaves
6 pieces allspice
6 cloves
one teaspoon salt
¼ teaspoon pepper

2. Remove fish when cooked. Strain liquid and return to pot. Now add while stirring

½ lb. crumbled "Ginger Snaps"
6 cooked prunes (pitted)
one tablespoon butter
¼ cup Karo Syrup (dark)
Juice of one lemon
½ CUP Blanched almonds
½ CUP Cooked raisins

3. Bring sauce to a boil. If it gets too thick, add water. If you wish to thicken, brown some flour in butter and add to sauce

4. Place fish steaks on plates and pour sauce over them. Can be served either hot or cold. The recipe feeds 8.

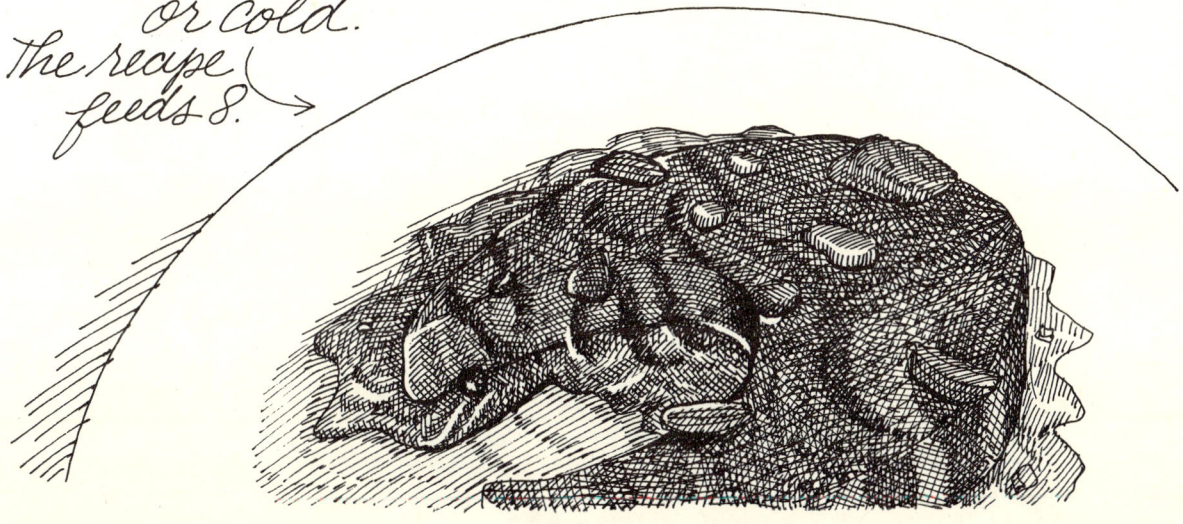

Captain Charlie Nappi stands on the bridge of his shark-emblazoned boat, the "Sea Witch II" which he moors at the Montauk Marine Basin in Montauk, New York.

In 1975, Charlie took a world record Fluke of 22 pounds, but his real dream is to break a world record with a "Monster" White Shark.

His recipe is for broiled Mako Shark steaks. You can also use it for Swordfish steaks. On a blindfold test, you would find it hard to tell them apart.

Mako Steak or Swordfish Steak, broiled in butter.

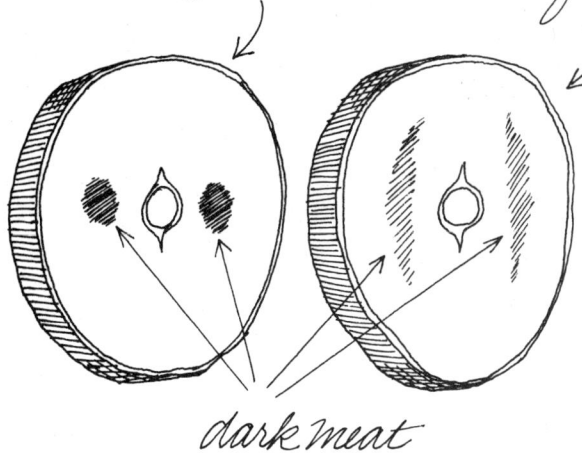

Now that you can tell the difference, which did you eat the last time?

1. Salt and pepper the steaks. Add two dashes of Paprika on each side.

2. Grease grill or broiler pan with a solid shortening like butter, margarine, Spry, Crisco, etc.

If you possibly can, charcoal broil your steaks.

solids somehow prevent sticking

3. Melt ¼ pound of butter in a saucepan. Squeeze half a lemon into it.

4. With a pastry brush, flow lemon butter on top side. After a few minutes turn and baste the lightly cooked side.

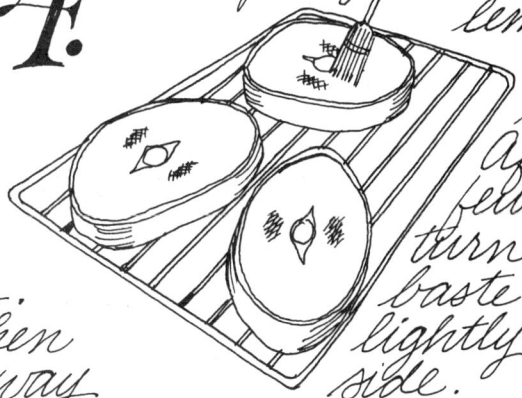

5. Continue basting throughout broiling. The steaks are done when they are opaque all the way through. Just before serving dot with more butter. Garnish with some finely chopped parsley. Serve with lemon wedges on the side.

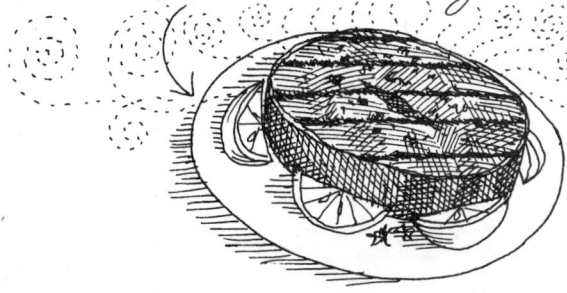

dark meat

You'll love it!

Hint: Leftovers make a great salad the next day.

Author's recipe

How to make broiled fresh Tuna because cookbooks don't tell you how to make broiled fresh Tuna.

1. Cut Tuna into portion-sized pieces about 1½ to 2 inches thick.

← Don't panic, it's supposed to be red.

For incredible results, make a charcoal fire; even if it's in a small hibachi, it's worth the trouble. →

Don't consider putting anything on the fire until briquettes are pure white. Drink Martinis while you wait.

2. Slice up an onion and put on bottom of a Pyrex dish (any pan will do). then lay tuna pieces on onion

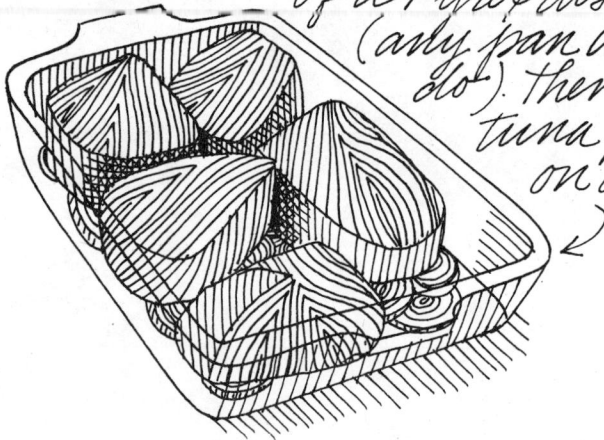

3. Dump in a bottle of your favorite prepared Italian salad dressing.

My favorite →

Italian dressing

↙ Let tuna marinate for about 10 minutes, then turn over for 10 minutes more.

4. Grease grill well with a solid shortening like

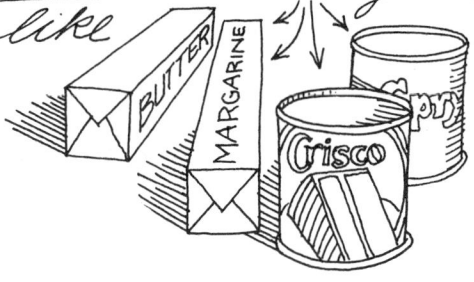

BUTTER
MARGARINE
Crisco

5. Place fish on grill. Try to avoid pieces touching.

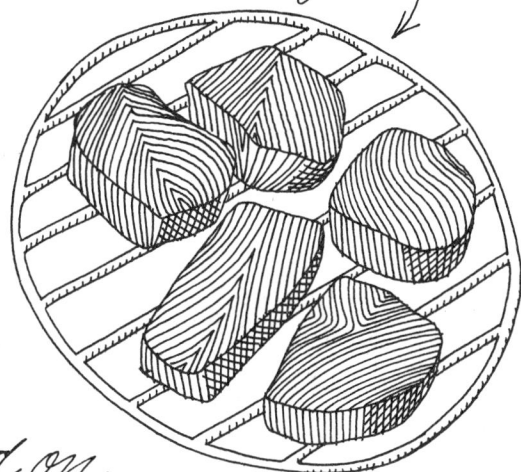

6. Brush on marinade throughout cooking

7. Grill till well seared on one side. Turn, baste, and cook meat until it is opaque throughout.

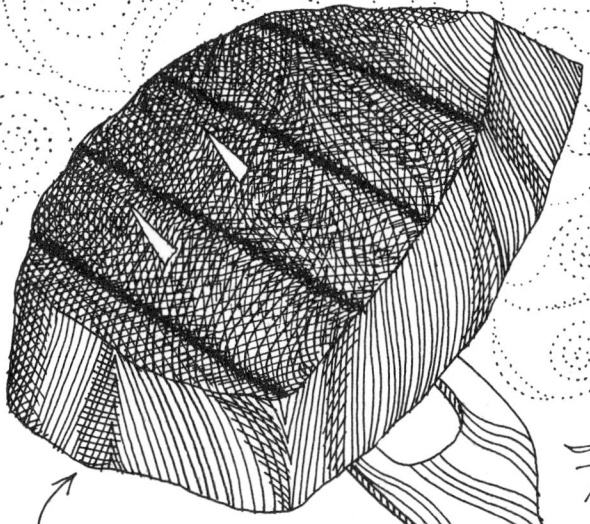

Place pieces back in marinade pan until serving time.

It doesn't taste like canned Tuna. It looks and tastes like a filet mignon. Save what's left (if any) and make a great cold salad.

Captain Don Imbriaco stands on the
stern of his brand-new 45 foot diesel-
powered sportsfisherman that's moored
at the Belmar Marine Basin on
Shark River in Belmar, New Jersey.

Specializing in both inshore and
offshore fishing, Don contributes
his recipe for the best of
Tuna salads. The salad's
made from real fresh Tuna.

Try it his way and see what you've
been missing all these years.

How to make a fresh Tuna Salad...or Bonito, or Albacore Salad.

1. Cut fish into fillets or chunks

Use as much as you feel you'll need. Remove the "dark" meat.

2. Add a tablespoon of salt to each quart of water (use enough water to cover fish) and bring to a boil

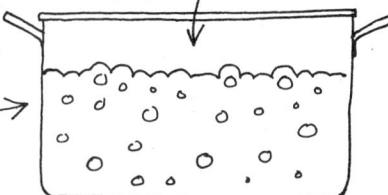

3. Put fish into boiling water and cook for 10 minutes and then dump into colander.

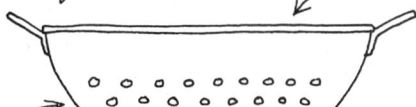

note the meat getting lighter

4. Repeat the entire procedure in fresh salted boiling water for another 10 minutes. Drain and refrigerate.

5. Chop up an onion, 2 or 3 radishes, a few stalks of celery, and mix together with the now white-meat tuna.

6. Add salt and pepper to taste and blend in enough mayonnaise to make mixture stick together. Garnish with sliced olives and hard-boiled eggs. You'll give up canned tuna forever.

Captain Jim Rizzuto is shown here holding a beautiful 55 pound Wahoo caught from Hawaiian waters. Jim runs his private "Rizzuto Maru" out of Kawaihai.

The Hawaiian word for Wahoo is "Ono," which is their same word for "delicious". That should tell you something about what to expect from this recipe for Wahoo, Japanese style. Its great!

Sliced raw Wahoo is a Hawaiian favorite whose origin is Japanese. If you can't get Wahoo, try it with fresh Tuna, Bonito, Sea Bass, Striped Bass, or almost any other species.

1. Cut Wahoo fillets into long "blocks" about 3" x 2" x 2".

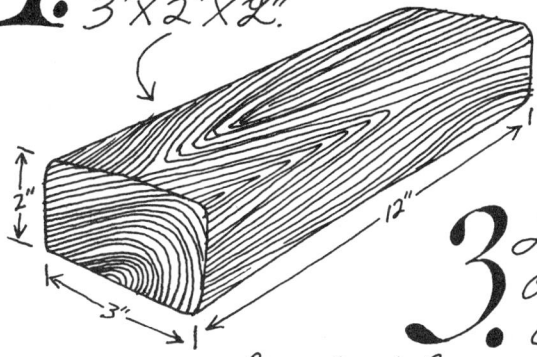

2. Cut straight through the "blocks" to make slices 1/8" thick

3. Lay slices in an overlapping manner on a bed of finely shredded cabbage. Include some purple cabbage with the green to enhance the appearance (which is very important in the Japanese tradition of serving any food). Make sure to cut fish within an hour of serving.

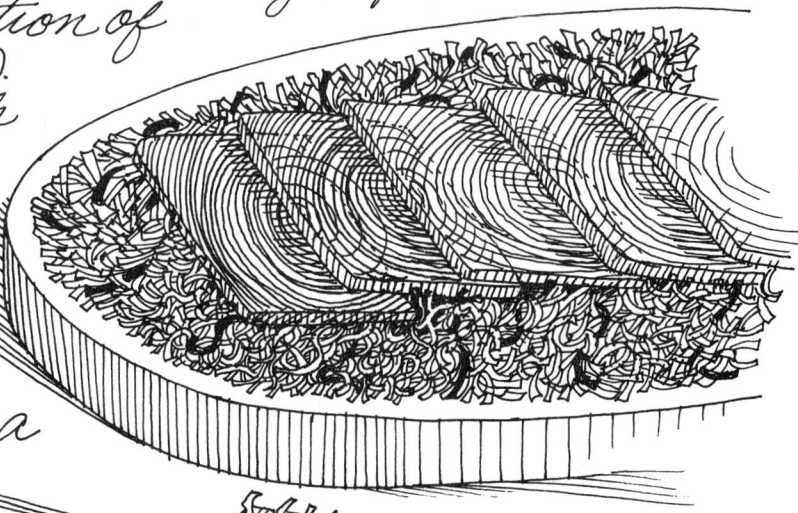

4. Prepare either one of these two sauces into which you will dip a slice of fish with a bit of cabbage with chopsticks

Sauce "A":
Mix a few drops of water to 1/4 teaspoon of dried Japanese mustard until a thick paste is formed. Now add 1/3 cup of Soy Sauce and 2 teaspoons of water and stir.

SOY SAUCE

Sauce "B"
Combine all these ingredients and let stand 1/2 hour.

1/4 CUP water
1/4 CUP soy sauce
1 clove of garlic smashed
1 thumb-nail-sized piece of ginger root smashed
1 tablespoon sugar
1 tablespoon toasted sesame seeds

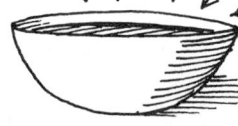

Sprinkle on two tablespoons sliced green onions.

Captain Danny Palm is the skipper of the "Red Rooster", an 85 foot long-range sportsfisherman that specializes in fabulous 4 to 21 day fishing trips out of San Diego around the entire Baja Peninsula and Gulf of California.

He has been Captain of the "Red Rooster" for 12 years and along with his father, Captain Lee Palm, has made these fishing excursions a real special experience. Ask anyone who's gone.

Barbecued California Yellowtail

1. Take a fillet of Yellowtail, leaving the skin on one side.

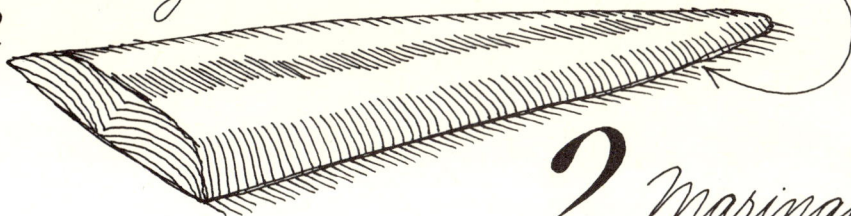

2. Marinate for 4 hours in one cup of oil, one-quarter cup of lemon juice, a diced-up onion and 2-3 tablespoons of snipped parsley.

(Adjust amounts to size of fillets).

3. Grease a grill with a solid shortening (for some reason it helps keep things from sticking).

4. Barbecue flesh side down first

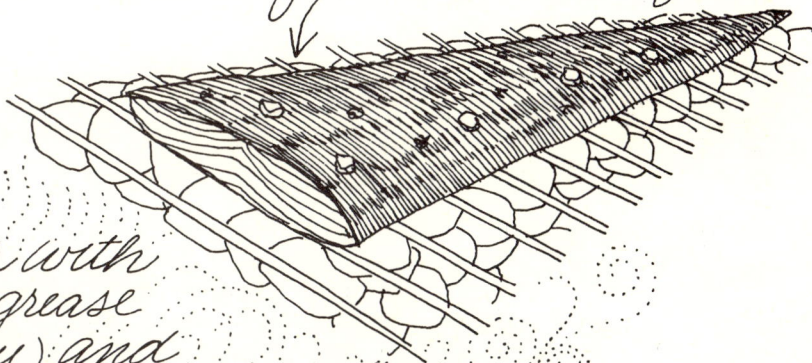

5. then turn over with a spatula (re-grease grill if necessary) and finish cooking skin side down.

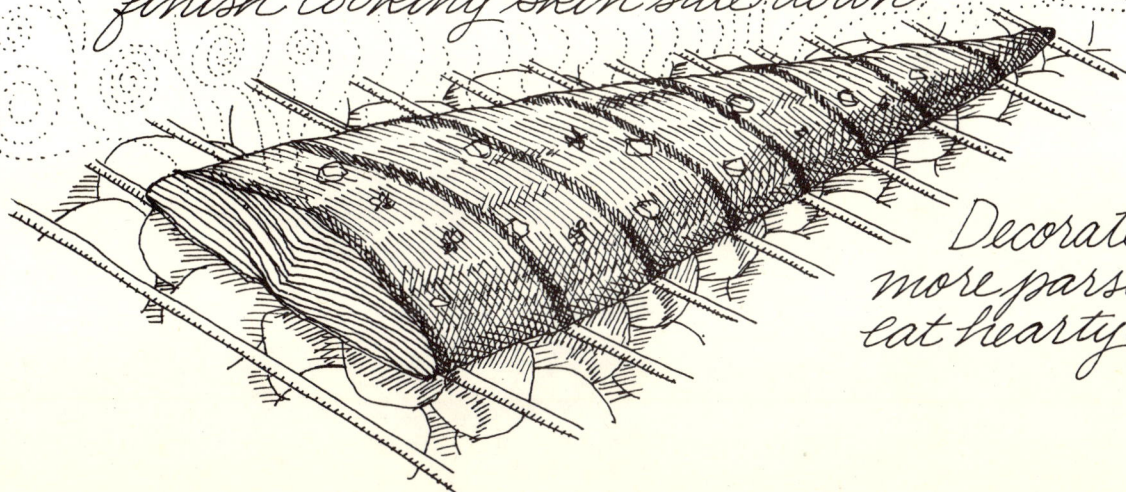

Decorate with more parsley and eat hearty!

210.

Index of Recipes

212.